ISBN: 9781313022101

Published by:
HardPress Publishing
8345 NW 66TH ST #2561
MIAMI FL 33166-2626

Email: info@hardpress.net
Web: http://www.hardpress.net

CORNELL
UNIVERSITY
LIBRARY

THE
HART MEMORIAL LIBRARY

DATE DUE

Cornell University Library
PR 3432.A17

The works of Sir George Etheredge:plays

3 1924 012 961 482

THE WORKS

OF

SIR GEORGE ETHEREDGE

PLAYS AND POEMS

PUBLISHER'S NOTE.

Five hundred copies of this book printed for England and America, and each numbered as issued. Type distributed.

No. 320,

THE WORKS
OF
SIR GEORGE ETHEREDGE

PLAYS AND POEMS

EDITED, WITH CRITICAL NOTES AND INTRODUCTION

BY

A. WILSON VERITY, B.A.

LATE SCHOLAR OF TRINITY COLLEGE, CAMBRIDGE

LONDON

JOHN C. NIMMO

14, KING WILLIAM STREET, STRAND

MDCCCLXXXVIII

PR
3432
A17

CHISWICK PRESS:—C. WHITTINGHAM AND CO., TOOKS COURT,
CHANCERY LANE.

CONTENTS.

	PAGE
INTRODUCTION	vii
THE COMICAL REVENGE; OR, LOVE IN A TUB . .	1
SHE WOULD IF SHE COULD	119
THE MAN OF MODE; OR, SIR FOPLING FLUTTER .	237
POEMS	375
INDEX	407

INTRODUCTION.

FROM the Restoration, or thereabout, down to the Revolution Sir George Etheredge seems to have held a conspicuous place among English men of letters. He is very frequently referred to, and generally in terms of praise; he was familiar with most of the well-known writers of the time, especially those who combined literary success with social distinction; and as a dramatist his reputation was considerable. It is strange, therefore, that so little should be known of his personal life. When and where he was born; when and where he died; what was his career: on these and other points our information is of the scantiest. That information, such as it is, was, in the main, brought together by Oldys in his article on the dramatist in the *Biographia Britannica* (1750); it may be given briefly.

Sir George Etheredge—or Etherege—was probably born in 1634;[1] possibly in 1635. The date is arrived at in a somewhat roundabout

---

[1] "About the year 1636," says Oldys.

fashion. Dryden, in the piece of rhymed octosyllabics which I have placed at the end of this volume, addresses Etheredge thus:—

> To you who live in chill degree,
> As map informs, of fifty-three,
> And do not much for cold atone
> By bringing[1] thither fifty-one.

Dryden's letter, it may be remembered, was written at the request of the Earl of Middleton as a reply to a similar epistle which Etheredge had addressed to the Secretary of State. Etheredge's lines,[2] as we find from the *Letterbook*[3] in the British Museum, were dated April 29th, 1686; Dryden's answer must be assigned to the same year. If, therefore, Etheredge was fifty-

---

[1] "Bringing" might imply that Etheredge was fifty-one when he was sent to Ratisbon, *i.e.* in 1685, not at the time when Dryden wrote.

[2] See the *Poems*.

[3] This volume, acquired by the British Museum in 1837, and described in the Catalogue of MS. Additions for that year, contains the drafts of some hundred letters written by Etheredge during his residence at Ratisbon to his friends in England and France; also copies of a few letters received by him from Dryden, Middleton, and others; several spiteful letters written by his own secretary, in which Etheredge is very sharply criticised; three or four copies of verse, some accounts, a crude Hudibrastic poem on the dramatist's life and character, and a catalogue of his books. Amongst the latter the number of French translations of the Classics is curious. The *Letterbook* was evidently known to Macaulay, see *History* (popular ed.), ii. 405, 487. I need hardly say that Mr. Gosse has made very extensive and effective use of its contents in his essay on Etheredge, *Seventeenth Century Studies*.

three in the spring of 1686 he must have been born in 1634, or early in 1635.

Beyond this single date we know nothing of Etheredge's origin and early life. Gildon, indeed, tells us that he came of an old Oxfordshire family—possibly that to which Dr. George Etheredge, the Greek scholar, belonged—and that for a time " his applications were to the law ;" Oldys thinks that he was at Cambridge. On none of these points is there any direct evidence whatever. That he entered at Cambridge seems unlikely ; no record of his residence there is preserved, the tone of his plays is decidedly unacademic, and Dennis[1] assures us that to his " certain knowledge he understood neither Greek nor Latin." What does appear quite certain is, that previous to the production of *The Comical Revenge* (1664) the dramatist must have spent

---

[1] In his anonymous *Defence of Sir Fopling Flutter*, 1722, defending Etheredge from the attacks of " the knight, his brother ;" the brother being Steele, who had passed very severe judgments on *She Would if She Could* and *Sir Fopling*. (" I allow it to be nature, but it is nature in its utmost corruption and degeneracy ") in the *Spectator*, Nos. 51 and 65. Dennis, by the way, was very fervent in his admiration of Etheredge : " 'Tis my humble opinion that there is no dialogue extant in any language which has half the charms of the Terentian dialogue ; what comes nearest to it is that of Etheredge in *Sir Fopling*."— Letter to Henry Cromwell on " Vis Comica," Oct. 11th, 1717. Again, in his criticism on Crown, he speaks of " that grace, that delicacy, that courtly air which make the charm of Etheredge ;" and there are similar allusions in a letter to Prior on the " Roman Satirists."—*Familiar Letters*, 1721.

some considerable time in France; no one can read that play, still less *Sir Fopling Flutter*, without seeing at once that the writer was familiar to a very remarkable degree with French life and ways. He displays at every turn a knowledge of the language and a close acquaintance with things Parisian that only a long residence in the French capital could have given.

Etheredge's first work, so far as we know, was the piece just alluded to—*The Comical Revenge, or Love in a Tub*, brought[1] upon the stage in 1664, and published[2] in the same year. It was

[1] As Mr. Gosse points out, it is important that we should be able to establish the fact that *The Comical Revenge* preceded all similar pieces; but this precedence depends on the date of the production of the play, not on the date of its publication, and the former can very easily be shown. It would have been a strange thing indeed if Samuel Pepys had been silent about the comedy to which all the town thronged, and Samuel Pepys is not silent: "Jan. 4, 1664: Mr. Moore and I to *Love in a Tubb*, which is very merry."—*Diary*, Mynors Bright's ed., iii. 98; see, too, iv. 138 and v. 263. Pepys, it will be noted, does not imply that he was present at the first representation of the play; yet he saw it so early in the year as Jan. 4th. Perhaps, therefore, it was really produced the end of 1663. Evelyn found the *Revenge* "facetious."—*Diary*, April 27, 1664. That it held the boards for some time is pretty clear from Langbaine's remark, "has succeeded admirably on the stage, it having always been acted with general applause." From some lines in Rochester's *Tunbridge Wells* we may conclude that the character of Sir Nicholas soon became proverbial.

[2] Of this scarce edition the Bodleian possesses two copies: the British Museum not one. The popularity of the piece is attested by the number of editions published—1664, 1669, 1689, 1690, etc.

dedicated to the Earl of Dorset, then Lord Buckhurst, was acted by a very strong cast,[1] which included Betterton and Harris, the first actors of the day, and achieved a great success. Etheredge indeed found himself famous; so famous that for a time he rested on his laurels, not hazarding another essay until 1668. *The Comical Revenge*, we should add, was partly written in rhymed couplets, an early use of the metre that afterwards became so popular.[2]

Etheredge's second play, *She Would if She Could*, appeared in 1668;[3] it marked a decided advance on his first effort. Rhyme has been discarded, and with it the serious, rather melodramatic element which in Etheredge's hands had a tendency to become farcical. The characterization is clearer and cleverer, the movement and lilt of the piece easier, and all through are bright, quick touches that suggest the ready hand of the practised playwright. Curiously

---

[1] See Downes' *Roscius Anglicanus*, pp. 24, 25, Mr. Knight's reprint (1886), where the full list of actors and actresses is given, with the doggerel remark:—

    Sir Nich'las, Sir Frederick, Widow and Dufoy
    Were not by any so well done, ma foy (*i.e. foi*).

The two girls, Graciana and Aurelia, were played by Mrs. Betterton and Mrs. Davies respectively.

[2] In his essay on heroic plays prefixed to the *Conquest of Granada* Dryden rather implies that the merit of the innovation lay with Davenant—the innovation being the employment of the couplet.

[3] Reprinted in quarto 1671 and 1693.

enough, the success of the comedy does not appear to have been in proportion to its merit: "took well, but inferior to *Love in a Tub*," is Downes' summary criticism, while Pepys, who assisted at the *première*, more than hints a partial failure. His account [1] is graphic: "My wife being gone before, I to the Duke of York's Playhouse; where a new play of Etheredge's called *She Would if She Could;* and though I was there by two o'clock, there were 1000 people put back that could not have room in the pit: and I, at last, because my wife was there, made shift to get into the 18*d.* box, and thus saw; but Lord! how full was the house." Everybody was present, the King in his box, Buckingham, with "my Lord Buckhurst and Sedley, and Etheredge the poet; the last of whom I did hear mightily find fault with the actors, that they were out of humour, and had not their parts perfect, and that Harris did do nothing." [2]

---

[1] Mynors Bright, vol. v. p. 180; also p. 456.

[2] Cf. Preface to *The Humorists*, 1671: "Imperfect action had like to have destroyed *She Would if She Could*, which I think, and I have the authority of some of the best judges in England for it, is the best comedy that has been written since the restoration of the stage. And even that, for the imperfect representation of it at first, received such prejudice, that had it not been for the favour of the Court, in all probability it had never got up again; and it suffers for it in a great measure to this very day." Shadwell's wife played the part of Lady Cockwood; Harris, the chief offender, was Sir Joslin Jolley.—Downes, pp. 28, 29.

INTRODUCTION.

From Pepys' remarks, as from those of Shadwell, we may conclude that Etheredge had cause to be dissatisfied with the reception of the play, and this, perhaps, combined with his habitual laziness, was the reason why for eight years his pen lay idle. This silence was broken in 1676, possibly at the rebuke administered by his friend Rochester, who, in the *Session of the Poets*, 1675 (wrongly assigned sometimes to Buckingham), more than hinted that a successor to *She Would if She Could* ought to be forthcoming:—

> Now Apollo had got gentle George in his eye,
> And frankly confessed that of all men that writ
> There's none had more fancy, sense, judgment and wit;
> But i' the crying sin, idleness, he was so hardened
> That his long seven years' silence was not to be pardoned.

Such an appeal was conclusive, and Etheredge responded with his final and most famous comedy, *The Man of Mode, or Sir Fopling Flutter*, produced at the Duke's Theatre in 1676. On this occasion, at any rate, nothing was to be left to chance. Etheredge dedicated his play to the Duchess of York, applied to Sir Car Scroope and Dryden for the prologue and epilogue respectively, secured for its representation the best possible company[1]—Betterton (Dorimant),

---

[1] From Downes' *Roscius Anglicanus*, p. 36: "This comedy," he says, "being well cloathed and well acted, got a great deal of money."

Harris (Medley), Mrs. Barry (Mrs. Loveit), and Mrs. Betterton as Belinda—and "met," in Gildon's words, "with extraordinary success." All London crowded to the Duke's House, the critics showered laurels on the author, and a fresh interest was added when someone (a friend, no doubt) happily discovered that Dorimant, the libertine of the piece, must be my Lord Rochester,[1] that Medley was evidently meant for Sir Charles Sedley, and that in the exquisite of exquisites, Sir Fopling himself, the dramatist had sketched to the life the most notorious fop of the day, the Beau Hewitt for whom Rochester and Dryden[2] have a passing sneer. It is in the main on *The Man of Mode* that Etheredge's reputation rests; the play illustrates

---

[1] So Oldys. Compare, too, St. Evremond, a letter on Rochester to the Duchess of Mazarin, prefixed to *The Works of the Earls of Rochester, Roscommon, Dorset, etc.*, 1721 : "Sir George Etherege wrote Dorimant in Sir Fopling in compliment to him." Spence in his *Anecdotes* mentions a different tradition ; he quotes Dean Lockier : " Sir George Etherege was as thorough a fop as ever I saw ; he was exactly his own Sir Fopling Flutter, and yet he designed Dorimant, the genteel rake of wit, for his own picture."

[2] *Essay on Satire:*—

>   Then o'er his cups this nightbird chirping sits
>   Till he takes Hewit or Jack Hall for wits.

— *Works*, vol. xv. p. 213, where Scott quotes from Rochester's *Farewell* :—

>   Scarce will their greater grief pierce every heart
>   Should Sir George Hewit or Sir Car (*i.e.* Scroope) depart.

the merits and defects of that peculiar type of comedy which Etheredge was the first to develop, and which for a century afterwards remained dominant. We shall have a word to say about it later on.

In this same year, 1676, we catch for the first time a glimpse of the personal life of the dramatist; and unfortunately the glimpse is not particularly pleasing. Etheredge, Rochester, and two friends were at Epsom one Sunday night—to be quite accurate, it was June 17th—and amongst other things they tossed sundry fiddlers in blankets and "skirmisht the watch," so effectually, however, that one of their party got run through with a pike, whereupon the other three had to abscond. How the affair was settled we are not told.[1] Another scanty item: Gildon informs us rather crudely that Etheredge "for marrying a fortune was knighted," and the marriage and knighthood must be referred to some time between the year 1676, when he was plain "Geo. Etheridge," and the year 1680,

---

[1] See the Hatton Correspondence, Camden Society publications, 1879; I owe the reference to Mr. Gosse. Apparently the event created rather a stir, as I find it alluded to in a letter in the Verney Papers—*Historical MSS. Commission Reports*, vol. vii. p. 467—"Mr. Downes, who (with Lord Rochester, Mr. William Jepson and Geo. Etheridge) skirmisht the watch at Epsom 12 days since, died last Tuesday of his hurts received from the rustics." Addison may have heard of the scandal, *Spectator*, 2.

when in the Hatton Correspondence he is referred to as "Sir George." That the marriage was perfunctory would appear from Buckingham's lines in *A Consolatory Epistle to Captain Julian* :—

> E'en gentle George (flux'd both in tongue and purse)
> Shunning one snare yet fell into a worse.
> A man may be relieved once in a life,
> But who can be relieved that has a wife.[1]

This almost brings us to the final, and, thanks to his letters, fairly tangible period in Etheredge's life. In March, 1685, he was appointed English Envoy—more technically, Resident—at Ratisbon.[2] There seems some reason to believe that he had previously held diplomatic posts, and a contemporary pasquil, quoted by Oldys, contains the couplet—

> Ovid to Pontus sent for too much wit;
> Etheredge to Turkey for the want of it;

from which we might conclude that he had once represented the English Court at Constantinople. However this may have been, he was now sent to Ratisbon, where we can follow his life for the

---

[1] *State Poems* (1703 collection), ii. 132.
[2] Mr. Gosse gives the following warrant from the Privy Signet Book : "Warrant to pay Sir Geo. Etheredge (whom his Maj. has thought fit to employ in his service in Germany) 3*l.* per diem." This was supplemented by bounties ; cf. the following extract from *The Secret Services of Charles II. and James II.*, published by the Camden Society, 1851 : "To Sir George Etheridge, bounty . . . . 200*l.*" ; date, Sept. 20th, 1685.

next two years with tolerable closeness. Up to this point Etheredge has been the vaguest, most elusive of personalities; it is pleasant now to turn to the letters (upon which we shall not scruple to draw freely), and to extract from them some idea of what our author really was.

At first the correspondence is not very promising: the poet-plenipotentiary is on his good behaviour and official, priding himself a little on the Cato-like firmness with which he had said good-bye to the pleasures of London, and only inveighing against the sheer dulness that drives him to bed at impossibly early hours—" is it not enough to breed an ill habit of body in a man who was used to sit up till morning to be forced, for want of knowing what to do with himself, to go to bed in the evening?" Obviously Ratisbon is *le monde où l'on s'ennuie*, and numerous are his complaints against the consuming dreariness of the place and people. In December—he had reached Ratisbon, by the way, on August 30th —he tells a friend in Paris that sleighing is their great amusement; in February the Carnival brings a little diversion, and we find him writing to a certain M. Purpurat of Vienna[1]: " Nous avons esté employer ici plus que d'ord^{re} le temps de ce Carnaval: autrement je n'avais pas manqué *devant* de vous faire mes recon-

---

[1] In the French extracts I have retained Etheredge's spelling.

naissances. Vous m'avez accabler d'une telle manière de compliments et de tabac, que je manque des paroles et des moyens en ce misérable endroit pour faire le retour que vostre generosité mérite." This M. Purpurat subsequently arrives at Ratisbon and swindles the English Resident out of ten thousand crowns at cards, which the latter has some difficulty in recovering; the secretary tells us the whole story in his pleasant way. During the spring of this year Etheredge's letters are almost entirely official; apparently his friends were lazy about writing. " Pray, my lord," he says to Middleton, " keep me alive in the memory of those you think convenient;" but notwithstanding this appeal, he has to complain in June that nothing has reached him for a whole week, "which is a thing that touches me here as nearly as ever a disappointment did in London with the woman I loved most tenderly." If his friends were fickle, the dulness of the Diet was constant: " si ce n'estoit "—he informs a French correspondent — " pour la maison de Monsieur le Comte de Crecy Ratisbonne serait un triste sejour ;" and then a characteristic little touch—"je n'ai pas veu la Dindonelle depuis vostre depart." The Comte de Crecy, we may explain, was the French Ambassador, to whom Barillon had given Etheredge letters of introduction.

At last in November something happens. A troupe of actors comes over from Nuremberg, and Etheredge, sinking the diplomatist in the Restoration courtier, finishes off his weekly despatch to Middleton with the assurance that the company includes "a comedian as handsome at least as the Fair Maid of the West, which you have seen at Newmarket, and makes as much noise in this little town, and gives as much jealousies to the ladies, as ever Mrs. Wright or Mrs. Johnson did in London." The secretary, always excellent at throwing a side-light on his master's idiosyncrasies, gives us a quaint, acid little account of the envoy's relations with the *comédienne;* she appears to have been singularly successful in setting all Ratisbon by the ears. In the same month Etheredge writes a long letter to Buckingham, speaking with unusual favour of his place of banishment. A short extract is worth giving: "Nov. 12, 1686: Ten years ago I as little thought that my stars designed to make a politician of me, and that it would come to my share to debate in public assemblies . . . . as the Grand Signior dreamed of losing Hungary. . . . . I live in one of the finest and best-mannered cities in Germany, where 'tis true we have not pleasure in that perfection as we see it in London and Paris, yet, to make amends, we enjoy a noble serene air that makes us as hungry as hawks; and though business, and even the worst sort of business, wicked politics, is the distinguishing commodity of the place, yet I will say that for the Germans, they manage it the best of any people in the world; they cut off and retrench all those idle preliminaries and useless ceremonies that clog the wheels of it everywhere else: and I find to this day they make good the observation that Tacitus made of their ancestors, I mean that their affairs, let them be ever so serious and pressing, never put a stop to good eating and drinking, and that they debate their weightiest negotiations over their cups." The excessive drinking of the Germans is a point to which he frequently recurs. With the new year comes a change of ministry in London, and Etheredge considers it expedient to write and bespeak the good favour of my Lord Godolphin, remarking, however, that he had always been "too lazy and too careless to be ambitious." In February (12th) he thinks that his rumoured appointment to the Swedish Court must be a mistake; later in the month (24th) he is "in great want of assistance," and, a notice having arrived from the Treasury that his expenses must be curtailed, complains to Middleton of hard treatment—" it is natural to think we are a little hardly dealt with when we are retrenched a bounty we have been used to.

. . . . You know it is very much for me to be three quarters of a year in arrears in a town where there is no credit." This was in March—the 10th. In another letter written at the same time we catch a glimpse of his way of spending his days: "I have good greyhounds, and coursing is one of my greatest recreations; we have such plenty of game that now and then I start a brace[1] of hares in a day." If only Charles Boyle were there to play chess with him: at any rate, business has cured his "passion for play." Earlier in the year (Feb. 17th) Dryden had written, and now Etheredge replies, reproaching the Laureate with his laziness: "I cannot endure you should arrogate a thing to yourself you have not the least pretence to. Is it not enough you should excel in so many eminent virtues, but you must be putting in for a vice which all the world knows is properly my province? If you persist in your claim to laziness you will be thought as affected in it as ——
. . . . I (whose every action of *my* life is a witness of *my* idleness) little thought that you, who have raised so many immortal monuments of your industry, durst have set up to be my rival." In April (21st) we note a long letter to the Duke of Berwick, and a month later, May 22nd, an inquiry after various friends in Eng-

[1] The copyist seems to have made some mistake.

land, "particularly my Lord Dunbar, and Ned Lee, whose prosperity I have always wished."

Four days later comes one of the pleasantest letters contained in the correspondence; it must be given in full:—

"To Betterton (the player): A poor man who has lost the enjoyment of his friends and the pleasures of London ought to have all the means he can to divert his chagrin, and pass away the time as easy as is possible; in order to [do] this I am often forced to trouble my acquaintance in England, and I do not doubt but you will forgive me my making bold with you among the rest. I have three in my family who now and then give me a little music; they play very well and at sight, and we have all the operas, and I have a correspondent at Paris who sends me what is new there: if you would do me the favour to procure me some of the best compositions with the several parts, and let them be given to Dr. Wynne, at my Lord Middleton's office, he will take care to send them to me. I shall esteem myself much obliged to you for this courtesy, and your kindness will be greater if now and then you give me an account of the stage, and of other matters which (you shall judge) I will be glad to hear of: you will not mistake if you have the same opinion you had of me formerly, for I assure you I am not changed in my inclination, and can never be otherwise than, etc. . . . .

" My humble service to Mrs. Betterton."

June brings us back to Dryden. " Yesterday," writes Etheredge to Wynne, June 23rd, " I received yours of the 27th of May, together with the part of *The Hind and Panther*. . . . . Pray let me know how this poem is approved by the Court." June 30th he receives parts ii. and iii. of the same work from England, but has not quite finished reading them before post time. July 3rd he has a short criticism to offer : " Mr. Wynne has sent me *The Hind and Panther*, by which I find John Dryden has a noble ambition to restore poetry to its ancient dignity in wrapping up the mysteries of religion in verse. What a shame it is to me to see him a saint, and remain still the same devil (*i.e.* myself)." The letter (to Middleton) ends with some complimentary allusions to Sir Charles Sedley, who " had always more wit than was enough for one man." A fortnight later, the 15th, he is annoyed to find that his letters don't reach regularly, though he writes twice a week, while about the same time a friend in Paris learns—no doubt, with satisfaction—that " la petite Stubenberg devient tous les jours plus jollie et plus meure (*i.e.* mûre), et je crois que les doux zephyres que soufflent les amants feront bientost épanouir le petit bouton de rose." This obviously is in the "gentle George" style of *Sir Fopling* days. The end of the month Etheredge writes for the first and last time (so far as the *Letterbook* is concerned) to Dorset, reviving the memory of " old (but not " unhappy ") far-off things ;" of how, in particular, they carried "the two draggle-tailed nymphs one bitter frosty night over the Thames to Lambeth." In the autumn he is ill: it happened in this way. The afternoon of October the 19th was delightfully fine—for Ratisbon, of course—and the Electoral College spent several hours in the pleasant grounds of the English envoy ; and—

> Flowing cups went freshly round
> With no allaying Danube.

Like Waller, Etheredge had always been but an amateur over his cups, so that next morning finds him suffering for his hospitality. " I write," he says on the 23rd, and the letter contains a pleasant little picture—" to let you see I am in a fair way of living again, though I was dangerously ill last week. . . . . Yesterday was the first I intended to take a little fresh air, and just as I was stepping into my coach, word was brought me the Duke of Berwick was arrived. I went immediately to see him, and saw him look so fresh and so well after his sickness, that the joy of it, I think, has forwarded much the recovery of my health. We stayed together till ten at night, and I took my leave of him at five this morning, not being able to prevail with him to stay a day and unweary himself." In a subsequent letter he praises the duke highly.

His correspondence just now is official and uninteresting, except perhaps to the historical student, but a letter written on December 19th has several characteristic touches and details of his personal life; as, for instance: "The women need not rail at our changing; few of us have the gift to be constant to ourselves. Sir C. S.[1] sets up for good hours and sobriety; my Lord D. has given over variety, and shuts himself up within my lady's arms, as you inform me." And then turning to himself: "I have a very convenient garden belonging to my house; I wish the rent of it may not cost me too dear. I have good horses and often go a hunting. Were I to write to —— (mentioning two unfamiliar names) this would afford me wherewithal to fill one side of paper. I bungle away now and then a morning at tennis; here is a pretty *carré* court and players so exactly sized to Sir C. (Sedley), that were he here he would live in it." The epistle concludes in very charming fashion: "I wear

---

[1] A marginal note in the *Letterbook* explains the initials—Sir Charles Sedley and Dorset.

flannel, sir; therefore, pray, talk no more to me of poetry."

One more extract and we have exhausted the resources of the *Letterbook*, with regard to which we may take this opportunity of saying that it is official to a most irritating degree. In a letter dated March 8, 1688, we light on some scraps of personal gossip: " Mrs. Barry "—he has been mentioning various actresses—" bears up as well as I myself have done ; my poor Lord Rochester[1] could not weather the Cape, and live under the Line fatal to puling constitutions. Though I have given up writing plays, I should be glad to read a good one, wherefore pray let Will Richards send me Mr. Shadwell's[2] as soon as it is printed, that I may know what follies are in fashion ; the fops I knew are grown stale. . . . . Our Carnival ends to-morrow, and I am just now going to a ball, where there will be a great many, and some pretty young women, though to tell you the truth I have of late lived as chaste as Lady Etheredge." Three days later comes the last letter contained in the *Letterbook*. We know,

[1] *i.e.* Hyde, Earl of Rochester. The more famous Earl, the author, died in 1680.
[2] *The Squire of Alsatia*, as Mr. Gosse notes ; it was extraordinarily successful—"had an uninterrupted run of 13 days together," says Downes, adding in a note : " the poet received for his third day in the house at Drury Lane at single prices £130, which was the greatest receipt they ever had at that house at single prices."

however, that Etheredge remained at Ratisbon for another year, until indeed the Revolution forced him, in the words of his secretary, "to seek an asylum among the French." Naturally he was much chagrined at the course events took in England: "his Majesty," he writes to Lord Preston, "has been so shamefully betrayed at home that our nation has justly lost the little reputation it had recovered; honour and honesty are looked upon by foreigners to be no more of the growth of our unhappy isle."[1] The letter in which this passage occurs is dated January 3rd, 1689. At the end of the month (28th) we find him complaining to the same correspondent that his position at the Diet is very uncomfortable, the Elector of Brandenburgh having circulated a libellous paper against James II. which he should do his best to counteract. And then the rest is silence; we catch no further glimpse of Etheredge. The story that he died by falling down stairs in a drunken fit is a mere legend, first mentioned by Oldys on the vague authority of a friend of Etheredge's family. The exact date of his death is not quite certain;[2] but I have found the following entry in Luttrell's

---

[1] *Historical MSS. Commission Report*, vol. vii. p. 428, where extracts from three letters are given.

[2] I say not certain because some verses in Southerne's lines to Congreve seem inconsistent with Luttrell's report. The verses are:—

Diary,[1] which may perhaps be accepted as fairly conclusive: "Those from France say that .... Sir George Etherege, the late King James's ambassador to Vienna, died lately at Paris." This is under date of February, 1691; it would agree with the fact mentioned by Mr. Gosse that Colonel Chester possesses "the record of administration to the estate of a Dame Mary Etheredge, widow, dated Feb. 1, 1692." By his wife Etheredge does not seem to have had any children; he was connected, however, with Mrs. Barry the actress, and she bore him a daughter who died young. His brother, Colonel Etheredge,[2] was a soldier of some note; he died in 1708, leaving a daughter who married Aaron Hill. Oldys, on the authority of Bowman the actor, who knew Etheredge, says that he was "a fair, slender man .... very affable and courteous, of a sprightly and generous temper." To his contemporaries he was always "gentle

> Loose, wand'ring Etherege, in wild pleasures tost,
> In foreign interests to his hopes long lost.
> Poor Lee and Otway dead, Congreve appears,
> The darling and last comfort of his years.

Lee did not die till 1692, and Congreve's *Old Bachelor* was produced in 1693. Perhaps the mistake is Southerne's; people had naturally lost sight of Etheredge.

[1] Vol. ii. p. 171. Vienna may be an error for Ratisbon. It is quite possible, however, that Etheredge was among the envoys sent by James to different European Courts to ask for help.

[2] Luttrell, vi. 254.

George" or "easy Etheredge," and he is generally coupled with Sir Charles Sedley.[1]

We must say a word upon Etheredge's claims to recognition. As a verse-writer he need not detain us; he rarely rises above mediocrity; careless and irregular, his lyrics, for the most part, are no whit superior to the reams of rhymed commonplace that lie entombed in the anthologies of the time. Indeed, his prose seems to me better than his verse; the former, as shown in his letters,[2] is generally clear and straightforward, with a good deal of balance and rhythm, thus illustrating the development in prose style after the Restoration which Mr. Matthew Arnold has somewhere remarked upon. It is as a dramatist that Etheredge must be known, if known at all; and here his services to English literature may be summed up in the statement that he initiated the school of prose comedy which reached its highest

---

[1] As in Fenton's *Epistle to Southerne* :—
  Etheredge and Sedley joined him in her cause,
  And all deserved, and all received applause;
the "him" being Wycherley.

[2] Besides the letters we have an amusing pamphlet, entitled, "An Account of the Rejoycing at the Dyet at Ratisbonne, Performed by Sir George Etherege, Kt. : Residing there from His Majesty of Great Britain, upon occasion of the Birth of The Prince of Wales. In a letter from Himself." A copy of this broadside is in the Bodleian. *A propos* of Etheredge's prose style a sentence in Dryden's already alluded-to letter is interesting—"for I will never enter the lists in prose with the undoubted best author of it which our nation has produced," the "best author" being Etheredge.

point in Congreve and ended with Sheridan. With *The Man of Mode* comedy ceased to be earnest and to point a moral; it ceased to be mere rough-and-tumble buffoonery. It aimed henceforth at a realistic representation of contemporary society; at pointed dialogue and the verbal pyrotechnics of which the author of *The Way of the World* is so incomparable a master; above all, at a vivid presentment of characters familiar to everyone—the scented exquisite in periwig and lace ruffles, who lounges in the pit, and is rather loud in his criticism of the play; the not too scrupulous fair (leaning from her box), who knows the advantages of masks and sedan-chairs; and so on. It is all very brilliant, very artificial, and, in the favourite epithet of last-century critics, very polite; and if the audience have to put up with a minimum of plot, should they not be content with the feeling that they are moving in unimpeachable society, and seeing life as it is at the Piazza, the Park, the New Exchange, and other approved *rendezvous* of fashion and intrigue? This was the type of comedy[1] introduced by Etheredge. To some extent he may have profited by what he had seen on the French stage;[2] to some extent

---

[1] "The dawn was in Etheredge, as its latest close was in Sheridan."—Hazlitt.

[2] Mr. Gosse has a good deal to say on this point; for instance,

the style of his works was determined by the conditions under which he wrote. Society under Charles II. was unlike anything that had gone before; and the theatre which held up the mirror to such a society had to undergo a corresponding change. Historically [1] Etheredge is interesting as the first of a long line of writers: intrinsically his plays possess considerable merit.

"it is certain to me that the movement of *She Would if She Could* is founded upon a reminiscence of *Tartuffe*."

[1] In connection with the history of Etheredge's three comedies it may be convenient to give the date of the last recorded performance of each. *The Comical Revenge* was acted at Drury Lane in 1726, November 26th, the cast including Colley Cibber (as Dufoy) and Mrs. Oldfield; the revival ran for three nights. *She Would if She Could* ("not acted ten years") was produced, with Macklin, Ryan, and Ridout, in 1750 (Dec. 21st) at Covent Garden; and *Sir Fopling Flutter*—Genest calls him "The Man of *the* Mode"—last saw the scene on March 15th, 1766. See Genest, iii. 185, iv. 333, and v. 108.

THE
COMICAL REVENGE:
OR,
LOVE IN A TUB.
ACTED AT HIS HIGHNESS
THE DUKE OF YORK'S THEATRE
IN
LINCOLN'S INN FIELDS.

TO THE HONOURABLE
CHARLES LORD BUCKHURST.[1]

MY LORD,

I COULD not have wished myself more fortunate than I have been in the success of this poem. The writing of it was a means to make me known to your lordship; the acting of it has lost me no reputation; and the printing of it has now given me an opportunity to show how much I honour you.

I here dedicate it, as I have long since dedicated myself, to your lordship; let the humble love of the giver make you set some value upon the worthless gift. I hope it may have some esteem with others, because the author knows how to esteem you, whose knowledge moves admiration, and goodness love, in all that know you. But I design this a dedication, not a panegyric; not to proclaim your virtues to the world, but to show your lordship how firmly they have obliged me to be,

My lord,
Your most humble and
faithful servant,
GEO. ETHEREDGE.

[1] *Lord Buckhurst*, *i.e.* Charles Sackville, sixth Earl of Dorset; best known, perhaps, as author of the famous song, "To all you ladies now at land." "The finest gentleman in the voluptuous court of Charles II.," says Horace Walpole.

THE PROLOGUE.

WHO could expect such crowding here to-day,
    Merely on the report of a new play?
A man would think you've been so often bit
By us of late, you should have learn'd more wit;
And first have sent a forlorn hope to spy
The plot and language of our comedy;
Expecting till some desperate critics had
Resolved you whether it were good or bad.
But yet we hope you'll never grow so wise;
For, if you should, we and our comedies
Must trip to Norwich, or for Ireland go;
And never fix, but, like a puppet-show,
Remove from town to town, from fair to fair,
Seeking fit chapmen to put off our ware.
For such our fortune is, this barren age,
That faction now, not wit, supports the stage:
Wit has, like painting, had her happy flights,
And in peculiar ages reach'd her heights,
Though now declined: yet, could some able pen
Match Fletcher's nature, or the art of Ben,
The old and graver sort would scarce allow
Those plays were good, because we writ them now.
Our author therefore begs you would forget,
Most reverend judges, the records of wit;

*And only think upon the modern way
Of writing, whilst you're censuring his play.
And, gallants, as for you, talk loud i' th' pit;
Divert yourselves and friends with your own wit;
 Observe the ladies, and neglect the play,
 Or else 'tis fear'd we are undone to-day.*

DRAMATIS PERSONÆ.

The LORD BEVILL, *father to* LOVIS, GRACIANA, *and* AURELIA.
The LORD BEAUFORT, *servant to* GRACIANA.
COLONEL BRUCE } *A cavalier, friend to* LOVIS, *in love with* GRACIANA.
LOVIS, *friend to* BRUCE.
SIR FREDERICK FROLLICK, *cousin to the* LORD BEAUFORT.
GRACIANA, *a young lady, in love with the* LORD BEAUFORT.
AURELIA, *her sister, in love with* COLONEL BRUCE.
MRS. RICH, } *A wealthy widow, sister to the* LORD BEVILL, *in love with* SIR FREDERICK.
LETITIA, *a girl waiting upon* AURELIA.
BETTY, *waiting-woman to the widow.*
DUFOY, } *A saucy impertinent Frenchman, servant to* SIR FREDERICK.
CLARK, *servant to the* LORD BEAUFORT.
SIR NICHOLAS CULLY, *knighted by* OLIVER.
WHEEDLE *and* PALMER, *gamesters.*
MRS. GRACE, *a wench kept by Wheedle.*
JENNY, *her maid.*
MRS. LUCY, *a wench kept by* SIR FREDERICK.
A Coachman belonging to the widow.
A Bellman.

Footmen, Linkboys, Drawers, and other Attendants.

Scene : LONDON.

THE COMICAL REVENGE;
OR,
LOVE IN A TUB.

ACT I.

SCENE I.—AN ANTE-CHAMBER TO SIR FREDERICK FROLLICK'S BED-CHAMBER.

Enter DUFOY, *with a plaister on his head, walking discontentedly; and* CLARK *immediately after him.*

Clark.

GOOD-MORROW, monsieur.
  Duf. Good-mor',——good-mor'.
Clark. Is Sir Frederick stirring?
Duf. Pox sturré himé.
Clark. My Lord has sent me——
Duf. Begar, me vil havé de revengé; me vil no stay two day in Englandé.
Clark. Good monsieur, what's the matter?
Duf. De matré! de matré is easy to be perceive. Dis Bedlamé, madcapé, *diable de* matré, vas drunké de last night; and vor no reason, but dat me did advisé him to go to bed, begar, he did striké, breaké my headé, Jernie.
Clark. Have patience, he did it unadvisedly.

Duf. Unadvisé! didé not me advise him justé when he did ité?

Clark. Yes; but he was in drink, you say.

Duf. In drinké; me vishé he had been over de head and de ear in drinké. Begar, in France de drink dat van man drinké do's not crack de noder man's brainé. Hark!——he is avake, [SIR FRED. *knocks.*] and none of the people are to attendé himé. Ian villain,¹ day are all gone, run to the *diable;* [*Knocks again.*] have de patience, I beseech you.

[*Pointing towards his master's chamber.*

Clark. Acquaint Sir Frederick I am here from my lord.

Duf. I vil, I vil; your ver umble *serviteur.*

[*Exeunt.*

SCENE II.—SIR FREDERICK'S BED-CHAMBER.

Enter SIR FREDERICK *in his nightgown, and after him* DUFOY.

Duf. Good-mor', good-mor' to your vorshippé; me am alvay ready to attendé your vorshippé, and your vorshippé's alvay ready to beaté and to abusé mé; you vare drunké de lasté nighté, and my head aké to-day morningé. See you here, [*Showing his head.*] if my brainé have no ver good raison to counsel you, and to mindé your bus'nessé.

Sir Fred. Thou hast a notable brain. Set me down a crown for a plaister; but forbear your rebukes.

¹ Meant for "damn villains"?

Duf. 'Tis ver couragious ting to breaké de head of your *serviteur*, is it noté? Begar, you vil never keepé de good *serviteur*, had me no love you ver vel——

Sir Fred. I know thou lovest me.

Duf. And darefore you do beaté me, is dat de raison?

Sir Fred. Prithee forbear; I am sorry for't.

Duf. Ver good satisfaction! Begar, it is me dat am sorrié for't.

Sir Fred. Well, well.

Duf. De *serviteur* of my lord, your cousin, be comé speak vid you.

Sir Fred. Bring him in. [*Exit* DUFOY. I am of opinion that drunkenness is not so damnable a sin to me as 'tis to many; sorrow and repentance are sure to be my first work the next morning. 'Slid, I have known some so lucky at this recreation, that, whereas 'tis familiar to forget what we do in drink, have even lost the memory, after sleep, of being drunk. Now do I feel more qualms than a young woman in breeding.

Enter DUFOY *and* CLARK; DUFOY *goes out again.*

Clark! What news from the god of love? he's always at your master's elbow, he has justled the devil out of service; no more! Mrs. Grace! Poor girl, Mrs. Graciana has flung a squib into his bosom, where the wild-fire will huzza for a time, and then crack, it flies out at his breeches.

Clark. Sir, he sent me before with his service; he'll wait on you himself when he's dressed.

Sir Fred. In very good time; there never was a girl more humorsome or tedious in the dressing of her baby. [*Exit* CLARK.

Enter DUFOY *and Footboy.*

Duf. Hayé! heré is de ver vine varké, begar, de ver vine varké!——

Sir Fred. What's the business?

Duf. De business! de devil také mé if dare be not de whole regiment army de Hackené cocheman, de linkeboy, de fydler, and de shambermaydé, dat havé beseegé de howsé; dis is de consequance of de drink vid a poxé.

Sir Fred. Well, the coachmen and linkboys must be satisfied. I suppose there's money due to 'em; the fiddlers, for broken heads and instruments, must be compounded with; I leave that to your care. But for the chambermaid, I'll deal with her myself; go, go, fetch her up.

Duf. De pimpé, begar, I vil be de pimpé to no man in de Christendome; do you go fetch her up; de pimpé—— [*Exit* DUFOY.

Sir Fred. Go, sirrah, direct her.
[*To the Footboy; exit Footboy.*
Now have I most unmanfully fallen foul upon some woman, I'll warrant you, and wounded her reputation shrewdly. Oh drink, drink! thou art a vile enemy to the civillest sort of courteous ladies.

Enter JENNY, *Wheedle's wench's maid.*

Oh Jenny, next my heart nothing could be more welcome.

Maid. Unhand me; are you a man fit to be trusted with a woman's reputation?

Sir Fred. Not when I am in a reeling condition; men are now and then subject to those infirmities in drink which women have when they're sober. Drunkenness is no good secretary, Jenny; you must not look so angry, good faith! you must not.

Maid. Angry! we always took you for a civil gentleman.

Sir Fred. So I am, i' troth, I think.——

Maid. A civil gentleman will come to a lady's lodging at two o'clock in the morning, and knock as if it were upon life and death; a midwife was never knocked up with more fury.

Sir Fred. Well, well, girl; all's well, I hope, all's well.

Maid. You have made such an uproar amongst the neighbours, we must be forced to change our lodging.

Sir Fred. And thou art come to tell me whither—— kind heart!

Maid. I'll see you a little better mannered first. Because we would not let you in at that unseasonable hour, you and your rude ranting companions hooped and hollo'd like madmen, and roared out in the streets, "A whore, a whore, a whore!" You need not have knocked good people out of their beds; you might have met with them had been good enough for your purpose abroad.

Sir Fred. 'Twas ill done, Jenny, indeed it was.

Maid. 'Twas a mercy Mr. Wheedle was not there, my mistress's friend; had he been there, she'd been quite undone. There's nothing got by your lewd doings. You are but scandals to a civil woman. We had so much the goodwill of the neighbours before, we had credit for what we would; and but this morning the chandler refused to score a quart of scurvy-grass.

Sir Fred. Hang reputation among a company of rascals; trust me not if thou art not grown most wondrous pretty. [*Offers to hug her.*

Maid. Stand off, or I protest I'll make the people in your lodging know what a manner of man you are.

Sir Fred. You and I have been intimate acquaintance;—why so coy now, Jenny?

Maid. Pray forbear.——You'll never leave till I shriek out;——your servants listen. [*Noise within.*] Hark——there's somebody coming.

Enter BEAUFORT.

My mistress charged me to tell you she will never see your eyes again; she never deserved this at your hands,——Poor gentlewoman!——You had a fling at me too; you did not whisper it, I thank you. 'Tis a miserable condition we women bring ourselves to for your sakes. [*Weeps.*

Beauf. How now, cousin! what, at wars with the women?

Sir Fred. I gave a small alarm to their quarters last night, my lord.

Beauf. Jenny in tears! what's the occasion, poor girl?

Maid. I'll tell you, my lord.

Sir Fred. Buzz; set not her tongue a going again. [*Clapping his hand before her mouth.*] She has made more noise than half-a-dozen paper-mills: London

Bridge at a low water[1] is silence to her. In a word, rambling last night, we knocked at her mistress's lodging; they denied us entrance, whereupon a harsh word or two flew out, "Whore," I think, or something to that purpose.

Maid. These were not all your heroic actions.

Enter DUFOY.

Pray tell the consequence, how you marched bravely at the rear of an army of linkboys; upon the sudden, how you gave defiance, and then waged a bloody war with the constable; and having vanquished that dreadful enemy, how you committed a general massacre on the glass-windows. Are not these most honourable achievements, such as will be registered to your eternal fame by the most learned historians of Hicks's Hall.[2]

Sir Fred. Good sweet Jenny, let's come to a treaty; do but hear what articles I'll propose.

---

[1] Partly explained by a passage which Cunningham quotes from Beaumont and Fletcher's *The Woman's Prize.*

> *Petruchio.* What, are they mad? have we another Bedlam? They do not talk, I hope?
> *Sophocles.* Oh terribly!
> Extremely fearfully! the noise at London Bridge
> Is nothing near her.

[2] The Sessions House of the County of Middlesex. Built in 1612; taken down in 1782. Referred to by Pepys (Mynors Bright's ed., i. 226); cf., too, *Hudibras,* iii. c. 3:

> An old dull sot who told the clock
> For many years at Bridewell dock;
> At Westminster and Hicks's Hall,
> And *hiccius-doctius* play'd in all.

Maid. A woman's heart's too tender to be an enemy to peace. [*They whisper.*

Duf. Your most humble *serviteur*, my lord.

Beauf. Monsieur, I perceive you are much to blame; you are an excellent governor indeed.

Duf. Begar, do you tinké dat I amé de Bedlamé? no tingé but Bedlamé can governé himé.

Sir Fred. Jenny, here's my hand; I'll come and make amends for all——pretty rogue.——

Duf. Ver pret roguée, vid a poxé.

Maid. What rude French rascal have you here?

Duf. Rascalé! begar, ver it nod vor de reverence of my matré I vod cut off your occupation. French rascalé! whore English.——

Sir Fred. Dufoy, be gone, and leave us.

Duf. I vil, I vil leave you to your recreation; I vishé you ver good pastime, and de poxé, begar.

[*Exit* DUFOY.

Maid. I never heard a ruder fellow.——Sir Frederick, you will not fail the time.

Sir Fred. No, no, Jenny.

Maid. Your servant, my lord.

Beauf. Farewell, Jenny. [*Exit* JENNY.

Sir Fred. Now did all this fury end in a mild invitation to the lady's lodging.

Beauf. I have known this wench's mistress ever since I came from travel, but never was acquainted with that fellow that keeps her; prithee, what is he?

Sir Fred. Why, his name is Wheedle; he's one whose trade is treachery, to make a friend, and then deceive him; he's of a ready wit, pleasant conversation, thoroughly skilled in men; in a word, he knows so much of virtue as makes him well accomplished for all manner of vice. He has lately insinuated himself into Sir Nicholas Cully, one whom Oliver, for the transcendent knavery and disloyalty of his father, has dishonoured with knighthood; a fellow as poor in experience as in parts, and one that has a vainglorious humour to gain a reputation amongst the gentry, by feigning good nature and an affection to the king and his party. I made a little debauch th'other day in their company, where I foresaw this fellow's destiny; his purse must pay for keeping this wench, and all other Wheedle's extravagances. But, pray, my lord, how thrive you in your more honourable adventures? Is harvest near? When is the sickle to be put i' th' corn?

Beauf. I have been hitherto so prosperous, my happiness has still outflown my faith.
Nothing remains but ceremonial charms,
Graciana's fix'd i' th' circle of my arms.

Sir Fred. Then you're a happy man for a season.
Beauf. For ever.
Sir Fred. I mistrust your mistress's divinity; you'll find her attributes but mortal. Women, like jugglers' tricks, appear miracles to the ignorant; but in themselves they're mere cheats.

Beauf. Well, well, cousin; I have engaged that you this day shall be my guest at my Lord Bevill's table; pray make me master of my promise once.

Sir Fred. Faith, I have engaged to dine with my dear Lucy; poor girl, I have lately given her occasion to suspect my kindness; yet for your sake I'll venture to break my word, upon condition you'll excuse my errors; you know my conversation has not been among ceremonious ladies.

Beauf. All modest freedom you will find allowed; formality is banished thence.

Sir Fred. This virtue is enough to make me bear with all the inconveniences of honest company.

Beauf. The freeness of your humour is your friend: I have such news to tell thee that I fear thou'lt find thy breast too narrow for thy joy.

Sir Fred. Gently, my lord, lest I find the thing too little for my expectation.

Beauf. Know that thy careless carriage has done more than all the skill and diligence of love could e'er effect.

Sir Fred. What, has the widow some kind thoughts of my body?

Beauf. She loves you, and dines on purpose at her brother's house this day, in hopes of seeing you.

Sir Fred. Some women, like fishes, despise the bait, or else suspect it, whilst still it's bobbing at their mouths; but subtilely waved by the angler's hand, greedily hang themselves upon the hook. There are many so critically wise, they'll suffer none to deceive them but themselves.

Beauf. Cousin, 'tis time you were preparing for your mistress.

Sir Fred. Well, since 'tis my fortune, I'll about it. Widow, thy ruin lie on thy own head. Faith, my lord, you can witness 'twas none of my seeking.

[*Exeunt.*

SCENE III.—WHEEDLE'S LODGING.

Enter WHEEDLE *and* PALMER.

Wheed. Come, bear thy losses patiently.

Palm. A pox confound all ordinaries, if ever I play in an ordinary again—— [*Bites his thumb.*

Wheed. Thou'lt lose thy money. Thou hast no power to forbear; I will as soon undertake to reclaim a horse from a hitch he has learned in his pace, or an old mastiff from worrying of sheep.

Palm. Ay, ay, there is nothing can do it but hemp.

Wheed. Want of money may do much.

Palm. I protest, I had rather still be vicious than owe my virtue to necessity. How commendable is chastity in an eunuch! I am grown more than half virtuous of late: I have laid the dangerous pad now quite aside; I walk within the purlieus of the law. Could I but leave this ordinary, this square, I were the most accomplished man in town.

Wheed. 'Tis pity, thou art master of thy art; such a nimble hand, such neat conveyance.

Palm. Nay, I should have made an excellent juggler, faith.

Wheed. Come, be cheerful; I've lodged a deer shall make amends for all; I lacked a mau to help me set my toils, and thou art come most happily.

Palm. My dear Wheedle, who is it?

Wheed. My new friend and patron, Sir Nicholas Cully.

C

Palm. He's fat, and will say well, I promise you. Well, I'll do his business most dextrously, else let me ever lose the honour of serving a friend in the like nature.

Wheed. No more words, but haste, prepare for the design; habit yourself like a good thrifty countryman; get tools, dice and money for the purpose, and meet me at the Devil about three exactly.

Enter Boy.

Boy. Sir, Sir Nicholas Cully is without.

Wheed. Desire him to walk in. Here Palmer, the back way, quickly, and be sure——

Palm. Enough, enough, I'll warrant thee.

[*Exit* PALMER.

Enter SIR NICHOLAS CULLY.

Wheed. Sir Nicholas, this visit is too great a favour: I intended one to you; how do you find yourself this morning?

Cul. Faith, much the drier for the last night's wetting.

Wheed. Like thirsty earth which gapes the more for a small shower; we'll soak you thoroughly to-day.

Cul. Excuse me, faith, I am engaged.

Wheed. I am sorry for't; I meant you a share in my good fortune. But since it cannot be——

Cul. What? what good fortune?

Wheed. Nay, 'twill but vex you to know it, since you have not leisure to pursue it.

Cul. Dear Wheedle, prithee tell me.

Wheed. Now do I want power to keep it from you. Just as you came in at that door, went out at this a waiting-gentlewoman, sent with a civil message from her lady, to desire the happiness of my company this afternoon, where I should have the opportunity of seeing another lovely brisk woman, newly married to a foolish citizen, who will be apt enough to hear reason from one that can speak it better than her husband. I returned my humble thanks for the honour she did me, and that I could not do myself so great an injury to disobey her will. This is the adventure; but since you've business——

Cul. A pox on business. I'll defer it.

Wheed. By no means, for a silly woman; our pleasures must be slaves to our affairs.

Cul. Were it to take possession of an estate, I'd neglect it. Are the ladies Cavaliers?

Wheed. Oh, most loyal-hearted ladies.

Cul. How merry will we be then!

Wheed. I say, mind your business.

Cul. I'll go and put it off immediately. Where shall I meet you in the afternoon?

Wheed. You'll find me at the Devil about three o'clock, where I expect a second summons as she passes toward the City.

Cul. Thither will I come without fail; be sure you wait for me.   [*Exit* CULLY.

Wheed. Wait for thee, as a cat does for a mouse she intends to play with and then prey upon. How eagerly did this half-witted fellow chap up the bait!

like a ravenous fish that will not give the angler leave to sink his line, but greedily darts up and meets it half-way. [*Exit, laughing.*

Scene IV.—The Lord Bevill's House.

Enter Graciana, *and* Aurelia *immediately after her, with a letter in her hand.*

Grac. The sun's grown lazy; 'tis a tedious space
Since he set forth, and yet's not half his race.
I wonder Beaufort does not yet appear;
Love never loiters, love sure brings him here.
 Aurel. Brought on the wings of love, here I present
         [*Presenting the letter.*
His soul, whose body prisons yet prevent;
The noble Bruce, whose virtues are his crimes.
       [Graciana *rejects the letter.*
Are you as false and cruel as the times?
Will you not read the stories of his grief,
But wilfully refuse to give relief?
 Grac. Sister, from you this language makes me start:
Can you suspect such vices in my heart?
His virtues I, as well as you, admire;
I never scorn'd, but pity much his fire.
 Aurel. If you did pity, you would not reject
     [Graciana *rejects the letter again.*
This messenger of love: this is neglect.

Grac. 'Tis cruelty to gaze on wounds, I'm sure,
When we want balsam to effect their cure.

Aurel. 'Tis only want of will in you; you have
Beauty to kill, and virtue too to save.

Grac. We of ourselves can neither love nor hate:
Heaven does reserve the power to guide our fate.

Aurel. Graciana,——

Enter LORD BEVILL, LOVIS, *and the Widow.*

Grac. Sister, forbear; my father's here.

Lord Bev. So, girl; what, no news of your lover yet? our dinner's ready, and I am afraid he will go nigh to incur the cook's anger.

Wid. I believe he has undertook a hard task; Sir Frederick, they say, is no easy man to be persuaded to come among us women.

Lov. Sir,—— [LOVIS *and* LORD BEVILL *whisper.*
Lord Bev. What now?

Wid. I am as impatient as thou art, girl. [*To* GRACIANA.] I long to see Sir Frederick here.

Lord Bev. Forbear, I charge you on my blessing. Not one word more of Colonel Bruce.

Lov. You gave encouragement, sir, to his love; the honour of our house now lies at stake.

Lord Bev. You find by your sister's inclinations Heaven has decreed her otherwise.

Lov. But, sir,——

Lord Bev. Forbear to speak, or else forbear the room.

Lov. This I can obey, but not the other.
[*Exit* LOVIS.

Enter Footboy.

Footboy. Sir, my Lord Beaufort's come.

Lord Bev. 'Tis well.

Wid. D'ye hear, are there not two gentlemen?

Footboy. Yes, madam, there is another proper handsome gentleman. [*Exit Footboy.*

Lord Bev. Come, let's walk in, and give them entertainment.

Wid. Now, cousin, for Sir Frederick, this man of men; there's nothing like him.

[*Exeunt all but* AURELIA.

Aurel. With curious diligence I still have strove
[*Holding the letter in her hand.*
During your absence, Bruce, to breath your love
Into my sister's bosom; but the fire
Wants force; fate does against my breath conspire:
I have obey'd, though I cannot fulfil,
Against myself, the dictates of your will;
My love to yours does yield; since you enjoin'd,
I hourly court my rival to be kind;
With passion, too, as great as you can do,
Taught by those wounds I have received from you.
Small is the difference that's between our grief;
Yours finds no cure, and mine seeks no relief.
You unsuccessfully your love reveal;
And I for ever must my love conceal:
Within my bosom I'll your letter wear,
[*Putting the letter in her bosom.*
It is a tomb that's proper for despair. [*Exit.*

ACT II.

Scene I.—The Lord Bevill's House.

Enter Clark *and* Dufoy.

Clark.

METHINKS the wound your master gave you last night makes you look very thin and wan, monsieur.

Duf. Begar, you are mistaké, it be de woundé dat my metresse did give me long ago.

Clark. What, some pretty little English lady's crept into your heart?

Duf. No, but damned little English whore is creepé into my bone, begar; me could vish dat de *diable* vould také her vid all my harté.

Clark. You have managed your business ill, monsieur.

Duf. It vas the raskal *chirurgien* English dat did manage de business illé; me did putté my businessé into his haundé. He did stop de tapé, and de liquor did varké, varké, varké, up into de headé, and de shoulder, begar.

Clark. Like soap clapped under a saddle.

Duf. Here come my matré; holdé your peacé.

[*Exit* Clark.

Enter SIR FREDERICK, *Widow, and Maid.*

Sir Fred. Whither, whither do ye draw me, widow? what's your design?

Wid. To walk a turn in the garden, and then repose in a cool arbour.

Sir Fred. Widow, I dare not venture myself in those amorous shades; you have a mind to be talking of love I perceive, and my heart's too tender to be trusted with such conversation.

Wid. I did not imagine you were so foolishly conceited; is it your wit or your person, sir, that is so taking?

Sir Fred. Truly, you are much mistaken. I have no such great thoughts of the young man you see. Who ever knew a woman have so much reason to build her love upon merit? Have we not daily experience of great fortunes, that fling themselves into the arms of vain idle fellows? Can you blame me then for standing upon my guard? No, let us sit down here; have each of us a bottle of wine at our elbows; so prompted, I dare enter into discourse with you.

Wid. Would you have me sit and drink hand to fist with you, as if we were in the Fleece,[1] or some other of your beloved taverns?

Sir Fred. Faith, I would have thee come as near as possible to something or other I have been used to converse with, that I may the better know how to entertain thee.

Wid. Pray which of those ladies you use to con-

---

[1] In Covent Garden. Pepys was often there. Aubrey speaks of the tavern as "very unfortunate for homicides."

verse with, could you fancy me to look like? Be merry, and tell me.

Sir Fred. 'Twere too great a sin to compare thee to any of them; and yet thou hast so incensed me, I can hardly forbear to wish thee one of them. Ho, Dufoy! Widow, I stand in awe of this gentleman; I must have his advice before I dare keep you company any further.——How do you approve the spending of my time with this lady?

Duf. Ver vel, begar; I could vish I had never spend my time in de vorsé *compagnie*.

Wid. You look but ill, monsieur; have you been sick lately?

Duf. I have de ver great affliction in my mindé, madam.

Wid. What is it?

Duf. Truly, I havé de ver great passion vor dis jentelwoman, and she have no compassion at all vor me; she do refusé me all my *amour* and my *adresse*.

Wid. Indeed, Betty, you are to blame.

Maid. Out upon him for a French dissembler, he never spake to me in his life, madam.

Duf. You see, madam, she scorné me vor her *serviteur*.

Maid. Pray, when did you make any of your French lové to mé?

Duf. It vil breké my hearté to remember de time ven you did refusé me.

Wid. Will you permit me to serve you in this business, monsieur?

Duf. Madam, it be d'honour vor de King dé France.

Wid. Betty, whither run you?

Maid. I'll not stay to be jeered by a sneaking *valet-de-chambre.* I'll be revenged if I live, monsieur.

[*Exit* BETTY.

Wid. I'll take some other time.

Duf. Van you have de leisuré, madam.

Sir Fred. By those lips,——

Wid. Nay, pray forbear, sir.

Sir Fred. Who is conceited now, widow? Could you imagine I was so fond to kiss them?

Wid. You cannot blame me for standing on my guard so near an enemy.

Sir Fred. If you are so good at that, widow, let's see what guard would you choose to be at, should the trumpet sound a charge to this dreadful foe?

Wid. It is an idle question amongst experienced soldiers; but if we ever have a war, we'll never trouble the trumpet; the bells shall proclaim our quarrel.

Sir Fred. It will be most proper; they shall be rung backwards.

Wid. Why so, sir?

Sir Fred. I'll have all the helps that may be to allay a dangerous fire. Widows must needs have furious flames; the bellows have been at work, and blown 'em up.

Wid. You grow too rude, sir: I will have my humour, a walk i' th' garden; and afterwards we'll take the air in the park.

Sir Fred. Let us join hands then, widow.

Wid. Without the dangerous help of a parson, I do not fear it, sir.   [*Exit* SIR FREDERICK *and Widow.*

Duf. Begar, I do no caré two *sous* if de shambermaid ver hangé; be it not great deal better pretendé d'affection to her, dan to tellé de hole varldé I do take de medicine vor de clapé? Begar, it be de ver great deal better. [*Exit* DUFOY.

SCENE II.—A GARDEN BELONGING TO MY LORD BEVILL'S HOUSE.

Enter BEAUFORT *and* GRACIANA.

Beauf. Graciana, why do you condemn your love?
Your beauty without that, alas! would prove
But my destruction, an unlucky star,
Prognosticating ruin and despair.
   Grac. Sir, you mistake; 'tis not my love I blame,
But my discretion; [*pointing to her breast*] here the active flame
Should yet a longer time have been conceal'd,
Too soon, too soon I fear it was reveal'd.
Our weaker sex glories in a surprise,
We boast the sudden conquests of our eyes;
But men esteem a foe that dares contend,
One that with noble courage does defend
A wounded heart; the victories they gain
They prize by their own hazard, and their pain.
   Beauf. Graciana, can you think we take delight
To have our happiness against us fight;
Or that such goodness should us men displease,
As does afford us Heaven with greater ease?

Enter Lovis, *walking discontentedly.*

See where your brother comes; his carriage has been strange of late to me; I never gave him cause of discontent; he takes no notice of our being here. I will salute him.

Grac. By no means. Some serious thoughts, you see, employ his mind.

Beauf. I must be civil. Your servant, sir.

Lov. You are my sister's servant, sir; go fawn upon your mistress. Fare you well.　　　[*Exit* Lovis.

Beauf. Fare you well, if you are no better company. Heavens! What is the matter?　　[Graciana *weeps.*
What saucy sorrow dares approach your heart?
Waste not these precious tears. Oh! weep no more.
Should Heaven frown, the world would be too poor,
(Robb'd of the sacred treasure of your eyes)
To pay for mercy one fit sacrifice.

Grac. My brother, sir, is growing mad, I fear.

Beauf. Your brother is a man whose noble mind
Was to severest virtue still inclined;
He in the school of honour has been bred,
And all her subtle laws with heed has read:
There is some hidden cause; I fain would know
From whence these strange disorders in him flow.
Graciana, shall I beg you to dispel
These mists which round my troubled reason dwell?

Grac. It is a story I could wish you'd learn,
From one whom it does not so much concern:
I am th' unhappy cause of what you've seen;
My brother's passion does proceed from mine.

Beauf. This does confound me more; it cannot be;
You are the joy of all your family :
Dares he condemn you for a noble love,
Which honour and your duty both approve?

Grac. My lord, those errors merit our excuse
Which an excess of virtue does produce.

Beauf. I know that envy is too base a guest
To have a lodging in his generous breast ;
'Tis some extreme of honour, or of love,
Or both, that thus his indignation move.

Grac. Ere I begin, you my sad story end ;
You are a rival to his dearest friend.

Beauf. Graciana, though you have so great a share
Of beauty, all that see you rivals are ;
Yet during this small space I did proclaim
To you and to the world my purer flame,
I never saw the man that durst draw near,
With his ambitious love t'assault your ear.
What Providence has kept us thus asunder?

Grac. When I have spoke you'll find it is no wonder.
He has a mistress more renown'd than me,
Whom he does court, his dearer loyalty ;
He on his legs does now her favour wear;
He is confined by her foul ravisher.
You may not know his person ; but his name
Is strange to none that have conversed with fame.
'Tis Bruce.

Beauf. The man indeed I ne'er did see,

But have heard wonders of his gallantry.

Grac. This gallant man my brother ever loved;
But his heroic virtues so improved
In time those seeds of love which first were sown,
That to the highest friendship they are grown.
This friendship first, and not his love to me,
Sought an alliance with our family.
My sister and myself were newly come
From learning how to live, to live at home:
When barren of discourse one day, and free
With's friend, my brother chanced to talk of me.
Unlucky accident! his friend replied,
He long had wish'd their blood might be allied;
Then press'd him that they might my father move
To give an approbation to his love:
His person and his merits were so great,
He granted faster than they could entreat;
He wish'd the fates that govern hearts would be
So kind to him to make our hearts agree,
But told them he had made a sacred vow
Never to force what love should disallow.

Enter SIR FREDERICK *and Widow.*

But see, Sir Frederick and my aunt—
My lord, some other time I will relate
The story of his love and of its fate.

Sir Fred. How now, my lord? so grave a countenance in the presence of your mistress? Widow, what would you give your eyes had power to make me such another melancholy gentleman?

Wid. I have seen e'en as merry a man as yourself,

Sir Frederick, brought to stand with folded arms, and with a tristful look tell a mournful tale to a lady.

Enter a Footboy, who whispers SIR FREDERICK.

Sir Fred. The devil owes some men a shame; the coach is ready. Widow, I know you are ambitious to be seen in my company.

Wid. My lord, and cousin, will you honour me with yours to the park; that may take off the scandal of his?

Enter AURELIA *and* LETITIA.

Beauf. Madam, we'll wait upon you; but we must not leave this lady behind us.

Wid. Cousin Aurelia,——

Aurel. Madam, I beg you will excuse me, and you, my lord; I feel a little indisposition, and dare not venture into so sharp an air.

Beauf. Your servant, madam.

[*Exeunt all but* AURELIA *and* LETITIA.

Aurel. Retire: I would not have you stay with me,
I have too great a train of misery.
If virtuous love in none be cause of shame,
Why should it be a crime to own the flame?
But we by custom, not by nature led,
Must in the beaten paths of honour tread:
I love thee, Bruce; but Heaven, what have I done!
Letitia, did I not command you hence?

Letit. Madam, I hope my care is no offence:
I am afflicted thus to see you take
Delight to keep your miseries awake.

Aurel. Since you have heard me, swear you will be true :
Letitia, none must know I love but you.
Letit. If I at any time your love declare,
May I of Heaven and serving you despair.
Though I am young, yet I have felt this smart ;
Love once was busy with my tender heart.
Aurel. Wert thou in love?
Letit. I was.
Aurel. Prithee, with whom?
Letit. With one that like myself did newly bloom :
Methought his actions were above his years.

[*She weeps.*

Aurel. Letitia, you confirm me by your tears :
Now I believe you loved. Did he love you?
Letit. That had been more than to my love was due ;
He was so much above my humble birth,
My passion had been fitter for his mirth.
Aurel. And does your love continue still the same?
Letit. Some sparks remain, but time has quench'd the flame ;
I hope 'twill prove as kind to you, and cure
These greater griefs which, madam, you endure.
Aurel. Time to my bleeding heart brings no relief :
Death there must heal the fatal wounds of grief.
Letitia, come, within this shady bower
We'll join our mournful voices, and repeat
The saddest tales we ever learn'd of love.

AURELIA *and* LETITIA *walk into an arbour, and sing this song in parts.*

SONG.

When Phyllis watch'd her harmless sheep
  Not one poor lamb was made a prey ;
Yet she had cause enough to weep,
  Her silly heart did go astray :
Then flying to the neighb'ring grove,
  She left the tender flock to rove,
And to the winds did breathe her love.
    She sought in vain
    To ease her pain ;
The heedless winds did fan her fire ;
    Venting her grief
    Gave no relief,
But rather did increase desire.
Then sitting with her arms across,
  Her sorrows streaming from each eye ;
She fix'd her thoughts upon her loss,
  And in despair resolved to die.

Aurel. Why should you weep, Letitia, whilst we sing? [*Walking out of the arbour.*
Tell me from whence those gentle currents spring.
Can yet your faded love cause such fresh showers?
This water is too good for dying flowers.

Letit. Madam, it is such love commands this dew
As cannot fade; it is my love to you.

Aurel. Letitia, I am weary of this place; and yet I know not whither I should go.

Letit. Will you be pleased to try if you can sleep? that may deceive you of your cares a while.

Aurel. I will. There's nothing here does give me ease,
But in the end will nourish my disease. [*Exeunt.*

SCENE III.—A TAVERN.

Enter WHEEDLE, *and immediately after him a Footboy.*

Wheed. The hour is come; where's your master, sirrah?

Footboy. He'll be here immediately, sir.

Wheed. Is he neatly dressed?

Footboy. In the very suit he won th'other day of the Buckinghamshire grazier.

Wheed. Take this letter, and give it me when you perceive me talking with Sir Nicholas Cully, with recommendations from a lady; lurk in some secret place till he's come, that he may not perceive you at his entrance. \Oh! here's Palmer. [*Exit Footboy.*
Thom, what's the price of a score of fat wethers?

Enter PALMER.

Palm. Do they not well become me, boy?

Wheed. Nature doubtless intended thee for a rogue, she has so well contrived thee for disguises. Here comes Sir Nicholas.

Enter SIR NICHOLAS.

Sir Nicholas, come, come; this is an honest friend and countryman of mine.

Sir Nich. Your servant, sir. Is not the lady come by yet?

Wheed. I expect her every moment,——Oh! here's her boy. Well, what news?

Enter Boy.

Boy. My lady presents her service to you, sir, and has sent you this. [*Delivers a letter;* WHEEDLE *reads, and seems much displeased.*

Sir Nich. What is the matter, man?

Wheed. Read, read. [*Gives* CULLY *the letter.*] I want patience to tell you. Fortune still jades me in all my expectations.

Sir Nich. (*reading the letter*). *The citizen's wife forced to go to Greenwich with her husband; will meet some time next week.* Come, come, Wheedle, another time will do; be not so passionate, man.

Wheed. I must abuse my friend upon an idle woman's words.

Sir Nich. Pish, 'tis an accident. Come, let us drink a glass of wine, to put these women out of our heads.

Palm. Women? ho, boys! women, where are the women?

Wheed. Here's your merry countryman.

PALMER *sings.*
He took her by the apron,
To bring her to his beck;
But as he wound her to him,
The apron-strings did break.

Enter Drawer with wine.

Sir Nich. A merry man, indeed. Sir, my service to you. [*Drinks to* PALMER.

Palm. Thank you, sir. Come, Mr. Wheedle, remembering my landlord, i' faith; would he were e'en among us now. Come, be merry, man. Lend [*To* SIR NICHOLAS.] me your hand, sir; you look like an honest man; here's a good health to all that are so. Tope ——here pledge me.

[*Drinks; gives* SIR NICHOLAS *the glass.*

Sir Nich. Mr. Wheedle, to you.

[*Drinks, and leaves some in the glass.*

Palm. I'll not abate you an ace. 'Slid, you're not so honest as I took you for.

[SIR NICHOLAS *drinks up the rest.*

PALMER *sings.*

If any man baulk his liquor
Let him never baulk the gallows,
But sing a psalm there wi' th' vicar,
Or die in a dirty alehouse.

Enter Drawer.

Drawer. There's a countryman below desires to speak with his master Palmer.

Palm. So, so, thank thee, lad; it is my man. I appointed him to call here; he's sold the cattle, I'll warrant you. I'll wait upon you again presently, gentlemen. [*Exit* PALMER.

Wheed. Is not this a very pleasant fellow?

Sir Nich. The pleasantest I ever met with; what is he?

Wheed. He's a Buckingham grazier, very rich; he has the fat oxen and fat acres in the vale. I met him here by chance, and could not avoid drinking a glass o' wine with him. I believe he's gone down to receive money; it were an excellent design to bubble[1] him.

Sir Nich. How 'twould change his merry note! will you try him?

Wheed. Do you. I cannot appear in it, because he takes me for his friend.

Sir Nich. How neatly I could tope upon him!

Wheed. All things will pass upon him. I'll go your half; talk of dice, you'll perceive if he's coming. What money have you about you?

Sir Nich. Ten pieces.

Wheed. I have about that quantity too; here, take it. If he should run us out of our ready money, be sure you set him deep upon tick, if he'll be at you, that we may recover it; for we'll not pay a farthing of what we lose that way. Hush, here he comes.

Enter PALMER *with a bag of money under his arm, and flings it upon the table.*

Palm. All my fat oxen and sheep are melted to this, gentlemen.

Wheed. Their grease is well tried, sir.

---

[1] *i.e.* cheat. A slang word, though Mr. Spectator uses it: "he tells me with great passion that she has bubbled him."—*Spectator*, No. 89.

Sir Nich. Come, sir, for all your riches you are in arrear here. [*Offers him a glass.*

Palm. I'll be soon out of your debts. My hearty love to you, sir. [*Drinks.*] Would I had you both in Buckinghamshire, and a pipe of this canary in my cellar; we'd roast an ox before we parted; should we not, boy?

PALMER *sings.*

We'd sing, and we'd laugh, and we'd drink all the day;
Our reason we'd banish, our senses should sway;
And every pleasure our wills should obey.

Palm. Come, drink to me a brimmer, if you dare now.

Sir Nich. Nay, if you provoke me you'll find me a bold man. Give me a bigger glass, boy: so, this is fit for men of worship. Hang your retail drinkers; have at thee, my brave countryman. [*Drinks.*

Palm. I'll do all I can for my guts to pledge thee. Ho, brave boys! that's he, that's he, i' faith. How I could hug thee now! Mr. Wheedle, to you.

Wheed. I protest, gentlemen, you'll fright me out of your company. Sir Nicholas, shall we have the other round?

Sir Nich. Let's pause a while. What say you, gentlemen, if to pass away the time and to refresh us, we should have a box and dice, and fling a merry main among ourselves in sport?

Wheed. 'Twill spoil good company; by no means, Sir Nicholas.

Palm. Hang play among friends; let's have a wench.

Sings.

And Jenny was all my joy,
She had my heart at her will;
But I left her and her toy
When once I had got my fill.

What say you, shall we have her?
Sir Nich. We are not drunk enough for a wench.
Palm. Let's sing a catch then.
Wheed., Cull. Agreed, agreed.
Wheed. Begin, Mr. Palmer.

PALMER *sings, standing in the middle with a glass of wine in his hand.*

Palm. I have no design here,
    But drinking good wine here.
Wheed. Nor I, boy.
Sir Nich. Nor I, boy.
Wheed. Th' art my boy.
Sir Nich. Th' art my boy.
All three. Our heads are too airy for plots.
    Let us hug then all three,
    Since our virtues agree,
    We'll hollo and cast up our hats.

    [*They hollo whilst* PALMER *drinks, and then change till it has gone round.*

Sir Nich. Enough, enough.

Palm. Very good boys all, very good boys all. Give me a glass of wine there; fill a brimmer. Sir Nicholas, your lady.

Sir Nich. Pray, sir, forbear: I must be forced to leave your company else. Prithee, Wheedle, let's have a box and dice.

Wheed. We shall grow dull. Mr. Palmer, what say you to the business?

Palm. I do not understand dice. I understand good pasture and drink——hang the devil's bones.

[WHEEDLE *whispers* CULLY *to send for dice;* CULLY *whispers the Drawer.*

PALMER *sings.*

He that leaves his wine for boxes and dice,
Or his wench for fear of mishaps,
May he beg all his days, cracking of lice,
And die in conclusion of claps.

Enter Drawer with dice.

Palm. Come, come, gentlemen; this is the harmlesser sport of the two; a merry glass round.

Sir Nich. Excuse me, sir; I'll pledge you here. [*Takes dice.*] Come, come, sir, on six; six is the main.

Palm. The main? what's the main?

Sir Nich. Do not you understand hazard.

Palm. I understand dice or haphazard!

Sir Nich. Can you play at passage?

Palm. You pass my understanding. I can fling most at a throw, for a shot, or a glass of wine.

Sir Nich. Passage is easily learned: the caster wins if he fling above ten with doublets upon three dice.

Palm. How doublets?

Sir Nich. Two of a sort; two cinques, two treys, or the like.

Palm. Ho, ho! I have you.

Sir Nich. Come, set then.

Palm. I set you this bottle.

Sir Nich. Nay, nay, set money.

Palm. Is it a fair play, Mr. Wheedle? I trust to you.

Wheed. Upon my word, a very fair square play; but this table is so wet, there's no playing upon it.

Drawer. Will you be pleased to remove into the next room, gentlemen?

Sir Nich. I think 'twill not be amiss.

Wheed. Much better. Come, Mr. Palmer.

Palm. I'll follow, sir.

PALMER sings.

If she be not as kind as fair,
 But peevish and unhandy,
Leave her, she's only worth the care
 Of some spruce jack-a-dandy.
I would not have thee such an ass,
 Hadst thou ne'er so much leisure,
To sigh and whine for such a lass,
 Whose pride's above her pleasure.

Sir Nich. Ho, brave boy!

Palm. March on, march on.

Sings.
Make much of ev'ry buxom girl,
  Which needs but little courting;
Her value is above the pearl,
  That takes delight in sporting.
                    [*Exeunt omnes.*

ACT III.

Scene I.—A Tavern.

Enter Sir Nicholas Cully, Wheedle, Palmer, *and Drawer.*

Palm.

NAY, Sir Nicholas, for all your haste, I must have a note under your hand for the thousand pounds you owe me.

Wheed. This must not be among friends, Mr. Palmer; Sir Nicholas shall not pay the money.

Sir Nich. I had been a madman to play at such a rate if I had ever intended to pay.

Palm. Though I am but a poor countryman, I scorn to be choused. I have friends in town.

Wheed. But hark you, Mr. Palmer.

Palm. Hark me no harks; I'll have my money.

Sir Nich. Drawer, take your reckoning.

Wheed. (*laughing*). Farewell, sir; haste into the country to mind your cattle.

Palm. But hark you, gentlemen; are you in earnest?

Wheed. Ay, indeed; fare you well, sir.

Palm. I took you for my friend, Mr. Wheedle; but now I perceive what you are. [*To* Cully.] Your ear, sir.

Wheed. Never fear him; he dares not go into the field, without it be among his sheep.

Cul. Agreed; to-morrow, about eight in the morning, near Pancridge.[1]

Wheed. I will have the honour to serve you, Sir Nicholas. Provide yourself a second, Mr. Palmer.

[*Exeunt* SIR NICHOLAS *and* WHEEDLE *laughing.*

Palm. So, laugh. This is the sheep that I must fleece. [*Exit.*

SCENE II.—COVENT GARDEN.

Enter SIR FREDERICK FROLLICK, *with Fiddlers before him, and six or eight Linkboys, dancing and singing.*

Sir Fred. Here, here, this is the window; range yourselves here.

Enter the Bellman.

Bellman. Good morrow, gentlemen.

Sir Fred. Honest Bellman, prithee lend me thy bell.

Bellman. With all my heart, master.

[SIR FREDERICK *rings the bell, and then repeats these verses.*

---

[1] *i.e.* St. Pancras, a part of the town disreputable for many reasons; amongst others, for the weddings celebrated at its church. Cf. *The Way of the World*, i. 1. The favourite duelling grounds were the fields behind Montagu House and Barns Elms.

Sir Fred.

You, widow, that do sleep dog-sleep,
And now for your dead husband weep,
Perceiving well what want you have
Of that poor worm has eat in grave;
Rise out of bed and ope the door;
Here's that will all your joys restore.
Good morrow, my mistress dear, good morrow.
Good morrow, widow.
　　　　　　　　　　[*He rings the bell again.*

The Chambermaid comes to the window unlaced, holding her petticoats in her hand.

Maid. Who's that comes at this unseasonable hour, to disturb my lady's quiet?

Sir Fred. An honest bellman to mind her of her frailty.

Maid. Sir Frederick, I wonder you will offer this; you will lose her favour for ever.

Sir Fred. You're mistaken; now's the time to creep into her favour.

Maid. I'm sure you've waked me out of the sweetest sleep. Heigho!——

Sir Fred. Poor girl! let me in, I'll rock thee into a sweeter.

Maid. I hear a stirring in my mistress's chamber; I believe you've frighted her. 　　　[*Exit Maid.*

Sir Fred. Sound a fresh alarm; the enemy's at hand. 　　　　　　　　　[*Fiddlers play.*

The Widow comes to the window in her nightgown.

Wid. Whose insolence is this, that dares affront me thus?

Sir Fred. (*in a canting tone*). If there be insolence
        in love, 'tis I
Have done you this unwilling injury.

Wid. What pitiful rhyming fellow's that? He speaks as if he were prompted by the fiddlers.

Sir Fred. Alas! what pains I take thus to unclose
Those pretty eyelids which lock'd up my foes!

Wid. A godly book would become that tone a great deal better. He might get a pretty living by reading Mother Shipton's prophecies, or some pious exhortation at the corner of a street; his mournful voice, I vow, has moved my compassion.

Sir Fred. Ay, ay, we should have a fellow-feeling of one another indeed, widow.

Wid. Sir Frederick, is it you?

Sir Fred. Yes, truly; and can you be angry, lady? Have not your quarters been beaten up at these most seasonable hours before now?

Wid. Yes; but it has been by one that has had a commission for what he did. I'm afraid, should it once become your duty, you would soon grow weary of the employment.

Sir Fred. Widow, I hate this distance: 'tis not the English fashion; prithee let's come to it hand to fist.

Wid. I give no entertainment to such lewd persons. Farewell, sir. [*Exit Widow.*

Sir Fred. I'll fetch thee again, or conjure the whole Garden up. Sing the catch I taught you at the Rose.[1]

[*Fiddlers sing.*

SONG.

He that will win a widow's heart
Must bear up briskly to her :
She loves the lad that's free and smart,
But hates the formal wooer.

The Widow runs to the window again, with her Maid.

Wid. Hold, hold, Sir Frederick; what do you imagine the neighbours will think?

Sir Fred. So ill, I hope, of thee, thou'lt be forced to think the better of me.

Wid. I am much beholden to you for the care you have of my reputation.

Sir Fred. Talk no more, but let the door be opened; or else fiddlers——

Wid. Pray hold! What security shall I have for your good behaviour?

Sir Fred. My word.

Wid. That's pawned at the tavern from whence you came.

---

[1] A not inglorious ordinary, in Russell Street, Covent Garden. Pepys "drank some burnt wine" there on Christmas Eve, or rather Christmas morning, 3 a.m. (*circa*) 1667. It was conveniently near to the theatres; you could slip out from the King's House during the performance, have "a tankard of cool drink," and be back *en moins de rien.* Cf. Pepys, May 14th (and 18th), 1668.

Sir Fred. Thy own honesty then ; is that engaged ?

Wid. I think that will go nigh to secure me. Give 'em entrance, Betty. [*Exit Widow and her Maid.*

Enter PALMER, *with a link before him.*

Sir Fred. Ha ! who goes there ?

Palm. An humble creature of yours, sir.

Sir Fred. Palmer in a disguise ! what roguery hast thou been about ?

Palm. Out of my loyal inclinations doing service to his majesty.

Sir Fred. What ? a plotting ?

Palm. How to destroy his enemies ; Mr. Wheedle and I are very vigilant.

Sir Fred. In bubbling of somebody, on my life.

Palm. We do not use to boast our services, nor do we seek rewards ; good actions recompense themselves.

Sir Fred. Oh ! the door opens ; farewell, sirrah. Gentlemen, wait you without, and be ready when I call. Honest Bellman, drink this.

[*Gives the Bellman money.*

Bellman. Thank you, noble master. [*Exit Bellman.*

Sir Fred. (*entering*). Here's something to stop thy mouth, too. [*The Maid shrieks.*

Maid. Out upon you, Sir Frederick ; you'll never leave your old tricks. [*Exeunt.*

SCENE III.—THE WIDOW'S HOUSE.

Enter SIR FREDERICK, *leading the Widow, followed by her Maid.*

Sir Fred. Little did I think I should have been brought to this pass: love never had the power to rob me of my rest before.

Wid. Alas, poor gentleman! he has not been used to these late hours.

Sir Fred. Widow, do not you be peevish now; 'tis dangerous jesting with my affection; 'tis in its infancy, and must be humoured.

Wid. Pray teach me how, sir.

Sir Fred. Why, with kisses, and such pretty little dalliances; thus, thus. [*Kisses her.*

Wid. Hold, hold, sir; if it be so froward, put it out to nurse; I am not so fond of it as you imagine. Pray how have you disposed of your brave *camarades?* Have you left them to the mercy of the beadle?

Sir Fred. No, you must be acquainted with their virtues. Enter, gentlemen.

Enter the Fiddlers, and a Masque of the Linkboys, who are dancing-masters disguised for the frolic.

Wid. (*after the masque*). These are men of skill.

Sir Fred. I disguised 'em for your entertainment.

Wid. Well, sir, now I hope you'll leave me to my rest.

E

Sir Fred. Can you in conscience turn a young man out of doors at this time o' th' night, widow? Fie, fie, the very thought on't will keep you waking.

Wid. So pretty, so well-favoured a young man; one that loves me.

Sir Fred. Ay, one that loves you.

Wid. Truly 'tis a very hard-hearted thing.

[*She sighs.*

Sir Fred. Come, come, be mollified. You may go, gentlemen, [*To the Masquers.*] and leave me here; you may go.

Wid. You may stay, gentlemen; you may stay, and take your captain along with you. You'll find good quarters in some warm hayloft.

Sir Fred. Merciless woman! Do but lend me thy maid; faith, I'll use her very tenderly and lovingly, even as I'd use thyself, dear widow, if thou would'st but make proof of my affection.

Wid. If the constable carry your suspicious person to the Compter,[1] pray let me have notice of it; I'll send my tailor to be your bail.

Sir Fred. Go, go to bed, and be idle, widow; that's worse than any misfortune I can meet with. Strike up, and give notice of our coming. Farewell, widow; I pity thy solitary condition.

[*Exeunt; Fiddlers playing.*

---

[1] Compter, or Counters; they were prisons in the Poultry and Wood Street.

Scene IV.—Sir Frederick's Lodging.

Enter Dufoy *and* Clark.

Clark. I wonder Sir Frederick stays out so late.

Duf. Dis is noting; six, seven o'clock in the morning is ver good hour.

Clark. I hope he does not use these hours often.

Duf. Some six, seven time a veek; no oftiner.

Clark. My lord commanded me to wait his coming.

Duf. Matré Clark, to divertise you, I vil tell you how I did get be acquainted vid dis Bedlam matré. About two, tree year ago me had for my conveniance dischargé myself from attending

Enter a Footboy.

as *maître d'hôtel* to a person of condition in Paris; it hapen after de despatch of my little *affaire*.

Footboy. That is, after he'd spent his money, sir.

Duf. Jan foutré de lacque; me vil have de vip and de belle vor your breeck, rogue.

Footboy. Sir, in a word, he was Jack-pudding to a mountebank, and turned off for want of wit. My master picked him up before a puppet-show, mumbling a halfpenny custard, to send him with a letter to the post.

Duf. Morbleu, see, see de insolance of de footboy English; *bougre* rascale, you lie; begar, I vil cutté your troaté.   [*Exit Footboy*.

Clark. He's a rogue; on with your story, monsieur.

Duf. Matré Clark, I am your ver humble *serviteur;* but begar, me have no patience to be abusé. As I did say, after de despatché of my *affaire*, van day being idele, vich does producé de mellanchollique, I did valké over de New Bridge[1] in Paris, and to divertise de time and my more serious toughté, me did look to see de *marionettes* and the Jack-puddinge, vich did play hundred pretty triké, time de collation vas come; and vor I had no company, I vos unvilling to go to de *cabaret*, but did buy a *dariole*, littel custardé, vich did satisfie my apetite ver vel. In dis time young Monsieùr de Grandvil (a jentelman of ver great quality, van dat vas my ver good friendé, and has done me ver great and insignal *faveur*) come by in his *caroche*, vid dis Sir Frollick, who did pension at the same academy, to learn de language, de *bonne mine*, de great horse,[2] and many oder triké. Monsieur seeing me did make de bowé, and did beken, beken me come to him. He did tellé me dat de Englis jentelman had de letré vor de posté, and did entreaté me (if I had de oppertunity) to see de letré deliver. He did tellé me too, it vold be ver great obligation. De memory of de *faveur* I had receive from his famelyé, beside de inclination I naturally have to servé de strangeré, made me returné de complemen vid ver great civility, and so I did take de letré and see it

---

[1] The Pont Neuf, begun by Henry III. in 1578 and finished in the next reign: "a stately bridge," according to Evelyn, who describes it at some length, *Diary*, i. 46, ed. 1879.

[2] Apparently a proverbial expression. Lord Herbert of Cherbury tells us in his Autobiography how riding "the great horse" was one of the accomplishments he acquired at Paris.

deliveré. Sir Frollick perceiving (by de management of dis *affaire*) dat I vas man *d'esprit*, and of vitté, did entreaté me to be his *serviteur;* me did take d'affection to his personé, and vas contenté to live vid him, to counsel and to advisé him. You see now de lie of de *bougre* de lacque Englishe, *morbleu*.

Enter a Footman.

Footman. Monsieur, the apothecary is without.

Duf. Dat news be no ver velcome, begar. Matré Clark, go and sit you down ; I vil but swal my breakface, and be vid you again presant. *Morbleu*, l'apothecaré ! [*Exeunt.*

SCENE V.—A FIELD.

Enter WHEEDLE *and* CULLY.

Cul. Dear Wheedle, this is too dangerous a testimony of thy kindness.

Wheed. I should be angry with you if you thought so ; what makes you so serious ?

Cul. I am sorry I did not provide for both our safeties.

Wheed. How so ?

Cul. Colonel Hewson is my neighbour and very good friend. I might have acquainted him with the business, and got him with a file of musketeers to secure us all.

Wheed. But this would not secure your honour. What would the world have judged ?

Cul. Let the world have judged what it would. Have we not had many precedents of late, and the world knows not what to judge?

Wheed. But you see there was no need to hazard your reputation; here's no enemy appears.

Cul. We have done our duty, let's be going then.

Wheed. We ought to wait a while.

Cul. The air is so bleak, I vow I can no longer endure it.

Wheed. Have a little patience, methinks I see two making towards us in the next close.

Cul. Where, where? 'Tis them.

Wheed. Bear up bravely now like a man.

Cul. I protest I am the worst dissembler in cases of this nature.

Wheed. Along; look like a man of resolution. Whither, whither go you?

Cul. But to the next house to make my will, for fear of the worst. Tell them I'll be here again presently.

Wheed. By no means; if you give 'em the least occasion to suspect you, they'll appear like lions.

Cul. Well, 'tis but giving security for the money; that will bring me off at last.

Enter PALMER *and his Second.*

Palm. I see you ride the fore-horse, gentlemen.
[*All strip but* CULLY, *who fumbles with his doublet.*

Wheed. Good morrow, sir.

Sec. Come, sir, let us match the swords.
[*To* Wheedle.
Wheed. With all my heart. [*They match the swords.*

Palmer *sings.*

He had and a good right Bilboe blade,
Wherewith he used to vapour;
Full many a stubborn foe had made
To wince and cut a caper.

Sec. Here's your sword, sir. [*To* Palmer.
Palm. Come, sir, are you ready for this sport?
[*To* Cully.
Cul. By-and-by, sir. I will not rend the buttons from my doublet for no man's pleasure.
Wheed. Death, you've spoiled all; make haste.
Cul. Hang 'em, the devil eggs 'em on; they will fight.
Palm. What, will you never have done fumbling?
Sec. This is a shame; fight him with his doublet on; there's no foul play under it.
Palm. Come, sir, have at you. [*Making to* Cully.
Sec. Here, here, sir. [*To* Wheedle.
Wheed. I am for you, sir.
[Wheedle *and the Second seem to fight.*
Cul. Hold, hold, I beseech you, Mr. Palmer; hear me, hear me.
Wheed. What's the matter?
Cul. My conscience will not let me fight in a wrong cause; I will pay the money, I have fairly lost it.
Wheed. How contemptible is man, overcome by

the worst of passions, fear! it makes him as much below beasts as reason raises him above them; I will myself fight you both; come on, if you dare.——

Cul. Prithee, dear Wheedle, do but hear me.

Wheed. I disown all the kindness I ever had for you. Where are these men of valour, which owe their virtue to this man's vice? Let me go, I will chastise their insolence myself. [CULLY *holds him.*

Cul. Dear Wheedle, bear with the frailties of thy friends.

Wheed. Death! what would you have me do? Can I serve you with anything more dear than my life?

Cul. Let us give them security.

Wheed. Do you know what it is you would do? Have you considered what a thousand pounds is? 'Tis a fortune for any one man.

Cul. I will pay it all, thou shalt be no loser.

Wheed. Do you hear, shepherd? How do you expect this money?

Palm. I expect such security for it as my friend shall advise.

Sec. A warrant to confess a judgment from you both.

Wheed. You shall be damned first; you shall have nothing.

Palm. and Sec. We'll have your bloods.

[*They proffer to fight;* CULLY *holds* WHEEDLE.

Wheed. Let me go.

Cul. Dear Wheedle, let it be so. You shall have a judgment, gentlemen.

Wheed. I will take care hereafter with whom I engage. [*The Second pulls papers out of his pocket.* What? you have your tacklings about you?

Sec. We have articles for peace, as well as weapons for war.

Wheed. Despatch, despatch then; put me to no more torment with delays.

Sec. Come, Sir Nicholas, to the book. You see we are favourable, we grant you the benefit of your clergy.
[CULLY *subscribes on* PALMER'S *back, and then* WHEEDLE.
Your helping hand, good Mr. Wheedle, to finish the work.

Wheed. Take that into the bargain. [*Kicks him.*

Palm. You shall have another, if you please, at the price.

Sec. We seldom quarrel under a thousand pounds.

Palm. and Sec. We wish you merry, gentlemen.

PALMER *sings.*

Come, let's to the tavern 'scape,
  And drink whilst we can stand;
We thirst more for the blood o' th' grape
  Than for the blood of man.
[*Exeunt* PALMER *and Second.*

Wheed. Do you see now what men of mighty prowess these are?

Cul. I was to blame indeed.

Wheed. I am in such a passion I know not what to

do. Let us not stand gazing here; I would not have this known for a kingdom.

Cul. No, nor I neither. [*Exeunt.*

Scene VI.—The Lord Bevill's House.

Enter my Lord Bevill *and* Lovis.

Lov. 'Tis yet within your power, sir, to maintain
Our honour, and prevent this threatening stain.

L. Bev. Forbear this wicked insolence; once more
I charge you think on your obedience.
[*Exit* Lord Bevill.

Lov. Beauty, what art thou we so much admire?
Thou art no real, but a seeming fire,
Which, like the glowworm, only casts a light
To them whose reason passion does benight.
Thou art a meteor, which but blazing dies,
Made of such vapours as from us arise.
Within thy guilty beams lurk cruel fates,
To peaceful families and warring states.
Unhappy friend, to dote on what we know——

Enter a Servant.

Serv. Sir, Colonel Bruce, unexpectedly released from his imprisonment, is come to wait upon you.
[*Exit Servant.*

Lov. What shall I do? Ye powers above be kind,
Some counsel give to my distracted mind.

Friendship and shame within me so contend,
I know not how to shun or meet my friend.

Enter BRUCE.

Bruce. Where is my generous friend? Oh, noble
    youth!
How long have I been robb'd of this content?
                              [*They embrace.*
Though deprivation be the greatest pain,
When Heaven restores our happiness again,
It makes amends by our increase of joy,
Perfecting that which it did once destroy.
Dear friend, my love does now exact its due;
Graciana must divide my heart with you.
Conduct me to your sister, where I may
Make this my morn of joy a glorious day.
What means this sad astonishment?

Lov. How can we choose but with confusion greet,
When I your joys with equal sorrows meet?

Bruce. O Heaven! must my afflictions have no end?
I 'scaped my foe, to perish by my friend.
What strange disaster can produce this grief?
Is Graciana dead? Speak, speak; be brief.

Lov. She lives; but I could wish her dead.

Bruce. Rash man! why should your envy swell so
    high,
To wish the world this great calamity?
Wish the whole frame of nature were dissolved,
That all things to a chaos were revolved.
There is more charity in this desire,
Since with our loss our sorrows would expire.

Enter AURELIA.

Lov. Here comes Aurelia, sent for my relief:
Heaven knows her tongue can best express this grief.
Examine her, and you shall find e'er long
I can revenge, though not relate your wrong,
　Bruce. For pity haste, Aurelia, and declare
　　　　　　　　　　　　　　　[*Kisses her hand.*
The reasons of your brother's frighting care:
My soul is rack'd with doubts until I know.
　　　　　　　　　　　　　　　[*After a pause.*
Your silence and your looks, Aurelia, show
As if your kindness made you bear a part
Of those great sorrows that afflict his heart.
　Aurel. His passion is so noble and so just,
No generous soul can know it but it must
Lay claim unto a portion, as its due:
He can be thus concern'd for none but you.
　Bruce. Kind maid, reveal what my misfortunes are;
Friendship must not engross them, though it share.
I would not willingly my love suspect;
And yet I fear 'tis answer'd with neglect.
　Aurel. My sister, by unlucky stars misled,
From you and from her happiness is fled;
Unskilful in the way, by passion press'd,
She has took shelter in another's breast.
　Bruce. Fate, thou hast done thy worst, thy triumph
　　　sing;
Now thou hast stung so home, thou'st lost thy sting.
I have not power, Graciana, to exclaim　[*After a pause.*
Against your fault; indeed you are to blame.

Lov. Tell me, did she her promise plight, or give
Your love encouragement enough to live?
  Bruce. It was her pity sure, and not her love,
That made her seem my passion to approve.
My story was unpleasant to her ear
At first; but time had made her apt to hear
My love. She told me that it grew her grief,
As much as mine, my pain found no relief;
Then promised she'd endeavour the decrease
Of that in her which warr'd against my peace.
'Twas in this joyful spring of love that I
Was ravish'd from her by our enemy.
My hopes grew strong, I banish'd all despair;
These glowing sparks I then left to the care
Of this fair maid, thinking she might inspire
My passion, and blow up the kindling fire.
  Lov. Alas! she to my knowledge has been true;
She's spoke and sigh'd all that she could for you.
  Aurel. When you were forced to end, I did proceed,
And with success the catching fire did feed;
Till noble Beaufort, one unlucky day,
A visit to our family did pay;
Newly arrived from foreign courts, and fraught
With all those virtues that in courts are taught;
He with his amorous tales so charm'd her ear,
That she of love from none but him would hear.
  Bruce. That heart which I so long with toil and
    pain
Besieged and used all stratagems to gain,

  Enter a Servant, who whispers with LOVIS.

Is now become within a trice we see
The triumph of another's victory.
There is a fate in love, as well as war;
Some, though less careful, more successful are.

   Lov. Do not this opportunity withstand;
These lovers now are walking hand in hand
I' th' garden; fight him there, and sacrifice
His heart to that false woman's cruelties.
If fate be so unjust to make thee fall,
His blood or mine shall wait thy funeral.

   Bruce. Young man, this rashness must have my
      excuse,
Since 'tis your friendship does your fault produce;
If powers above did not this passion sway,
But that our love our reason did obey,
Your sister I with justice might accuse,
Nor would I this occasion then refuse.

   Lov. Does Bruce resolve thus tamely to decline
His interest and like foolish women pine?
Can that great heart which in your breast does dwell,
Let your fond griefs above your courage swell?

   Bruce. My passions grow unruly, and I find
Too soon they'll raise a tempest in my mind.
Graciana, like fond parents, you're to blame,
You did not in its youth correct my flame;
'Tis now so headstrong, and so wild a fire,
I fear to both our ruins 'twill conspire.
I grow impatient, friend; come lead me where
I may to her my injured love declare.
Graciana, yet your heart shall be my prize,
Or else my heart shall be your sacrifice.

Despair's the issue of ignoble minds,
And but with cowards entertainment finds.
					[*Exeunt* Lovis *and* Bruce.
Aurel. Heaven grant some moderation to this rage,
That reason their swell'd passions may assuage.
Oh, Bruce! thou little think'st the fates in me
Have to the full revenged thy injury.			[*Exit.*

Scene VII.—A Garden belonging to my Lord Bevill's House.

Enter Beaufort *and* Graciana.

Beauf. Madam, what you have told so much must move
All that have sense of honour or of love,
That for my rival I could shed a tear,
If grief had any power when you are near.
	Grac. Leave this discourse; your mistress you neglect,
And to your rival all your thoughts direct.

Enter Bruce *and* Lovis *and stand undiscovered.*

Beauf. Forgive me, dear Graciana, I have been
By my compassion sooth'd into a sin:
The holiest man that to the altar bows,
With wandering thoughts too often stains his vows.
	Bruce. Graciana, you are alter'd much. I find,
					[*Surprising her by the hand.*

Since I was here you've learn'd how to be kind,
The god of love, which subtly let you sway,
Has stol'n your heart and taught it to obey.
 Grac. Heavens! what strange surprise is this!
 Bruce. Hither I'm come to make my lawful claim;
You are my mistress and must own my flame.
 Beauf. Forbear, bold man, and do not tempt thy
   fate.   [*Taking her by the other hand.*
Thou hast no right; her love does right create.
Thy claim must to my title here give place:
'Tis not who loves, but whom she's pleased to grace.
 Grac. Hear me but speak, Bruce. You divide my
   care;
Though not my love, you my compassion share;
My heart does double duty; it does mourn
For you, brave Bruce; for you, brave Beaufort, burn.
 Bruce. Your pity but destroys; if you would save,
It is your love, Graciana, I must have.
 Beauf. Her love is mine, she did it now declare;
Name it no more, but vanish and despair.
 Bruce. Death, do you think to conjure me away!
I am no devil that am forced t'obey:
If you're so good at that, here are such charms
     [*Laying his hand on his sword.*
Can fright y'into the circle of her arms.
    [GRACIANA *takes* BEAUFORT *in her arms.*
 Beauf. Here is a sword more fit for my defence;
This is not courage, Bruce, but insolence.
Graciana, let me go, my heart wants room.
 Grac. My arms till now were ne'er thought trouble-
   some.

Bruce. Beaufort, I hope you've courage to appear
Where sacred sanctuary is not near.
I'll leave you now within that happy state,
Which does provoke my fury and my hate.
      [*Exeunt* BRUCE *and* LOVIS.
 Grac. You must not meet him in the field, to prove
A doubtful combat for my certain love.
Beside, your heart is mine; will you expose
The heart you gave me to its raging foes?
Those men want honour who stake that at play
Which to their friends their kindness gave away.
 Beauf. Graciana, why did you confine me so
Within your arms? You should have let me go:
We soon had finish'd this our hot debate,
Which now must wait a longer time on fate.
 Grac. None in combustions blame such as desire
To save their precious goods from raging fire.
Banish this passion now, my lord, and prove
Your anger cannot overcloud your love.
 Beauf. Your glorious presence can this rage control,
And make a calm in my tempestuous soul;
But yet there must be time; the sun does bear
Awhile with the fierce tempests of the air,
Before he makes those stormy conflicts cease,
And with his conquering beams proclaims a peace.
         [*Exeunt.*

F

ACT IV.

Scene I.

Enter LORD BEAUFORT *and* LOVIS.

Lovis.

FAREWELL, my lord, I'll to my friend declare
How generous you in your acceptance were.

Beauf. My honour is as forward as my love,
On equal wings of jealousy they move:
I to my rival will in neither yield;
I've won the chamber, and will win the field.

Lov. Your emulation, sir, is swoln so high,
You may be worthy of his victory:
You'll meet with honour blown, not in the bud,
Whose root was fed with vast expense of blood.

[*Exit* LOVIS.

Enter SIR FREDERICK.

Sir Fred. What, my lord, as studious as a country vicar on a Saturday in the afternoon? I thought you had been ready for the pulpit.

Beauf. I am not studying of speeches for my mistress; 'tis action that I now am thinking on, wherein there's honour to be gained; and you, cousin, are come luckily to share it.

Sir Fred. On my life, a prize to be played for your

mistress. I had notice of your quarrel, which brought me hither so early with my sword to serve you. But dares so zealous a lover as your lordship break the commandment of your mistress? I heard, poor lady, she wept, and charged you to sleep in a whole skin; but young men never know when they're well.

Beauf. Cousin, my love to her cannot make me forget my duty to my family.

Sir Fred. Pray, whose body must I exercise my skill upon?

Beauf. You met the man; Graciana's brother.

Sir Fred. An expert gentleman, and I have not fenced of late, unless it were with my widow's maids; and they are e'en too hard for me at my own weapon.

Beauf. Cousin, 'tis time we were preparing for the field.

Sir Fred. I wait to serve you, sir.

Beauf. But yet with grief, Graciana, I must go,
Since I your brother there shall meet my foe:
My fate too near resembles theirs, where he
Did wound himself that hurt his enemy.   [*Exeunt.*

Scene II.

Enter WHEEDLE, *and* PALMER *dressed like the* LORD BEVILL.

Wheed. So, my Proteus, exactly dressed! Dexterous rogue! Is Grace ready in her gears, and settled in my Lady Dawbwell's house?

Palm. Every trap is baited.

Wheed. I'll warrant thee then we catch our Cully. He's gone to put himself into a fantastic garb, in imitation of Sir Frederick Frollick; he's almost frantic with the very conceit of gaining the rich widow. But, hark! I hear him coming; slip down the back way, and to your charge. [*Exit* PALMER.

Enter CULLY.

Sir Nich. Wheedle, and what think you of this habit? is it not very modish?

Wheed. As any man need wear. How did you furnish yourself so suddenly?

Sir Nich. Suddenly? I protest I was at least at sixteen brokers before I could put myself exactly into the fashion; but now I defy Sir Frederick; I am as fine as he, and will be as mad as he, if that will carry the widow, I'll warrant thee.

Wheed. Is it not better pushing thus for a fortune before your reputation's blasted with the infamous names of coward and gamester, and so become able to pay the thousand pounds without noise, than going into the country, selling your land, making a havoc among your woods, or mortgaging your estate to a scrupulous scrivener that will whisper it into the ears of the whole town by inquiring of your good behaviour?

Sir Nich. Excellent Wheedle! And will my Lord Bevill speak my commendations to his sister?

Wheed. She is impatient till she see you, sir; for in my hearing, upon the account I gave him of you, he told her you were the prettiest, wittiest, wildest gentleman about the town, and a Cavalier in your heart, the only things that take her.

Sir Nich. Wheedle, come; I will go to the tavern and swallow two whole quarts of wine instantly, and when I am drunk ride on a drawer's back to visit her.

Wheed. Some less frolic to begin with.

Sir Nich. I will cut three drawers over the pate then, and go with a tavern-lantern before me at noonday. Come away.   [*Exeunt,* CULLY *singing.*

SCENE III.

Enter PALMER *and* GRACE.

Palm. Do not I look like a very reverend lord, Grace?

Grace. And I like a very fine lady, Mr. Palmer?

Palm. Yes, in good faith, Grace. What a rogue is that Wheedle, to have kept such a treasure to himself, without communicating a little to his friends!

[*Offers to kiss her.*

Grace. Forbear; you'll be out in your part, my lord, when Sir Nicholas comes.

Palm. The truth is, my lady, I am better prepared at this time to act a lover than a relation.

Grace. That grave dress is very amorous indeed.

Palm. My virtues, like those of plants in the winter, are retired; your warm spring would fetch 'em out with a vengeance.

Enter JENNY *in haste.*

Jenny. Mr. Wheedle and Sir Nicholas are come.
Palm. Away, away then; sister, expect your cue.

Enter WHEEDLE, *and* SIR NICHOLAS *kicking a tavern-boy before him, who has three bottles of wine on a rope hanging at his back.*

Cul. (*singing*). Then march along, boys;
　　　　　　　Valiant and strong, boys.
So, lay down the bottles here.
Wheed. My lord, this is the worthy gentleman that I told you was ambitious to be your sister's servant.
Cul. Hither am I come, my lord, to drink your sister's health, without offence, I hope.
Palm. You are heartily welcome, sir.
Cul. Here's a brimmer then to her, and all the fleas about her.
Palm. Sir, I'll call her to pledge it.
Cul. Stay, stay, my lord, that you may be able to tell her you have drunk it. [PALMER *drinks, and exit.* Wheedle, how do you like this? [*Draws his sword.* Shall I break the windows?
Wheed. Hold, hold; you are not in a house of evil reputation.
Cul. Well admonished, Sir Frederick Frollick.

Enter PALMER *and* GRACE.

Palm. This is Sir Nicholas, sister.
Cul. Ay, madam, I am Sir Nicholas, and how do you like me?

Grace. A pretty gentleman. Pray, sir, are you come a house-warming, that you bring wine with you?

Cul. If you ask such pert questions, madam, I can stop your mouth. [*Kisses her.*] Hither I am come to be drunk, that you may see me drunk; and here's a health to your flannel petticoat. [*Drinks.*

Grace. Mr. Wheedle, my service to you; a health to Sir Nicholas's great-grandfather's beard-brush.

[*She drinks part.*

Cul. Nay, pledge me; ha——

Grace. You are not quarrelsome in your drink, I hope, sir?

Cul. No, faith; I am wondrous loving. [*Hugs her.*

Grace. You are a very bold lover.

Cul. Widow, let you and I go upon the ramble to-night.

Grace. Do you take me for a nightwalker, sir?

Cul. Thou shalt be witness how many constables' staves I'll break about the watchmen's ears; how many bellmen I'll rob of their verses, to furnish a little apartment in the back side of my lodging.

Grace. I believe you're an excellent man at quarter-staff, sir?

Cul. The odds was on my head against any warrener in all our country; but I have left it off this two year. My lord, what say you? Do you think your sister and I should not furnish a bed-chamber as well as two soberer people? What think you, my lord?

Grace. Ay, and a nursery too, I hope, sir.

Cul. Well said, widow, i' faith; I will get upon thy body a generation of wild cats, children that shall waw, waw, scratch their nurses, and be drunk with their sucking-bottles.

Wheed. Brave Sir Nicholas!

Cul. Wheedle, give me a brimmer; the widow shall drink it to our progeny. [*Exit* GRACE. Where, where is she gone?

Palm. You have frighted her hence, sir.

Cul. I'll fright her worse if I find her in a corner. Ha, widow! I'll follow you, I'll follow you, ha!

[*Exit* CULLY.

Wheed. The wine makes the rogue witty; he overacts the part I gave him; Sir Frederick is not half so mad. I will keep him thus elevated till he has married Grace, and we have the best part of his estate at our mercy.

Palm. Most ingenious Wheedle!

Wheed. I was not born to ease nor acres; industry is all my stock of living. [*The women shriek within.*

Palm. Hark! he puts them to the squeak.

Wheed. We must go and take him off; he's as fierce as a bandog that has newly broke his chain.

[*Exeunt, laughing.*

SCENE IV.—A FIELD.

Enter BRUCE *and* LOVIS, *and traverse the stage.*

Then enter four or five Men in disguises.

1 *Man.* This way they went; be sure you kill the villain. Let pity be a stranger to your breasts.

2 Man. We have been bred, you know, unacquainted with compassion.

3 Man. But why, colonel, should you so eagerly pursue his life? He has the report of a gallant man.

1 Man. He murdered my father.

3 Man. I have heard he killed him fairly in the field at Naseby.

1 Man. He killed him, that's enough; and I myself was witness. I accused him to the Protector, and suborned witness to have taken away his life by form of law; but my plot was discovered, and he yesterday released; since which I've watched an opportunity, without the help of seeming justice, for my revenge. Strike home.——

3 Man. We are your hired slaves; and since you'll have it so, we'll shed his blood, and never spare our own. [*Exeunt, drawing their swords.*

Enter BEAUFORT *and* SIR FREDERICK, *and traverse the stage.*

Enter BRUCE *and* LOVIS *at another door.*

Bruce. Your friendship, noble youth, 's too prodigal;
For one already lost you venture all,
Your present happiness, your future joy;
You for the hopeless your great hopes destroy.

Lov. What can I venture for so brave a friend?
I have no hopes but what on you depend.
Should I your friendship and my honour rate
Below the value of a poor estate,
A heap of dirt? Our family has been
To blame; my blood must here atone the sin.

Enter the five Villains with drawn swords.

Heavens! what, is there an ambuscado laid!
Draw, dearest friend! I fear we are betray'd.

 1 *Vil.* Bruce, look on me, and then prepare to die.
          [*Pulling off his vizard.*

 Bruce. O treacherous villain!

 1 *Vil.* Fall on, and sacrifice his blood to my revenge.

 Lov. More hearts than one shall bleed if he must die.   [*They fight.*

Enter BEAUFORT *and* SIR FREDERICK.

 Beauf. Heavens! what's this I see! Sir Frederick, draw; their blood's too good to grace such villains' swords. Courage, brave men; now we can match their force.

 Lov. We'll make you, slaves, repent this treachery.
            [*The Villains run.*

 Beauf. So.

 Bruce. They are not worth pursuit; we'll let them go.
Brave men! this action makes it well appear
'Tis honour, and not envy, brings you here.

 Beauf. We come to conquer, Bruce, and not to see
Such villains rob us of our victory.
Your lives our fatal swords claim as their due;
We'd wrong'd ourselves had we not righted you.

 Bruce. Your generous courage has obliged us so,
That to your succour we our safety owe.

 Lov. You've done what men of honour ought to do,

What in your cause we would have done for you.
　Beauf. You speak the truth, we've but our duty done ;
Prepare : duty's no obligation.　　　　　[*He strips.*
　Bruce. My honour is dissatisfied ; I must,
　　　　　[Lovis *and* Sir Frederick *strip.*
My lord, consider whether it be just
To draw my sword against that life which gave
Mine but e'en now protection from the grave.
　Beauf. None come into the field to weigh what's right,
This is no place for counsel, but for fight :
Despatch.
　Bruce.　I am resolved I will not fight.
　Beauf. Did I come hither then only to fright
A company of fearful slaves away ?
My courage stoops not at so mean a prey.
Know, Bruce, I hither come to shed thy blood.
　Bruce. Open this bosom, and let out a flood.
　Beauf. I come to conquer bravely in the field,
Not to take poor revenge on such as yield.
Has nothing power, too backward man! to move
Thy courage ?　Think on thy neglected love :
Think on the beauteous Graciana's eyes ;
'Tis I have robb'd thee of that glorious prize.
　Bruce. There are such charms in Graciana's name,
　　　　　　　　　　　　[*Strips hastily.*
My scrupulous honour must obey my flame :
My lazy courage I with shame condemn :
No thoughts have power streams of blood to stem.
　Sir Fred. Come, sir, out of kindness to our friends,

you and I must pass a small compliment on each other. [*They all fight.*

[BEAUFORT, *after many passes, closes with* BRUCE; *they fall;* BEAUFORT *disarms him.*

Beauf. Here, live! [*Giving* BRUCE *his sword again.*
Bruce. My lord, you've gain'd a perfect victory;
You've vanquish'd and obliged your enemy.
Beauf. Hold, gallant men!
[BRUCE *and* BEAUFORT *part* LOVIS *and* SIR FREDERICK.

Lov. Before we bleed? Do we here fight a prize,
Where handsome proffers may for wounds suffice?
I am amazed! what means this bloodless field!
Bruce. The stoutest heart must to his fortune yield.
Brave youth! here honour did with courage vie,
[*To* BEAUFORT.
And both agree to grace your victory.
Heaven does with such a conquest favour few:
'Tis easier to destroy than to subdue.
Our bodies may by brutish force be kill'd;
But noble minds alone to virtue yield.
My lord, I've twice received my life from you;
Much is to both those generous actions due:
The noble giver I must highly prize,
Though I the gift, Heaven knows! as much despise.
Can I desire to live, when all the joy
Of my poor life its ransom does destroy?
No, no, Graciana's loss I'll ne'er survive:
I pay too dear for this unsought reprieve.
[*Falls on his sword, and is desperately wounded.*

Beauf. Hold, gallant man! Honour herself does bleed;
[*Running to him, takes him in his arms.*
All generous hearts are wounded by this deed.
Lov. He does his blood for a lost mistress spend;
And shall not I bleed for so brave a friend?
[Lovis *offers to fall on his sword, but is hindered by* Sir Frederick.
Sir Fred. Forbear, sir, the frolic's not to go round, as I take it.
Beauf. 'Twere greater friendship to assist me here; I hope the wound's not mortal, though I fear——
Bruce. My sword, I doubt, has fail'd in my relief; 'T has made a vent for blood, but not for grief.
[Bruce *struggling,* Lovis *and* Sir Frederick *help to hold him.*
Let me once more the unkind weapon try:
Will ye prolong my pain? oh, cruelty!
Lov. Ah, dearest Bruce, can you thus careless be
Of our great friendship and your loyalty?
Look on your friend; your drooping country view;
And think how much they both expect from you.
You for a mistress waste that precious blood
Which should be spent but for our master's good.
Sir Fred. Expense of blood already makes him faint; let's carry him to the next house, till we can procure a chair to convey him to my Lord Bevill's, the best place for accommodation.
[*They all take him up.*
Beauf. Honour has play'd an after game; this field
The conqueror does unto the conquer'd yield. [*Exeunt.*

Scene V.

Enter GRACIANA *weeping.*

Grac. Farewell all thoughts of happiness, farewell!
My fears together with my sorrows swell:
While from my eyes there flows this crystal flood
From their brave hearts there flow such streams of blood.
Here I am lost, while both for me contend;
With what success can this strange combat end?
Honour with honour fights for victory,
And love is made the common enemy.

Enter LORD BEVILL.

L. Bev. Weeping! Ah, child!——
Grac. Kill me not with expectation, sir.
L. Bev. The generous Bruce has killed himself for you. Being disarmed and at his rival's mercy, his life and sword were given him by the noble youth. He made a brave acknowledgment for both; but then, considering you were lost, he scorned to live; and, falling on his sword, has given himself a mortal wound. [*Exit* LORD BEVILL.

Enter AURELIA *weeping.*

Aurel. Cruel Graciana, go but in and see
The fatal triumph of your victory.

The noble Bruce, to your eternal shame,
With his own blood has quench'd his raging flame,
   Grac. (*weeping*). My carriage shall in these misfor-
      tunes prove
That I have honour too, as well as love.
   Aurel. (*aside*). Thy sorrows, sad Aurelia, will declare
At once, I fear, thy love and thy despair:
These streams of grief straight to a flood will rise;
I can command my tongue, but not my eyes.
                              [*Exit* AURELIA.
   Grac. In what a maze, Graciana, dost thou tread!
Which is the path that doth to honour lead?
I in this labyrinth so resolve to move,
That none shall judge I am misled by love.

           Enter BEAUFORT.

   Beauf. Here conquerors must forget their victories,
And homage pay to your victorious eyes.
Graciana, hither your poor slave is come
After his conquest to receive his doom:
Smile on his victory; had he proved untrue
To honour, he had then proved false to you.
   Grac. Perfidious man, can you expect from me
An approbation of your treachery?
When I, distracted with prophetic fears,
Blasted with sighs, and almost drown'd in tears,
Begg'd you to moderate your rage last night,
Did you not promise me you would not fight?
Go now and triumph in your victory;
Into the field you went my enemy,
And are return'd the only man I hate,

The wicked instrument of my sad fate.
My love has but dissembled been to thee,
To try my generous lover's constancy. [*Exit* GRACIANA.
    Beauf. Oh, Heaven! how strange and cruel is my fate!
Preserved by love, to be destroy'd by hate!
                                 [*Exit* BEAUFORT.

SCENE VI.—THE WIDOW'S HOUSE.

Enter BETTY *and* LETITIA (*the two chambermaids*) *severally.*

Betty. Oh, Lettice, we have stayed for you.

Letit. What hast thou done to the Frenchman, girl? He lies yonder neither dead nor drunk; nobody knows what to make of him.

Betty. I sent for thee to help make sport with him; he'll come to himself, never fear him. Have you not observed how scurvily he's looked of late?

Letit. Yes; and he protests it is for love of you.

Betty. Out upon him, for a dissembling rascal! he's got the foul disease; our coachman discovered it by a bottle of diet-drink he brought and hid behind the stairs, into which I infused a little opium.

Letit. What dost intend to do with him?

Betty. You shall see.

Enter Coachman with a tub without a bottom, which should at the top be locked, and a hole to put one's head out at, made easy to be borne on one's shoulders.

Coachman. Here's the tub; where's the Frenchman?

Betty. He lies behind the stairs; haste and bring him in, that he may take quiet possession of his wooden tenement; for 'tis near his time of waking.

[*The Coachman and another servant bring in* DUFOY, *and put him into the tub.*

Is the fiddler at hand that used to play at the blind alehouse?

Coachman. He's ready.

Enter a Fiddler.

Betty. Well, let's hear now what a horrible noise you can make to wake this gentleman.

[*Fiddler plays a tune.*

Letit. He wants a helping hand; his eyelids are sealed up; see how the wax sticks upon 'em.

[DUFOY *begins to wake.*

Let me help you, monsieur.

Duf. Vat aré you? Jernie! vat is dis? Am I Jack in a boxé? Begar, who did putté me here?

Betty. Good-morrow, monsieur; will you be pleased to take your pills this morning?

Duf. Noé; but I vo'd have de *diable* take youé; it vas youé dat did abusé me dus, vas it noté? Begar, I vil killé ale de shambermaid in Englandé.

Letit. Will you be pleased to drink, monsieur? There's a bottle of your diet-drink within.

Duf. Are youé de littel *diable* come to tormenté mé? *Morbleu!* vas ever man afronté in dis naturé!

Betty. Methinks he has *fort bonne mine,* monsieur.

G

Now, if you please to make your little *adresse* and your *amour*, you will not find me so coy.

Duf. Begar, I vil no marié de cousin-germane of de *diable*.

Letit. What should he do with a wife? He has not house-room for her.

Betty. Why do you not keep your head within doors, monsieur?

Letit. Now there's such a storm abroad.

Duf. Why did not youé keep your maidenheadé vid in dooré? Begar; tellé me daté.

Coachman. Have you any fine French commodities to sell—gloves and ribbons? You've got a very convenient shop, monsieur.

Duf. I do hope you vil have verié convenient halteré, begar. Jernie! can I not taré dis tingé in de picés?

Betty. You begin to sweat, monsieur; the tub is proper for you.

Duf. I have no more patiencé; I vil breaké dis prison, or I vil breaké my neké, and ye shall alé be hangé. [*Struggles to get out.*

Letit. He begins to rave; bless the poor man!

Betty. Some music quickly to compose his mind!
[*The music plays, and they dance about him.*
How prettily the snail carries his tenement on his back!
[*He walks with the tub on his back.*
I'm sorry I am but his mistress: if I had been your wife, monsieur, I had made you a complete snail; your horns should have appeared.

Duf. I vil have de patiencé, dere is no oder

remedé; you be alé de raskalé whore; de *diable* take you alé; and I vil say no more, begar.

Betty. This is a very fine vessel and would swim well; let's to the horse-pond with him.

Letit. Come, come, he looks as sullenly as a hare in her form; let's leave him.

Coachman. Your *serviteur très humble*, monsieur.

[*Exeunt all but* DUFOV.

Duf. Bougre! I canno hangé myselfé; begar, I canno drowné myselfé; I vil go hidé myselfé, and starvé to dyé; I vil no be de laughé for every jackanapé Englishé. *Morbleu!*

SCENE VII.

SIR FREDERICK *is brought in upon a bier, with a mourning cloth over him, attended by a Gentleman in a mourning cloak. Four Fiddlers carry the corpse, with their instruments tucked under their cloaks.*

Enter the Widow weeping.

Mourner. Madam,[1] you must expect a bloody consequence
When men of such prodigious courage fight.
The young Lord Beaufort was the first that fell,
After his sword too deeply had engaged
His rival not to stay behind him long.
Sir Frederick with your nephew bravely fought;
Death long did keep his distance, as if he

[1] The speech is printed as verse in the old copies.

Had fear'd excess of valour; but when they,
O'erloaded with their wounds, began to faint,
He with his terrors did invade their breasts.
Fame soon brought many to the tragic place,
Where I found my dearest friend, Sir Frederick,
Almost as poor in breath as blood :
He took me by the hand, and all the stock he'd left
He spent, madam, in calling upon you.
He first proclaim'd your virtues, then his love ;
And having charged me to convey his corpse hither,
To wait on you, his latest breath expired with
The command.

Wid. The world's too poor to recompense this loss.
Unhappy woman ! why should I survive
The only man in whom my joys did live?
My dreadful grief !   [*The Fiddlers prepare.*

Enter DUFOY *in his tub.*

Duf. Oh, my matré, my matré ! who has kill my matré?   *Morbleu!* I vil——
              [*The Widow shrieks and runs out; all the
                        Fiddlers run out in a fright.*
Oh, de *diable*, de *diable !*
       [SIR FREDERICK *starts up, which frights* DUFOY.
Sir Fred. What devilish accident is this ? Or has the widow undermined me?

Enter the Widow and her Maid laughing.

I shall be laughed to death now, indeed, by chambermaids. Why have you no pity, widow ?

Wid. None at all for the living; ha, ha, ha! You see we're provided for your frolic, sir; ha, ha!

Sir Fred. Laugh but one minute longer, I will forswear thy company, kill thy tabby cat, and make thee weep for ever after.

Wid. Farewell, sir; expect at night to see the old man, with his paper lantern and cracked spectacles, singing your woeful tragedy to kitchenmaids and cobblers' 'prentices.

[*Widow offers to go,* SIR FREDERICK *holds her by the arm.*

Sir Fred. Hark you, hark you, widow. By all those devils that have hitherto possessed thy sex——

Wid. No swearing, good Sir Frederick.

Sir Fred. Set thy face then; let me not see the remains of one poor smile. So now I will kiss thee and be friends. [*Widow falls out a-laughing.* Not all thy wealth shall hire me to come within smell of thy breath again. Jealousy and, which will be worse for thee, widow, impotence light upon me, if I stay one moment longer with thee. [*Offers to go.*

Wid. Do you hear, sir; can you be so angry with one that loves you so passionately she cannot survive you?

Sir Fred. Widow, may the desire of man keep thee waking till thou art as mad as I am.

[*Exit* SIR FREDERICK.

Wid. How lucky was this accident! How he would have insulted over my weakness else!
Sir Frederick, since I've warning, you shall prove
More subtile ways, before I own my love. [*Exeunt.*

ACT V.

Scene I.—The Lord Bevill's House.

Enter LOVIS, *a Surgeon, Servants carrying* BRUCE *in a chair.*

Surgeon.

COURAGE, brave sir; do not mistrust my art.
   Bruce. Tell me, didst thou e'er cure a wounded heart?
Thy skill, fond man! thou here employ'st in vain;
The ease thou giv'st does but increase my pain.
   Lov. Dear Bruce, my life does on your life depend;
Though you disdain to live, yet save your friend.
   Bruce. Do what you please; but are not those unkind
That ease the body to afflict the mind?
                               [The Surgeon dresses him.
Oh, cruel love! thou shoot'st with such strange skill,
The wounds thou mak'st will neither heal nor kill:
Thy flaming arrows kindle such a fire
As will not waste thy victims, nor expire!

Enter AURELIA.

   Lov. Is the wound mortal? tell me, [*To the Surgeon.*] or may we cherish hopes of his recovery?

Surg. The danger is not imminent. Yet my prognostic bodes a sad event; for though there be no great vessel dissected, yet I have cause to fear that the *parenchyma* of the right lobe of the lungs, near some large branch of the *asperia arteria,* is perforated.

Lov. Tell me, in English, will he live or die?

Surg. Truly, I despair of his recovery.

[*Exit Surgeon.*

Aurel. (aside). Forgive me, ladies, if excess of love
Me beyond rules of modesty does move,
And, against custom, makes me now reveal
Those flames my tortured breast did long conceal;
'Tis some excuse, that I my love declare
When there's no medicine left to cure despair.

[*Weeps by the chair-side.*

Bruce. Oh, Heaven! can fair Aurelia weep for me?
This is some comfort to my misery.
Kind maid, those eyes should only pity take
Of such as feel no wounds but what they make:
Who for another in your sight does mourn
Deserves not your compassion, but your scorn.

Aurel. I come not here with tears to pity you;
I for your pity with this passion sue.

Bruce. My pity! tell me, what can be the grief
That from the miserable hopes relief?

Aurel. Before you know this grief, you feel the pain.

Bruce. You cannot love, and not be loved again:
Where so much beauty does with love conspire,
No mortal can resist that double fire.

Aurel. When proud Graciana wounded your brave
  heart,

On poor Aurelia's you revenged the smart :
While you in vain did seek those wounds to cure,
With patience I their torture did endure.

Bruce. My happiness has been so long conceal'd,
That it becomes my misery reveal'd :
That which should prove my joy, now proves my grief,
And that brings pain, which, known, had brought relief.
Aurelia, why would you not let me know,
While I had power to pay, the debt I owe?
'Tis now too late; yet all I can I'll do,
I'll sigh away the breath I've left for you.

Aurel. You yet have power to grant me all I crave;
'Tis not your love I court, I court your grave.
I with my flame seek not to warm your breast,
But beg my ashes in your urn may rest :
For since Graciana's loss you scorn'd t'outlive,
I am resolved I'll not your death survive.

Bruce. Hold, you too generous are; yet I may live:
Heaven for your sake may grant me a reprieve.

Aurel. Oh, no ; Heaven has decreed, alas ! that we
Should in our fates, not in our loves agree.

Bruce. Dear friend, my rashness I too late repent;
I ne'er thought death till now a punishment.

[*To* Lovis.

Enter GRACIANA.

Grac. Oh, do not talk of death ! the very sound
Once more will give my heart a mortal wound :
Here on my knees, I've sinn'd, I must confess,

Against your love and my own happiness;
I, like the child, whose folly proves his loss,
Refused the gold and did accept the dross.

Bruce. You have in Beaufort made so good choice,
His virtue's such, he has his rival's voice;
Graciana, none but his great soul could prove
Worthy to be the centre of your love.

Grac. You to another would such virtue give,
Brave sir, as in yourself does only live.
If to the most deserving I am due,
He must resign his weaker claim to you.

Bruce. This is but flattery; for I'm sure you can
Think none so worthy as that generous man :
By honour you are his.

Grac. Yet, sir, I know
How much I to your generous passion owe;
You bleed for me; and if for me you die,
Your loss I'll mourn with vow'd virginity.

Bruce. Can you be mindful of so small a debt,
And that which you to Beaufort owe forget?
That will not honour but injustice be :
Honour with justice always does agree.
This generous pity which for me you show,
Is more than you to my misfortunes owe :
These tears, Graciana, which for me you shed,
O'erprize the blood which I for you have bled :
But now I can no more——
My spirits faint within my wearied breast.

Lov. Sister, 'tis fit you give him leave to rest.
Who waits?

Enter Servants.

With care convey him to his bed.
Bruce. Hold——
Dearest Aurelia, I will strive to live,
If you will but endeavour not to grieve.
    Lov. Brave man! The wonder of this age thou'lt prove,
For matchless gratitude and generous love.
                             [*Exeunt all but* GRACIANA.
    Grac. How strangely is my soul perplex'd by fate!
The man I love I must pretend to hate,
And with dissembled scorn his presence fly,
Whose absence is my greatest misery!

Enter BEAUFORT.

    Beauf. Hear me, upon my knees I beg you'll hear.
She's gone.   [*Exit* GRACIANA.
There was no need, false woman! to increase
My misery with hopes of happiness.
This scorn at first had to my love and me
But justice been; now it is cruelty.
Was there no way his constancy to prove,
But by your own inconstancy in love?
To try another's virtue could you be,
Graciana, to your own an enemy?
Sure 'tis but passion which she thus does vent,
Blown up with anger and with discontent;
Because my honour disobey'd her will,
And Bruce for love of her his blood did spill.
I once more in her eyes will read my fate;
I need no wound to kill me, if she hate.

Scene II.

Enter Cully *drunk, with a blind Fellow led before him playing on a cymbal, followed by a number of Boys holloing and persecuting him.*

Cul. Villains, sons of unknown fathers, tempt me no more. [*The Boys shout at him, he draws his sword.* I will make a young generation of cripples to succeed in Lincoln's Inn Fields [1] and Covent Garden. The barbarous breeding of these London boys!

[*Frights the Boys away.*

Boy that leads the Cymbal. Whither do you intend to go, sir?

Cul. To see the wealthy widow, Mrs. Rich.

Boy. Where does she dwell, sir?

Cul. Hereabouts; inquire; I will serenade her at noonday. [*Exeunt.*

Enter the Widow and her Maid Betty.

Wid. Where is this poor Frenchman, girl? he's done me good service.

Betty. The butler has got him down into the cellar,

---

[1] "Frequented," says Cunningham, *Handbook to London*, "from a very early period down to the year 1735, by wrestlers, bowlers, cripples, beggars, and idle boys." Gay warns his readers:

> Where Lincoln's Inn, wide space, is railed around
> Cross not with venturous step.

madam, made him drunk, and laid him to sleep among his empty casks.

Wid. Pray, when he wakes let him be released of his imprisonment. Betty, you use your servant too severely. Hark! what ridiculous noise is that?

[*The Cymbal plays without.*

It sets my teeth on edge worse than the scraping of trenchers.

Enter a Servant.

Serv. Madame, a rude drunken fellow, with a cymbal before him, and his sword in his hand, is pressed into your house.

Enter CULLY *and Cymbal; the Women shriek.*

Cul. Sirrah, play me a bawdy tune, to please the widow. Have at thee, widow!

Betty. 'Tis one of Oliver's knights,[1] madam, Sir Nicholas Cully; his mother was my grandmother's dairymaid.

Enter Servants; they lay hands on him, and take away his sword.

Cul. Let me go; I am not so drunk but I can stand without your help, gentlemen. Widow, here is music; send for a parson, and we will dance Barnaby within this half-hour.

Wid. I will send for a constable, sir.

---

[1] Compare scene 2 in the first act: "one whom Oliver . . . has dishonoured with knighthood." Fifty years earlier James I.'s knights had been a butt for satire. Etheredge lets us know periodically that he was a Royalist.

Cul. Hast a mind to see me beat him? How those rogues dread me! Did not Wheedle tell thee upon what conditions I would condescend to make thee my bedfellow; widow, speak!

Wid. This is some drunken mistake; away with him; thrust him out of door.

Enter a Servant; clashing of swords and noise without.

Serv. Help, help, for Sir Frederick!

Wid. What's the matter?

Serv. He is fighting, madame, with a company of bailiffs that would arrest him at the door.

Wid. Haste everyone and rescue him quickly.
[*Exeunt all but* CULLY.

Cul. Widow, come back. I say, widow, I will not stir one foot after thee. Come back, I say, widow.
[*Falls down and sleeps.*

Enter DUFOY.

Duf. Vat de *diable* be de matré? here is de ver strange varké in dis house; de vemen day do cry, ha, ha, ha; de men day do run, day do take de baton, de dung-vorké, and de vire-vorké; vat is here, van killé? [*Looking on* CULLY.

Enter BETTY.

Betty. You are a trusty servant, indeed. Here you are locked up, while your poor master is arrested and dragged away by unmerciful bailiffs.

Duf. My matré? Jernie! Metres Bet, letté me go;

begar, I vil kill allé de *bougres* de bailié, and recover my matré. *Bougres* de bailié!

Betty. So, make all the haste you can.

[*She helps him out of the tub.*

Duf. Morbleu! bougres de bailié! I vil go prepare to killé a tousand bailié, begar. *Bougres* de bailié! [*Exit.*

Enter the Widow and Servant severally.

Wid. Well, what news?

Serv. Madam, they have arrested him upon an execution for two hundred pounds, and carried him to a bailiff's house hard by.

Wid. If that be all, Betty, take my key and give him the money in gold; do you content the bailiffs, but let Sir Frederick know nothing of it; and then let them bring him to my house as their prisoner. Despatch. [*Exeunt* BETTY *and Servant.*

Enter a Footboy.

Footboy. Pray, madam, is there not a stray gentleman here, misled by drink?

Wid. There lies the beast you look for; you had best remove him quickly, or I shall cause him to be put into the pound. [*Exit Widow.*

Footboy. If I do not get this fool clear off before he comes to himself, our plot is quite spoiled. This summer livery may chance to hover over my shivering limbs next winter. Yonder sits honest Palmer, my poor master, in a coach, quaking for fear; all that see him in that reverend disguise will swear he has got the palsy. Ho, Sir Nicholas! [*Pulls him.*

Cul. I will drink three beer-glasses to the widow's health before I go.

Footboy. The widow stays for you to wait upon her to the Exchange.

Cul. Let her go into her bedchamber and meditate; I am not drunk enough to be seen in her company.

Footboy. I must carry him away upon my back; but since things may go ill, 'tis good to make sure of something. I'll examine his pockets first. So, for this I thank my own ingenuity; in this way of plain dealing I can live without the help of my master.

Enter a Servant.

Pray, sir, will you help me up with my burden?

Serv. I am sure your master has his load already.

[*They lift him up.*

Cul. Carry me to my widow, boy. Where is my music?

Enter Sir Frederick *with the Bailiffs, who are Fiddlers disguised, with their fiddles under their coats, at one door, and the Widow at another.*

Boy. There is no hopes now; I'll shift for myself.

[*Exit Boy.*

Sir Fred. Widow, these are old acquaintance of mine; bid them welcome. I was coming to wait upon you before; but meeting them by the way, they pressed me to drink——

[Cully *reels against* Sir Frederick.

Cul. Sir Frederick! Widow, bid him welcome; he is a very good friend of mine, and as mad a fellow as myself. Kiss, kiss the widow, man; she has a plump under-lip and kisses smartly.

Sir Fred. What's here? Cully drunk, transformed into a gallant, and acquainted with the spring and proportion of the widow's lips!

Cul. Ay, I am drunk, sir; am I not, widow? I scorn to be soberer than yourself. I will drink with you, swear with you, break windows with you, and so forth.

Sir Fred. Widow, is this your champion?

Wid. You have no exceptions against him, I hope; he has challenged you at your own weapons.

Cul. Widow, Sir Frederick shall be one of our bridemen; I will have none but such mad fellows at our wedding; but before I marry thee, I will consider upon it. [*He sits down and sleeps.*

Sir Fred. Pray, widow, how long have you been acquainted with this mirror of knighthood?[1]

Wid. Long enough, you hear, sir, to treat of marriage.

Sir Fred. What? You intend me for a reserve, then? You will have two strings to your bow, widow. I perceive your cunning, and, faith, I think I shall do you the heartier service if thou employest me by the by.

Wid. You are an excellent gallant indeed. Shake off these lousy companions; come carry your mistress to the Park, and treat her at the Mulberry Garden[2] this glorious evening.

---

[1] So in *The Old Bachelor*, ii. 1: "The mirror of knighthood and pink of courtesy." The expression, of course, was borrowed from the title of the old romance.

[2] Often mentioned. It served as the title of one of Sedley's

Sir Fred. Widow, I am a man of business; that ceremony's to be performed by idle fellows.

Wid. What would you give to such a friend as should despatch this business now, and make you one of those idle fellows.

Sir Fred. Faith, pick and choose; I carry all my wealth about me; do it, and I am all at thy service, widow.

Wid. Well, I have done it, sir; you are at liberty, and a leg now will satisfy me.

Sir Fred. Good faith, thou art too reasonable, dear widow; modesty will wrong thee.

Wid. Are you satisfied?

Fiddler. Yes, madam.

Enter DUFOY, *with a helmet on his head, and a great sword in his hand.*

Duf. Vare are de *bougres* de bailié? Tête-bleu, *bougres* rogues. [*He falls upon the Fiddlers.*

Fiddlers. Help, help, Sir Frederick; murder, murder! Alas! sir, we are not bailiffs; you may see we are men of an honester vocation. [*They show their instruments.*

Sir Fred. Hold, hold, thou mighty man-at-arms!

Duf. Morbleu, de fiddler! and is my matré at liberty? Play me de trichaté, or de jegg Englishé,

---

comedies. Pepys found the gardens "a silly place," May 20th, 1668. Evelyn speaks of them—writing in 1654—"as the only place of refreshment about the town for persons of the best quality,—Cromwell and his partisans having shut up and seized on Spring Garden." The grounds ceased to be a public resort somewhere about 1673.

quickly, or I will make you all dance vidout your fiddle; quiké!

Wid. I am overreached, I perceive.

[DUFOY *dances a jig.*

Sir Fred. Kind widow, thank thee for this release. Laugh, widow. [*Shakes his pockets.* Ha, ha, ha! where is your counterplot, widow? Ha, ha, ha! Laugh at her, Dufoy. Come, be not so melancholy; we'll to the park. I care not if I spend a piece or two upon thee in tarts and cheesecakes. Pish, widow, why so much out of humour? 'Tis no shame to love such a likely young fellow.

Wid. I could almost find in my heart to punish myself to afflict thee, and marry that drunken sot I never saw before.

Sir Fred. How came he hither?

Wid. Inquire elsewhere; I will not answer thee one question, nor let thee see me out of a mask any more this fortnight.

Sir Fred. Go, go into thy closet, look over thy old receipts, and talk wantonly now and then with thy chambermaid; I shall not trouble thee much till this is spent; and by that time thy foolish vow will be near over. [*Shakes his pockets.*

Wid. I want patience to endure this insolence. Is my charity rewarded thus?

Sir Fred. Pious widow, call you this charity? 'Twill get thee little hereafter; thou must answer for every sin it occasions. Here is wine and women in abundance. [*Shakes his pockets.*

Wid. Avoid my house, and never more come near me.

Sir Fred. But hark you, hark you, widow; do you think this can last always?

Wid. Ungrateful man! [*Exit Widow.*

Sir Fred. She's gone; impatience for these two hours possess her, and then I shall be pretty well revenged.

Duf. Begar, matré, have you not de ver faithful *serviteur?* you do never take notice of my merit.

Sir Fred. Dufoy, thou art a man of courage and hast done bravely; I will cast off this suit a week sooner than I intended, to reward thy service.

Duf. Begar, I have several time given you ver dangerous testimonié of my affection.

Enter a Servant, who takes up CULLY *in his arms.*

Sir Fred. Whither do you carry him?

Serv. Sir, there is an old gentleman below in a coach, very like my Lord Bevill, who, hearing what a condition Sir Nicholas was in, desired me to bring him to him in my arms.

Cul. Let me go; where is the widow?

Sir Fred. What widow?

Cul. Mrs. Rich; she is to be my wife.

Sir Fred. But do you hear, Sir Nicholas? how long have you courted this widow?

Cul. Mr. Wheedle can tell you. Trouble me not with idle questions, Sir Frederick; you shall be welcome at any time; she loves men that will roar, and drink, and serenade her.

Sir Fred. This is some strange mistake; sure Wheedle, intending to chouse him, has showed him some counterfeit widow, and he being drunk has been misguided to the true widow's house. The fellow in the coach may discover all; I will step and see who it is. Hold him here, Dufoy, till I return. Gentlemen, come you with me.

[*Exit* SIR FREDERICK *and Fiddlers.*

Cul. Where is my mistress?

Duf. Vat metres?

Cul. The widow.

Duf. She be de metres of my matré.

Cul. You lie, sirrah.

Duf. Begar, you be be jackanape to tellé me I do lyea.

Cul. You are a French rascal, and I will blow your nose without a handkerchief.

[*He pulls* DUFOY *by the nose.*

Duf. Helpé, helpé me! *Morbleu!* I vil beat you vid my fisté and my footé, tellé you aské me de pardon. Take dat and daté; aské me de pardon.

[CULLY *falls down, and* DUFOY *beats him.*

Cul. I ask your pardon, sirrah?

Duf. Sirrah! *Tête-bleu!* [*Offers to strike.*

Enter SIR FREDERICK *and Fiddlers, leading in* PALMER *trembling.*

Sir Fred. Hold, hold, Dufoy.

Duf. Begar, he do merite to be beaté; he swaré he vil marré youré metres.

Palm. I beseech you, Sir Frederick.

Cul. My Lord Bevill!

Sir Fred. So, he takes him for my Lord Bevill;

now the plot will out. 'Tis fit this rascal should be cheated; but these rogues will deal too unmercifully with him. I'll take compassion upon him and use him more favourably myself.

Cul. My lord, where is the mad wench your sister?

[SIR FREDERICK *pulls off* PALMER's *disguise.*

Sir Fred. Look you, Sir Nicholas, where is my Lord Bevill now?

Cul. My merry countryman, Mr. Palmer! I thought you had been in Buckinghamshire. [*Sings.*

And he took her by the apron,
To bring her to his beck.

Never a catch now, my merry countryman? Sir Frederick, I owe this gentleman a thousand pounds.

Sir Fred. How so?

Cul. He won it of me at dice; Wheedle went my halves, and we have given him a judgment for it.

Sir Fred. This was the roguery you had been about the other night, when I met you in disguise, Palmer. You'll never leave your cheating and your robbing; how many robberies do I know of your committing?

Palm. The truth is, sir, you know enough to hang me; but you are a worthy gentleman and a lover of ingenuity.

Sir Fred. This will not pass. Produce the judgment.

Palm. Alas, sir! Mr. Wheedle has it.

Sir Fred. Produce it, or——Fetch the constable, boy.

Palm. Sir Frederick, be merciful to a sorrowful rascal: here is a copy of the judgment, as it is entered.

Sir Fred. Well, who is this counterfeit widow? Confess.

Palm. Truly, 'twas Wheedle's contrivance; a pox on him! Never no good comes on't when men are so unconscionable in their dealings.

Cul. What, am I cheated, Sir Frederick? Sirrah, I will have you hanged.

Sir Fred. Speak; who is this widow?

Palm. 'Tis Grace, sir, Wheedle's mistress, whom he has placed in my Lady Dawbwell's house. I am but a poor instrument, abused by that rascal.

Sir Fred. You see, Sir Nicholas, what villains these are; they have cheated you of a thousand pounds, and would have married you to a wench, had I not discovered their villainy.

Cul. I am beholding to you, Sir Frederick; they are rogues—villainous rogues. But where is the widow?

Sir Fred. Why, you saw the true widow here a little while ago.

Cul. The truth is, methought she was something comelier than my mistress; but will not this widow marry me?

Sir Fred. She is my mistress.

Cul. I will have none of her then.

Sir Fred. Well, I have discovered this cheat, kept you from marrying a wench, and will save you the thousand pounds too. Now, if you have a mind to marry, what think you of my sister? She is a plain brown girl, and has a good portion; but not out[1]

---

[1] Not more than.

twenty thousand pounds. This offer proves I have a perfect kindness for you.

Cul. I have heard she is a very fine gentlewoman; I will marry her forthwith and be your brother-in-law.

Sir Fred. Come then, I'll carry you where you may see her and ask her consent. Palmer, you must go along with us, and by the way assign this judgment to me. Do you guard him, gentlemen.

[*To the Fiddlers.*

Sir Fred. Come, Sir Nicholas.

Cul. How came I hither?

Sir Fred. You will be satisfied in that hereafter.

Palm. What cursed accident was this? What mischievous stars have the managing of my fortune? Here's a turn with all my heart, like an after-game at Irish!

Duf. Allons! marchez! shentelmen, *marchez!* You make de mouthé of de honest shentelmen: begar, you vil make de wry mouthé ven you be hangé.

[*Exeunt.*

Scene III.—A Garden.

Enter Graciana *and* Letitia *severally;* Letitia *with a nosegay in her hand.*

Grac. Letitia, what hast thou been doing here?

Letit. Cropping the beauty of the youthful year.

Grac. How innocently dost thou spend thy hours, Selecting from the crowd the choicest flowers! Where is thy mistress?

Letit. Madam, she's with the wounded colonel.
Grac. Come then into this arbour, girl, and there
With thy sweet voice refresh my wearied soul.
            [*They walk into an arbour;* LETITIA *sings.*

SONG.

Ladies, though to your conquering eyes
Love owes his chiefest victories,
And borrows those bright arms from you
With which he does the world subdue,
    Yet you yourselves are not above
    The empire nor the griefs of love.

Then rack not lovers with disdain,
Lest Love on you revenge their pain;
You are not free because you're fair;
The Boy did not his Mother spare:
    Beauty's but an offensive dart;
    It is no armour for the heart.

Grac. Dear girl, thou art my little confidante;
I oft to thee have breathed my discontent;
And thy sweet voice as oft has eased my care:
But now thy breath is like infectious air.

Enter BEAUFORT.

It feeds the secret cause of my disease,
And does enrage what it did use t'appease.
    Beauf. (*starting*). Hark! that was Graciana's voice.
    Grac. Oh, Beaufort!
    Beauf. She calls on me, and does advance this way:

I will conceal myself within this bower; she may
The secret causes of my grief betray.

          [BEAUFORT *goes into an arbour, and* GRACIANA
                and LETITIA *come upon the stage.*

  Grac. Too rigidly my honour I pursue;
Sure something from me to my love is due:
Within these private shades for him I'll mourn,
Whom I in public am obliged to scorn.
  Letit. Why should you, madam, thus indulge your
      grief?
Love never yet in sorrow found relief:
These sighs, like northern winds to th' early spring,
Destruction to your blooming beauty bring.
  Grac. Letitia, peace; my beauty I despise:
Would you have me preserve these fatal eyes?
  Letit. Had you less beauteous been, you'd known
      less care:
Ladies are happiest moderately fair:
But now should you your beauty waste, which way
Could you the debt it has contracted pay?
  Grac. Beaufort, didst thou but know I weep for thee,
Thou wouldst not blame my scorn, but pity me.
  Letit. When honour first made you your love decline,
You from the centre drew a crooked line:
You were to Beaufort too severe, I fear,
Lest to your love you partial might appear.
  Grac. I did what I in honour ought to do:
I yet to Beaufort and my love am true:
And if his rival live I'll be his bride;
Joy shall unite whom grief does now divide.
But if for love of me brave Bruce does die,

I am contracted to his memory.
Oh, Beaufort!

Beauf.   Oh, Graciana! here am I!
By what I've heard fix'd in an ecstasy.

Grac. We are surprised.   Unlucky accident!
Fresh sorrow's added to my discontent.

[*Exeunt* GRACIANA *and* LETITIA *leisurely*.
BEAUFORT *enters*.

Beauf. Graciana, stay; you can no more contend,
Since fortune joins with love to be my friend;
There is no fear of Bruce's death; the wound
By abler surgeons is not mortal found.
She will not stay.
My joys, like waters swell'd into a flood,
Bear down whate'er their usual streams withstood.

[*Exit* BEAUFORT.

SCENE IV.—MY LADY DAWBWELL'S HOUSE.

Enter WHEEDLE *and* GRACE.

Wheed. I wonder we have yet no tidings of our knight nor Palmer. Fortune still crosses the industrious, girl; when we recover him you must begin to lie at a little openerward; 'tis dangerous keeping the fool too long at bay, lest some old woodman drop in by chance and discover thou art but a rascal deer. I have counterfeited half-a-dozen mortgages, a dozen bonds, and two scriveners to vouch all; that will satisfy him in thy estate. He has sent into the country for his writings; but see, here he comes.

Enter Sir Nicholas.

Sir Nicholas, I must chide you, indeed I must; you neglect your duty here. Nay, madam, never blush; faith, I'll reveal all. You're the happiest, the luckiest man——

Enter Sir Frederick.

We're betrayed. Death! what makes him here? Sir Frederick, your humble servant, you're come in the luckiest time for mirth. [*To* Sir Frederick.] Will you but lend me your ear? Do not you see Sir Nicholas and Grace? Yonder; look, look!

Sir Fred. Yes.

Wheed. I am persuading him to keep her; she's a pretty deserving girl. Faith, let us draw off awhile and laugh among ourselves, for fear of spoiling the poor wench's market; let us, let us.

Sir Fred. With all my heart.

[*Bailiffs meet* Wheedle *at the door, and arrest him.*

Bailiffs. We arrest you, sir.

Wheed. Arrest me? Sir Frederick, Sir Nicholas!

Sir Fred. We are not provided for a rescue at present, sir.

Wheed. At whose suit?

Bailiffs. At Sir Frederick Frollick's.

Wheed. Sir Frederick Frollick's? I owe him never a farthing.

Sir Fred. You're mistaken, sir; you owe me a thousand pounds. Look you, do you know Mr.

Palmer's hand? He has assigned such a small debt over to me.

Enter PALMER *and* JENNY.

Wheed. How was I bewitched to trust such a villain! Oh! rogue, dog, coward, Palmer.

Palm. Oh! thou unconscionable Wheedle; a thousand pounds was too small a bubble!

Sir Fred. Away with him, away with him.

Wheed. Nay, Sir Frederick, 'tis punishment enough to fall from my expectation: do not ruin a young man.

Grace. I beseech you, sir.

Sir Fred. Thou hast moved me, Grace. Do not tremble, chuck; I love thy profession too well to harm thee. Look you, sir, what think you of a rich widow? [*Proffering him the whore.* Was there no lady to abuse, Wheedle, but my mistress? no man to bubble but your friend and patron, Sir Nicholas? But let this pass; Sir Nicholas is satisfied. Take Grace: here, marry her, we are all satisfied. She's a pretty deserving girl, and a fortune now in earnest; I'll give her a thousand pounds.

Wheed. Pray, sir, do but consider——

Sir Fred. No consideration; despatch, or to limbo.

Wheed. Was there ever such a dilemma? I shall rot in prison. Come hither, Grace; I did but make bold, like a young heir with his estate, before it come into his hands. Little did I think, Grace, that this pasty, when we first cut it up, should have been preserved for my wedding feast. [*Stroking her belly.*

Sir Nich. You are the happiest, the luckiest man, Mr. Wheedle.

Palm. Much joy, Mr. Wheedle, with your rich widow.

Wheed. Sir Frederick, shall that rogue Palmer laugh at me?

Sir Fred. No, no; Jenny, come hither; I'll make thee amends, as well as thy mistress, for the injury I did thee th'other night. Here is a husband for thee, too. Mr. Palmer, where are you?

Palm. Alas! Sir Frederick, I am not able to maintain her.

Sir Fred. She shall maintain you, sir. Do not you understand the mystery of stiponie, Jenny?

Maid. I know how to make democuana, sir.

Sir Fred. Thou art richly endowed, i' faith. Here, here, Palmer; no "shall I? shall I?": this or that, which you deserve better.

Palm. This is but a short reprieve; the gallows will be my destiny.

Sir Fred. Sir Nicholas, now we must haste to a better solemnity; my sister expects us. Gentlemen, meet us at the Rose; I'll bestow a wedding dinner upon you, and there release your judgment, Mr. Wheedle. Bailiffs, wait upon them thither.

Sir Nich. I wish you much joy with your fair brides, gentlemen.

Wheed. A pox on your assignment, Palmer.

Palm. A pox on your rich widow, Wheedle; come, spouse, come. [*Exeunt.*

SCENE V.—THE LORD BEVILL'S HOUSE.

Enter LORD BEVILL, BRUCE *led in*, LOVIS, BEAUFORT, GRACIANA, *and* AURELIA.

Bruce. Graciana, I have lost my claim to you,
And now my heart's become Aurelia's due;
She all this while within her tender breast
The flame of love has carefully suppress'd,
Courting for me, and striving to destroy
Her own contentment to advance my joy.

Aurel. I did no more than honour press'd me to;
I wish I'd woo'd successfully for you.

Bruce. You so excel in honour and in love,
You both my shame and admiration move.
Aurelia, here, accept that life from me,
Which Heaven so kindly has preserved for thee.
My lord, I hope you will my choice allow,
  [*To* LORD BEVILL.
And with your approbation seal our vow.

L. Bev. In generous minds this to the world will prove
That gratitude has power to conquer love.
It were, brave man! impiety in me
Not to approve that which the heavens decree.

Bruce. Graciana, on my generous rival you
Must now bestow what to his merit's due.

Grac. Since you recovering, Bruce, your claim decline,

To him with honour I my heart resign.

Beauf. Such honour and such love as you have shown
Are not in the records of virtue known.
My lord, you must assist us here once more;
         [*To* LORD BEVILL.
The god of love does your consent implore.

L. Bev. May love in you still feed your mutual fire.
    .   [*Joining their hands.*

Beauf. And may that flame but with our breaths expire.

Lov. My lord, our quarrel now is at an end;
You are not Bruce's rival, but his friend.

Beauf. In this brave strife your friendship soar'd above
The active flames of our aspiring love.

Bruce. Dear friend, thy merits fame cannot express.

Lov. They are rewarded in your happiness.

Bruce. Come all into my arms before I rest;
Let's breathe our joys into each other's breast:
Thus mariners rejoice when winds decrease,
And falling waves seem wearied into peace.

Enter SIR FREDERICK *and* DUFOY *at one door, and the Widow and* BETTY *at another.*

Sir Fred. Haste, Dufoy, perform what I commanded you.

Duf. I vil be ver quick, begar; I am more den half de Mercury.

Sir Fred. Ho, widow! the noise of these nuptials brought you hither; I perceive your mouth waters.

Wid. Were I in a longing condition, I should be apt enough to put myself upon you, sir.

Sir Fred. Nay, I know thou'rt spiteful, and wouldst fain marry me in revenge; but so long as I have these guardian angels about me, I defy thee and all thy charms. Do skilful falconers thus reward their hawks before they fly the quarry?

Wid. When your gorge is empty you'll come to the lure again.

Sir Fred. After I have had a little more experience of the vanity of this world, in a melancholy humour I may be careless of myself.

Wid. And marry some distressed lady that has had no less experience of that vanity.

Sir Fred. Widow, I profess the contrary; I would not have the sin to answer for of debauching any from such worthy principles. Let me see; if I should be good-natured now and consent to give thee a title to thy own wealth again, you would be stubborn, and not esteem the favour, widow.

Wid. Is it possible you can have thoughts of gratitude? Do you imagine me so foolish as yourself, who often venture all at play to recover one inconsiderable parcel?

Sir Fred. I told you how 'twould be, widow. Less providence attend thee, else I shall do no good upon thee. Farewell.

Wid. Stay, sir; let us shake hands at parting.

Sir Fred. Nay, if thou once art acquainted with my constitution, thou'lt never let me go. Widow, here; examine, examine. [*Holding out his hand.*

L. Bev. Sister, I long have known your inclinations; give me leave to serve you. Sir Frederick, here, take her; and may you make each other happy.

Wid. Now I have received you into my family, I hope you will let my maids go quietly about their business, sir.

Sir Fred. Upon condition there be no twits of the good man departed; no prescription pleaded for evil customs on the wedding night. Widow, what old doings will be anon! I have coupled no less than a pair-royal myself. This day, my lord, I hope you'll excuse the liberty I have taken to send for them; the sight will much increase your mirth this joyful day.

L. Bev. I should have blamed you, sir, if you had restrained your humour here. These must needs be pleasant matches that are of his making.

Enter DUFOY.

Sir Fred. What, are they come?

Duf. Day be all at de dooré, begar; every man vid his pret metres, brid, whore. *Entrez*, jentelmen, vid your lady, *entrez* vid your great fortuné: ha, ha, ha!

Enter SIR NICHOLAS *and his Bride,* WHEEDLE *and his Bride,* PALMER *and his Bride.*

Sir Nich. Brother, do you see how sneakingly Wheedle looks yonder, with his rich widow?

Wid. Brother! is this fellow your brother?

Sir Nich. Ay, that I am.

I

Sir Fred. No, no, Sir Nicholas.

Sir Nich. Did not I marry your sister, sir?

Sir Fred. Fie, fie, Sir Nicholas; I thought you'd been a modester man.

Sir Nich. Is my wife no kin to you, sir?

Sir Fred. Not your wife; but your son and heir may, if it prove so. Joy be with thee, [*To* Lucy.] old acquaintance. Widow, resolving to lead a virtuous life, and keep house altogether with thee, I have disposed of my own household stuff, my dear Mrs. Lucy, to this gentleman.

Wheed. and Palm. We wish you joy with your fair bride, Sir Nicholas.

Sir Nich. I will go and complain, and have you all clapped up for a plot immediately.

Sir Fred. Hold, hold, Sir Nicholas; there are certain coach-poles without. You cannot 'scape, without you've a thousand pounds in your pocket. Carry her into the country. Come, your neighbours' wives will visit her, and vow she's a virtuous well-bred lady; and, give her her due, faith, she was a very honest wench to me, and I believe will make a very honest wife to you.

Sir Nich. If I discover this I am lost; I shall be ridiculous even to our own party.

Sir Fred. You are in the right. Come, take her, make much of her, she shall save you a thousand pounds.

Sir Nich. Well, Lucy, if thou canst but deceive my old mother and my neighbours in the country, I shall bear my fortune patiently.

Sir Fred. I'll warrant you, sir : women so skilled in vice can dissemble virtue.

Duf. Fie, fie ; maké de much of your lady, shentelmen ; begar, you vil find dem ver civil.

Sir Fred. Dufoy, I had almost forgot thee.

Duf. Begar, my merit is ver seldom in your memorié.

Sir Fred. Now I will reward thy services ; here, enjoy thy mistress.

Duf. Ver vel, begar ; you will give me two tree oldé gowné vor all my diligence.

Betty. Marry, come up ! Is that a despicable portion for your greasy pantaloons ?

Duf. Peace, peace, Metres Bet ; ve vil be ver good friend upon occasion ; but ve vil no marrié : dat be ver much better, begar.

Sir Fred. Did you bring the bailiffs with you ?

Duf. Day be vidout. Begar, shentelmen, you have bin made ver sad ; and now you shall be made ver mer vid de fidler.

Wheed. Ha ! cozened with fiddlers for bailiffs ! I durst have sworn false dice might as soon have passed upon me.

Sir Fred. Bid them strike up ; we will have a dance, widow, to divert these melancholy gentlemen.

[*They dance.*

L. Bev. (*after the dance*). Sir Frederick, you shall
        command my house this day ;
Make all those welcome that are pleased to stay.

Sir Fred. Sir Nicholas, and Mr. Wheedle, I release you both of your judgment, and will give it you under my hand at any time. Widow, for all these bloody preparations, there will be no great massacre of maidenheads among us here. Anon I will make you all laugh with the occasion of these weddings.

On what small accidents depends our fate,
While chance, not prudence, makes us fortunate!

THE EPILOGUE.

Spoken by the Widow.

SIR FREDERICK, now I am revenged on you ;
   For all your frolic wit, you're cozen'd too :
I have made over all my wealth to these
Honest gentlemen ; they are my trustees.
Yet, gentlemen, if you are pleased you may
Supply his wants, and not your trust betray.

Spoken by Wheedle.

Poor Wheedle hopes he's given you all content ;
Here he protests 'tis that he only meant :
If you're displeased we're all cross-bit to-day,
And he has wheedled us that writ the play.
Like prisoners conscious of th'offended law,
When juries after th'evidence withdraw,
So waits our author between hope and fear,
Until he does your doubtful verdict hear.
Men are more civil than in former days ;
Few now in public hiss or rail at plays :
He bid me therefore mind your looks with care,
And told me I should read your sentence there ;
But I, unskill'd in faces, cannot guess
By this first view what is the play's success ;
  Nor shall I ease the author of his fear,
    Till twice or thrice, at least, I've seen you here.

SHE WOULD IF SHE COULD

A COMEDY.

ACTED AT HIS HIGHNESS

THE DUKE OF YORK'S THEATRE.

DRAMATIS PERSONÆ.

SIR OLIVER COCKWOOD
    and } *Two country knights.*
SIR JOSLIN JOLLEY,
MR. COURTAL
    and } *Two honest gentlemen of the town.*
MR. FREEMAN,
The LADY COCKWOOD.
ARIANA
    and } *Two young ladies, kinswomen of* SIR JOSLIN JOLLEY.
GATTY,
MRS. SENTRY, *the* LADY COCKWOOD'S *gentlewoman.*
MRS. GAZETTE
    and } *Two Exchange women.*
MRS. TRINKET,
MR. RAKEHELL, *a knight of the industry.*
THOMAS, SIR OLIVER COCKWOOD'S *man.*
A Servant belonging to MR. COURTAL.

Waiters, Fiddlers, and other Attendants.

Scene: LONDON.

SHE WOULD IF SHE COULD.

ACT I.

Scene I.—A Dining-Room.

Enter Courtal *and* Freeman, *and a Servant brushing* Courtal.

Court.

So, so, 'tis well; let the coach be made ready.

Serv. It shall, sir. [*Exit Servant.*

Court. Well, Frank, what is to be done to-day?

Free. Faith, I think we must e'en follow the old trade; eat well, and prepare ourselves with a bottle or two of good Burgundy, that our old acquaintance may look lovely in our eyes. For, for aught as I see, there is no hopes of new.

Court. Well, this is grown a wicked town! it was otherwise in my memory; a gentleman should not have gone out of his chamber but some civil officer or other of the game would have been with him, and have given him notice where he might have had a course or two in the afternoon.

Free. Truly, a good motherly woman of my acquaintance t'other day, talking of the sins of the times, told me, with tears in her eyes, that there are a company of higgling rascals, who partly for themselves, but more especially for some secret friends, daily forestall the markets; nay, and that many gentlemen who formerly had been persons of great worth and honour, are of late, for some private reasons, become their own purveyors, to the utter decay and disencouragement of trade and industry.

Court. I know there are some wary merchants who never trust their business to a factor; but for my part I hate the fatigue, and had rather be bound to back my own colts, and man my own hawks, than endure the impertinences of bringing a young wench to the lure.

Enter Servant.

Serv. Sir, there is a gentlewoman below desires to speak with you.

Court. Ha! Freeman, this may be some lucky adventure.

Serv. She asked me if you were alone.

Court. And did not you say, Ay?

Serv. I told her I would go see.

Court. Go, go down quickly, and tell her I am. Frank, prithee let me put thee into this closet awhile.

Free. Why, may not I see her?

Court. On my life, thou shalt have fair play and go halves, if it be a purchase that may with honour be divided; you may overhear all; but for decency sake, in, in, man.

Free. Well, good fortune attend thee!

Enter MISTRESS SENTRY.

Court. Mistress Sentry, this is a happiness beyond my expectation.

Sent. Your humble servant, sir.

Court. I hope your lady's come to town?

Sent. Sir Oliver, my lady, and the whole family. Well, we have had a sad time in the country! My lady's so glad she's come to enjoy the freedom of this place again, and I dare say longs to have the happiness of your company.

Court. Did she send you hither?

Sent. Oh, no! if she should but know that I did such a confident trick, she would think me a good one, i' faith; the zeal I have to serve you made me venture to call in my way to the Exchange, to tell you the good news, and to let you know our lodgings are in James Street[1] at the Black Posts, where we lay the last summer.

Court. Indeed, it is very obligingly done.

Sent. But I must needs desire you to tell my lady that you came to the knowledge of this by some lucky chance or other; for I would not be discovered for a world.

Court. Let me alone, I warrant thee.

Enter Servant.

Serv. Sir Oliver Cockwood, sir, is come to wait on you.

---

[1] The most fashionable street in London at that time. Waller lived there, 1660-1687.

Sent. O heaven! my master! my lady and myself are both undone, undone——

Court. 'Sdeath! why did you not tell him I was busy?

Sent. For heaven's sake, Mr. Courtal, what shall I do?

Court. Leave, leave trembling, and creep into the wood-hole here. [*She goes into the wood-hole.*

Enter SIR OLIVER.

Court. Sir Oliver Cockwood! [*Embraces him.*

Sir Oliv. Honest Ned Courtal, by my troth I think thou tak'st me for a pretty wench, thou hugg'st me so very close and heartily.

Court. Only my joy to see you, Sir Oliver, and to welcome you to town.

Sir Oliv. Methinks, indeed, I have been an age absent, but I intend to redeem the time; and how, and how stand affairs, prithee now? is the wine good? are the women kind? Well, faith, a man had better be a vagabond in this town than a justice of peace in the country. I was e'en grown a sot for want of gentlemanlike recreations; if a man do but rap out an oath, the people start as if a gun went off; and if one chance but to couple himself with his neighbour's daughter without the help of the parson of the parish, and leave a little testimony of his kindness behind him, there is presently such an uproar that a poor man is fain to fly his country. As for drunkenness, 'tis true, it may be used without scandal, but the drink is so abominable, that a man would forbear it, for fear of being made out of love with the vice.

Court. I see, Sir Oliver, you continue still your old

humour, and are resolved to break your sweet lady's heart.

Sir Oliv. You do not think me, sure, so barbarously unkind to let her know all this; no, no, these are secrets fit only to be trusted to such honest fellows as thou art.

Court. Well may I, poor sinner, be excused, since a woman of such rare beauty, such incomparable parts, and of such an unblemished reputation, is not able to reclaim you from these wild courses, Sir Oliver.

Sir Oliv. To say the truth, she is a wife that no man need be ashamed of, Ned.

Court. I vow, Sir Oliver, I must needs blame you, considering how tenderly she loves you.

Sir Oliv. Ay, ay, the more is her misfortune, and mine too, Ned. I would willingly give thee a pair of the best coach-horses in my stable, so thou couldst but persuade her to love me less.

Court. Her virtue, and my friendship, sufficiently secure you against that, Sir Oliver.

Sir Oliv. I know thou wert never married; but has it never been thy misfortune to have a mistress love thee thus entirely?

Court. It never has been my good fortune, Sir Oliver. But why do you ask this question?

Sir Oliv. Because then, perchance, thou mightst have been a little sensible what a damned trouble it is.

Court. As how, Sir Oliver?

Sir Oliv. Why look thee, thus: for a man cannot be altogether ungrateful, sometimes one is obliged to kiss, and fawn, and toy, and lie fooling an hour or two, when a man had rather, if it were not for the disgrace sake, stand all that while in the pillory pelted with rotten eggs and oranges.

Court. This is a very hard case, indeed, Sir Oliver.

Sir Oliv. And then the inconvenience of keeping regular hours; but, above all, that damned fiend jealousy does so possess these passionate lovers, that I protest, Ned—under the rose be it spoken—if I chance to be a little prodigal in my expense on a private friend or so, I am called to so strict an account at night that for quietness sake I am often forced to take a dose of *cantharides* to make up the sum.

Court. Indeed, Sir Oliver, everything considered, you are not so much to be envied as one may rashly imagine.

Sir Oliv. Well, a pox of this tying man and woman together, for better, for worse! Upon my conscience, it was but a trick that the clergy might have a feeling in the cause.

Court. I do not conceive it to be much for their profit, Sir Oliver, for I dare lay a good wager, let 'em but allow Christian liberty, and they shall get ten times more by christenings than they are likely to lose by marriages.

Sir Oliv. Faith, thou hast hit it right, Ned; and now thou talk'st of Christian liberty, prithee let us dine together to-day, and be swingingly merry, but with all secresy.

Court. I shall be glad of your good company, Sir Oliver.

Sir Oliv. I am to call on a very honest fellow,

whom I left here hard by making a visit, Sir Joslin Jolley, a kinsman of my wife's, and my neighbour in the country. We call brothers;[1] he came up to town with me, and lodgeth in the same house; he has brought up a couple of the prettiest kinswomen, heiresses of a very good fortune: would thou hadst the instructing of them a little. Faith, if I am not very much mistaken, they are very prone to the study of the mathematics.

Court. I shall be beholding to you for so good an acquaintance.

Sir Oliv. This Sir Joslin is in great favour with my lady, one that she has an admirable good opinion of, and will trust me with him anywhere; but to say truth, he is as arrant a sinner as the best of us, and will boggle at nothing that becomes a man of honour. We will go and get leave of my lady; for it is not fit I should break out so soon without her approbation, Ned.

Court. By no means, Sir Oliver.

Sir Oliv. Where shall we meet about an hour hence?

Court. At the French house, or the Bear.[2]

Sir Oliv. At the French house, by all means.

---

[1] *i.e.* call each other "brother."

[2] Perhaps the former was the ordinary mentioned by Pepys, Jan. 19th, 1660. The latter was near London Bridge; Pepys records the distressing fate of the landlady thereof—"which was a most beautiful woman, as most I have seen"—Feb. 24th, 1667. For Etheredge the tavern had pleasant associations. "Remember me," he writes in one of his letters from Ratisbon, "to all my friends at the Rose (cf. *ante*, p. 47), and do not forget the lily at the Bear."

Court. Agreed, agreed.

Sir Oliv. Would thou couldst bring a fourth man.

Court. What think you of Frank Freeman?

Sir Oliv. There cannot be a better: well—— Servant, Ned, servant, Ned! [*Exit* SIR OLIVER.

Court. Your servant, Sir Oliver.—Mistress Sentry!

Sentry (*in the hole*). Is he gone?

Court. Ay, ay! You may venture to bolt now.

Sent. (*crawling out*). Oh, heavens! I would not endure such another fright.

Court. Come, come, prithee be composed.

Sent. I shall not be myself again this fortnight; I never was in such a taking all the days of my life. To have been found false, and to one who, to say truth, has been always very kind and civil to me; but, above all, I was concerned for my lady's honour——

Court. Come, come——there's no harm done.

Sent. Ah! Mr. Courtal, you do not know Sir Oliver so well as I do; he has strange humours sometimes, and has it enough in's nature to play the tyrant, but that my lady and myself awe him by our policy.

Court. Well, well, all's well; did you not hear what a tearing blade Sir Oliver is?

Sent. Ah! 'tis a vile dissembling man. How fairly he carries it to my lady's face! but I dare not discover him, for fear of betraying myself.

Court. Well, Mistress Sentry, I must dine with 'em, and after I have entered them with a beer-glass or two, if I can I will slip away, and pay my respects to your lady.

Sent. You need not question your welcome, I assure you, sir.——Your servant, sir.

Court. Your servant, Mistress Sentry. I am very sensible of this favour, I assure you.

Sent. I am proud it was in my power to oblige you, sir. [*Exit* SENTRY.

Court. Freeman! Come, come out of thy hole. How hast thou been able to contain?

Free. Faith, much ado, the scene was very pleasant; but, above all, I admire thy impudence. I could never have had the face to have wheedled the poor knight so.

Court. Pish, pish! 'twas both necessary and honest: we ought to do all we can to confirm a husband in the good opinion of his wife.

Free. Pray how long, if without offence a man may ask you, have you been in good grace with this person of honour? I never knew you had that commendable quality of secresy before.

Court. You are mistaken, Freeman; things go not as you wickedly imagine.

Free. Why, hast thou lost all sense of modesty? Dost thou think to pass these gross wheedles on me too? Come, come, this good news should make thee a little merrier. Faith, though she be an old acquaintance, she has the advantage of four or five months' absence. 'Slid, I know not how proud you are, but I have thought myself very spruce e'er now in an old suit that has been brushed and laid up awhile.

Court. Freeman, I know in cases of this nature thou art an infidel; but yet methinks the knowledge thou

K

hast of my sincere dealing with my friends should make thee a little more confiding.

Free. What devilish oath could she invent to fright thee from a discovery?

Court. Wilt thou believe me, if I swear the preservation of her honour has been my fault, and not hers?

Free. This is something.

Court. Why then, know that I have still been as careful to prevent all opportunities as she has been to contrive 'em; and still have carried it so like a gentleman, that she has not had the least suspicion of unkindness. She is the very spirit of impertinence, so foolishly fond and troublesome, that no man above sixteen is able to endure her.

Free. Why did you engage thus far, then?

Court. Some conveniences which I had by my acquaintance with the sot her husband made me extraordinary civil to her, which presently by her ladyship was interpreted after the manner of the most obliging women. This wench came hither by her commission to-day.

Free. With what confidence she denied it!

Court. Nay, that's never wanting, I assure you. Now is it expected I should lay by all other occasions, and watch every opportunity to wait upon her; she would by her goodwill give her lover no more rest than a young squire that has newly set up a coach does his only pair of horses.

Free. Faith, if it be as thou say'st, I cannot much blame the hardness of thy heart. But did not the oaf talk of two young ladies?

Court. Well remembered, Frank, and now I think on't, 'twill be very necessary to carry on my business with the old one, that we may the better have an opportunity of being acquainted with them. Come, let us go and bespeak dinner, and by the way consider of these weighty affairs.

Free. Well, since there is but little ready money stirring, rather than want entertainment, I shall be contented to play awhile upon tick.

Court. And I, provided they promise fair, and we find there's hopes of payment hereafter.

Free. Come along, come along. [*Exeunt.*

SCENE II.—SIR OLIVER COCKWOOD'S LODGING.

Enter LADY COCKWOOD.

Lady Cock. 'Tis too late to repent. I sent her, but yet I cannot but be troubled to think she stays so long. Sure, if she has so little gratitude to let him, he has more honour than to attempt anything to the prejudice of my affection——Oh !——Sentry, are you come?

Enter SENTRY.

Sent. Oh, madam ! there has been such an accident !

Lady Cock. Prithee do not fright me, wench——

Sent. As I was discoursing with Mr. Courtal, in came Sir Oliver.

Lady Cock. Oh !——I'm ruined——undone for ever !

Sent. You'll still be sending me on these desperate errands.

Lady Cock. I am betrayed, betrayed——by this false——What shall I call thee?

Sent. Nay but, madam——have a little patience——

Lady Cock. I havè lost all patience, and will never more have any.——

Sent. Do but hear me, all is well.——

Lady Cock. Nothing can be well, unfortunate woman.

Sent. Mr. Courtal thrust me into the wood-hole.

Lady Cock. And did not Sir Oliver see thee?

Sent. He had not the least glimpse of me.——

Lady Cock. Dear Sentry——and what good news?

Sent. He intends to wait upon you in the afternoon, madam.

Lady Cock. I hope you did not let him know I sent you.

Sent. No, no, madam——I'll warrant you I did everything much to the advantage of your honour.

Lady Cock. Ah, Sentry! if we could but think of some lucky plot now to get Sir Oliver out of the way.

Sent. You need not trouble yourself about that, madam; he has engaged to dine with Mr. Courtal at the French house, and is bringing Sir Joslin Jolley to get your goodwill: when Mr. Courtal has fixed 'em with a beer-glass or two, he intends to steal away and pay his devotion to your ladyship.

Lady Cock. Truly, he is a person of much worth and honour.

Sent. Had you but been there, madam, to have overheard Sir Oliver's discourse, he would have made you bless yourself; there is not such another wild man in the town; all his talk was of wenching, and swearing, and drinking, and tearing.

Lady Cock. Ay, ay, Sentry, I know he'll talk of strange matters behind my back; but if he be not an abominable hypocrite at home—and I am not a woman easily to be deceived—he is not able to play the spark abroad thus, I assure you.

Enter SIR OLIVER *and* SIR JOSLIN; SIR JOSLIN *singing.*

My dearest dear, this is kindly done of thee to come home again thus quickly.

Sir Oliv. Nay, my dear, thou shalt never have any just cause to accuse me of unkindness.

Lady Cock. Sir Joslin, now you are a good man, and I shall trust you with Sir Oliver again.

Sir Jos. Nay, if ever I break my word with a lady, I will be delivered bound to Mistress Sentry here, and she shall have leave to carve me for a capon.

Sent. Do you think I have a heart cruel enough for such a bloody execution?

Sir Jos. Kindly spoke, i' faith, girl; I'll give thee a buss for that.   [*Kisses her.*

Lady Cock. Fie, fie, Sir Joslin; this is not seemly in my presence.

Sir Jos. We have all our failings, lady, and this is mine. A right bred greyhound can as well forbear running after a hare when he sees her, as I can mumbling a pretty wench when she comes in my way.

Lady Cock. I have heard indeed you are a parlous man, Sir Joslin.

Sir Jos. I seldom brag, lady, but for a true cock of the game little Joslin dares match with the best of 'em.

Sir Oliv. Sir Joslin's merry, my dear.

Lady Cock. Ay, ay, if he should be wicked, I know thou art too much a gentleman to offer an injury to thine own dear lady.

Sir Jos. Faith, madam, you must give my brother Cockwood leave to dine abroad to-day.

Lady Cock. I protest, Sir Joslin, you begin to make me hate you too; well, you are e'en grown as bad as the worst of 'em, you are still robbing me of the sweet society of Sir Oliver.

Sir Jos. Come, come, your discipline is too severe, i' faith, lady.

Lady Cock. Sir Oliver may do what he pleases, sir; he knows I have ever been his obedient lady.

Sir Oliv. Prithee, my dear, be not angry; Sir Joseph was so earnest in his invitation that none but a clown could have refused him.

Sir Jos. Ay, ay, we dine at my uncle Sir Joseph Jolley's, lady.

Lady Cock. Will you be sure now to be a good dear, and not drink, nor stay out late?

Sir Jos. I'll engage for all, and if there be no harm in a merry catch or a waggish story——

Enter ARIANA *and* MISTRESS GATTY.

Ha, ha! Sly girl and madcap, are you got up? I

know what you have been meditating on; but never trouble your heads, let me alone to bring you consolation.

Gat. We have often been beholding to you, sir; for every time he's drunk he brings us home a couple of fresh servants.

Sir Oliv. Well, farewell, my dear; prithee do not sigh thus, but make thee ready, visit, and be merry.

Lady Cock. I shall receive most satisfaction in my chamber.

Sir Jos. Come, come along, brother. Farewell, one and all, lady and sly girl, sly girl and madcap, your servant, your servant.——

[*Exeunt* Sir Oliver *and* Sir Joslin *singing.*

Lady Cock. (*to* Sentry, *aside*). Sentry, is the new point[1] I bought come home, and is everything in a readiness?

Sent. Everything, madam.

Lady Cock. Come, come up quickly then, girl, and dress me. [*Exeunt* Lady Cockwood *and* Sentry.

Aria. Dost not thou wonder, Gatty, she should be so strangely fond of this coxcomb?

Gat. Well, if she does not dissemble, may I still be discovered when I do. Didst thou not see how her countenance changed as soon as ever their backs were turned, and how earnestly she whispered with her woman? There is some weighty affair in hand, I warrant thee. My dear Ariana, how glad am I we are in this town again.

Aria. But we have left the benefit of the fresh

[1] *i.e.* lace.

air, and the delight of wandering in the pleasant groves.

Gat. Very pretty things for a young gentlewoman to bemoan the loss of, indeed, that's newly come to a relish of the good things of this world.

Aria. Very good, sister!

Gat. Why, hast not thou promised me a thousand times to leave off this demureness?

Aria. But you are so quick.

Gat. Why, would it not make anyone mad to hear thee bewail the loss of the country? Speak but one grave word more, and it shall be my daily prayers thou may'st have a jealous husband; then you'll have enough of it, I warrant you.

Aria. It may be, if your tongue be not altogether so nimble, I may be conformable. But I hope you do not intend we shall play such mad reaks as we did last summer?

Gat. 'Slife, dost thou think we come here to be mewed up, and take only the liberty of going from our chamber to the dining-room, and from the dining-room to our chamber again? And like a bird in a cage, with two perches only, to hop up and down, up and down?

Aria. Well, thou art a mad wench.

Gat. Wouldst thou never have us go to a play but with our grave relations, never take the air but with our grave relations? to feed their pride, and make the world believe it is in their power to afford some gallant or other a good-bargain.

Aria. But I am afraid we shall be known again.

Gat. Pish! the men were only acquainted with our vizards and our petticoats, and they are wore out long since. How I envy that sex! Well, we cannot plague 'em enough when we have it in our power for those privileges which custom has allowed 'em above us.

Aria. The truth is, they can run and ramble here and there and everywhere, and we poor fools rather think the better of 'em.

Gat. From one playhouse to the other playhouse, and, if they like neither the play nor the women, they seldom stay any longer than the combing of their periwigs or a whisper or two with a friend; and then they cock their caps and out they strut again.

Aria. But whatsoever we do, prithee now let us resolve to be mighty honest.

Gat. There I agree with thee.

Aria. And if we find the gallants like lawless subjects, who the more their princes grant, the more they impudently crave——

Gat. We'll become absolute tyrants and deprive 'em of all the privileges we gave 'em.

Aria. Upon these conditions I am contented to trail a pike under thee——March along, girl.

[*Exeunt.*

ACT II.

SCENE I.—THE MULBERRY GARDEN.

Enter COURTAL *and* FREEMAN.

Court.

WAS there ever a couple of fops better matched than these two knights are?

Free. They are harp and violin; Nature has so tuned 'em, as if she intended they should always play the fool in concert.

Court. Now is Sir Oliver secure, for he dares not go home till he's quite drunk, and then he grows valiant, insults and defies his sweet lady; for which, with prayers and tears, he's forced to feign a bitter repentance the next morning.

Free. What do we here idling in the Mulberry Garden? Why do not we make this visit then?

Court. Now art thou as mad upon this trail as if we were upon a hot scent.

Free. Since we know the bush, why do we not start the game?

Court. Gently, good Frank. First, know that the laws of honour prescribed in such nice cases will not allow me to carry thee along with me; and next, hast thou so little wit to think that a discreet lady that has had the experience of so much human frailty, can have so good an opinion of the constancy of her servant as to lead him into temptation?

Free. Then we must not hope her ladyship should make us acquainted with these gentlewomen?

Court. Thou may'st as reasonably expect that an old rook should bring a young snap acquainted with his bubble; but advantages may be hereafter made, by my admission into the family.

Free. What is to be done then?

Court. Why, look you, thus I have contrived it: Sir Oliver, when I began to grow restiff, that he might incline me a little more to drunkenness, in my ear discovered to me the humour of his dear friend, Sir Joslin. He assured me that when he was in that good-natured condition, to requite their courtesy, he always carried the good company home with him and recommended them to his kinswomen.

Free. Very good!

Court. Now, after the fresh air has breathed on us awhile, and expelled the vapours of the wine we have drunk, thou shalt return to these two sots whom we left at the French house, according to our promise, and tell 'em I am a little stayed by some unlucky business and will be with 'em presently; thou wilt find 'em tired with long fight, weak and unable to observe their order; charge 'em briskly, and in a moment thou shalt rout 'em, and with little or no damage to thyself gain an absolute victory.

Free. Very well!

Court. In the meantime, I will make my visit to the

longing lady, and order my business so handsomely, that I will be with thee again immediately, to make an experiment of the good-humour of Sir Joslin.

Free. Let's about it.

Court. 'Tis yet too early; we must drill away a little time here, that my excuses may be more probable, and my persecution more tolerable.

Enter ARIANA *and* GATTY *with vizards, and pass nimbly over the stage.*

Free. Ha, ha !——how wantonly they trip it! There is temptation enough in their very gait to stir up the courage of an old alderman. Prithee, let us follow 'em.

Court. I have been so often baulked with these vizard-masks that I have at least a dozen times forsworn 'em; they are a most certain sign of an ill face, or, what is worse, an old acquaintance.

Free. The truth is, nothing but some such weighty reason is able to make women deny themselves the pride they have to be seen.

Court. The evening's fresh and pleasant, and yet there is but little company.

Free. Our course will be the better; these deer cannot herd. Come, come, man, let's follow.

Court. I find it is a mere folly to swear anything; it does but make the devil the more earnest in his temptation. [*They go after the Women.*

Enter Women again, and cross the stage.

Aria. Now if these should prove two men-of-war that are cruising here to watch for prizes.

Gat. Would they had courage enough to set upon us! I long to be engaged.

Aria. Look, look yonder, I protest, they chase us.

Gat. Let us bear away then; if they be truly valiant, they'll quickly make more sail and board us.

> [*The Women go out, and go about behind the scenes to the other door.*

Enter COURTAL *and* FREEMAN.

Free. 'Sdeath, how fleet they are! whatsoever faults they have, they cannot be broken-winded.

Court. Sure, by that little mincing step they should be country fillies that have been breathed a course at park and barley-break. We shall never reach 'em.

Free. I'll follow directly, do thou turn down the cross walk and meet 'em.

Enter the Women, and after them COURTAL *at the lower door, and* FREEMAN *at the upper on the contrary side.*

Court. By your leave, ladies.

Gat. I perceive you can make bold enough without it.

Free. Your servant, ladies.

Aria. Or any other ladies that will give themselves the trouble to entertain you.

Free. 'Slife, their tongues are as nimble as their heels.

Court. Can you have so little good-nature to dash a couple of bashful young men out of countenance, who came out of pure love to tender you their service?

Gat. 'Twere pity to baulk 'em, sister.

Aria. Indeed, methinks they look as if they never had been slipped before.

Free. Yes, faith, we have had many a fair course in this paddock, have been very well fleshed, and dare boldly fasten. [*They kiss their hands with a little force.*

Aria. Well, I am not the first unfortunate woman that has been forced to give her hand where she never intends to bestow her heart.

Gat. Now, do you think 'tis a bargain already?

Court. Faith, would there were some lusty earnest given, for fear we should unluckily break off again.

Free. Are you so wild that you must be hooded thus?

Court. Fie, fie! put off these scandals to all good faces.

Gat. For your reputation's sake we shall keep 'em on. 'Slife, we should be taken for your relations if we durst show our faces with you thus publicly.

Aria. And what a shame that would be to a couple of young gallants! Methinks, you should blush to think on't.

Court. These were pretty toys, invented first merely for the good of us poor lovers to deceive the jealous and to blind the malicious; but the proper use is so wickedly perverted, that it makes all honest men hate the fashion mortally.

Free. A good face is as seldom covered with a vizard-mask as a good hat with an oiled case. And yet, on my conscience, you are both handsome.

Court. Do but remove 'em a little, to satisfy a foolish scruple.

Aria. This is a just punishment you have brought upon yourselves by that unpardonable sin of talking.

Gat. You can only brag now of your acquaintance with a Farendon[1] gown and a piece of black velvet.

Court. The truth is, there are some vain fellows whose loose behaviour of late has given great discouragement to the honourable proceedings of all virtuous ladies.

Free. But I hope you have more charity than to believe us of the number of the wicked.

Aria. There's not a man of you to be trusted.

Gat. What a shame is it to your whole sex that a woman is more fit to be a privy councillor than a young gallant a lover!

Court. This is a pretty kind of fooling, ladies, for men that are idle; but you must bid a little fairer if you intend to keep us from our serious business.

Gat. Truly you seem to be men of great employment, that are every moment rattling from the eating-houses to the playhouses, from the playhouses to the Mulberry Garden; that live in a perpetual hurry and have little leisure for such an idle entertainment.

Court. Now would not I see thy face for the world; if it should be but half so good as thy humour thou wouldst dangerously tempt me to dote upon thee, and, forgetting all shame, become constant.

Free. I perceive by your fooling here that wit and good-humour may make a man in love with a blackamoor: that the devil should contrive it so that we should have earnest business now!

[1] More correctly *Farendine.*

Court. Would they would but be so kind to meet us here again to-morrow.

Gat. You are full of business, and 'twould but take you off of your employments.

Aria. And we are very unwilling to have the sin to answer for, of ruining a couple of such hopeful young men.

Free. Must we then despair?

Aria. The ladies you are going to will not be so hard-hearted.

Court. (*to* FREEMAN). On my conscience they love us and begin to grow jealous already.

Free. Who knows but this may prove the luckier adventure of the two?

Court. Come, come, we know you have a mind to meet us. We cannot see you blush; speak it out boldly.

Gat. Will you swear, then, not to visit any other women before that time?

Aria. Not that we are jealous, but because we would not have you tired with the impertinent conversation of our sex and come to us dull and out of humour.

Court. Invent an oath, and let it be so horrid 'twould make an atheist start to hear it.

Free. And I will swear it readily, that I will not so much as speak to a woman till I speak to you again.

Gat. But are you troubled with that foolish scruple of keeping an oath?

Free. O most religiously!

Court. And may we not enlarge our hopes upon a little better acquaintance?

Aria. You see all the freedom we allow.

Gat. It may be we may be entreated to hear a fiddle, or mingle in a country dance, or so.

Court. Well! we are in too desperate a condition to stand upon articles, and are resolved to yield on any terms.

Free. Be sure you be punctual now!

Aria. Will you be sure?

Court. Or else may we become a couple of credulous coxcombs, and be jilted ever after. Your servants, ladies. [*Exeunt Men.*

Aria. I wonder what they think of us!

Gat. You may easily imagine; for they are not of a humour so little in fashion to believe the best. I assure you the most favourable opinion they can have is, that we are still a little wild and stand in need of better manning.

Aria. Prithee, dear girl, what dost think of 'em?

Gat. Faith, so well, that I'm ashamed to tell thee.

Aria. Would I had never seen 'em!

Gat. Ha! is it come to that already?

Aria. Prithee, let's walk a turn or two more and talk of 'em.

Gat. Let us take care then we are not too particular in their commendations, lest we should discover we intrench upon one another's inclinations, and so grow quarrelsome. [*Exeunt.*

L

SCENE II.—SIR OLIVER'S LODGINGS.

Enter LADY COCKWOOD *and* SENTRY.

Sent. Dear madam, do not afflict yourself thus unreasonably; I dare lay my life it is not want of devotion, but opportunity that stays him.

Lady Cock. Ungrateful man! to be so insensible of a lady's passion!

Sent. If I thought he were so wicked I should hate him strangely——But, madam,——

Lady Cock. Do not speak one word in his behalf, I am resolved to forget him; perfidious mortal, to abuse so sweet an opportunity!

Sent. Hark! here is somebody coming upstairs.

Lady Cock. Peace, he may yet redeem his honour.

Enter COURTAL.

Court. Your humble servant, madam.

Lady Cock. (*starting*). Mr. Courtal, for heaven's sake, how came you hither?

Court. Guided by my good fortune, madam—— Your servant, Mistress Sentry.

Sent. Your humble servant, sir; I protest you made me start too, to see you come in thus unexpectedly.

Lady Cock. I did not imagine it could be known I was in town yet.

Court. Sir Oliver did me the favour to make me a visit and dine with me to-day, which brought me to the knowledge of this happiness, madam; and as soon as I could possibly, I got the freedom to come hither and enjoy it.

Lady Cock. You have ever been extreme obliging, sir.

Sent. (aside). 'Tis a worthy gentleman; how punctual he is to my directions!

Lady Cock. Will you be pleased to repose, sir? Sentry, set some chairs. [*Exit* SENTRY.

Court. With much difficulty, madam, I broke out of my company, and was forced by the importunity of one Sir Joslin Jolley, I think they call him, to engage my honour I would return again immediately.

Lady Cock. You must not so soon rob me of so sweet a satisfaction.

Court. No consideration, madam, could take me from you, but that I know my stay at this time must needs endanger your honour; and how often I have denied myself the greatest satisfaction in the world, to keep that unblemished, you yourself can witness.

Lady Cock. Indeed, I have often had great trials of your generosity, in those many misfortunes that have attended our innocent affections.

Court. Sir Oliver, madam, before I did perceive it, was got near that pitch of drunkenness which makes him come reeling home and unmanfully insult over your ladyship; and how subject he is then to injure you with an unjust suspicion, you have often told me; which makes me careful not to be surprised here.

Lady Cock. Repose yourself a little, but a little, dear sir. These virtuous principles make you worthy to be trusted with a lady's honour. Indeed, Sir Oliver has his failings; yet I protest, Mr. Courtal, I love him dearly, but cannot be altogether insensible of your generous passion.

Court. (*aside*). Ay, ay, I am a very passionate lover!—Indeed, this escape has only given me leisure to look upon my happiness.

Lady Cock. Is my woman retired?

Court. Most dutifully, madam.

Lady Cock. Then let me tell you, sir——yet we may make very good use of it.

Court. (*aside*). Now am I going to be drawn in again.

Lady Cock. If Sir Oliver be in that indecent condition you speak of, to-morrow he will be very submissive, as it is meet for so great a misdemeanour; then can I, feigning a desperate discontent, take my own freedom without the least suspicion.

Court. This is very luckily and obligingly thought on, madam.

Lady Cock. Now if you will be pleased to make an assignation, sir.

Court. To-morrow about ten o'clock in the lower walk of the New Exchange,[1] out of which we can quickly pop into my coach.

Lady Cock. But I am still so pestered with my woman, I dare not go without her; on my conscience,

---

[1] In the Strand: opened in 1609 and destroyed in 1737. It was a kind of bazaar and promenade, and served the dramatists as an excellent scene. Lovers met in the Lower Walk; ladies from the country, ambitious of being fashionable, lodged in the houses near. Pepys often walked there, sometimes with Mrs. Pepys.

she's very sincere, but it is not good to trust our reputations too much to the frailty of a servant.

Court. I will bring my chariot, madam, that will hold but two.

Lady Cock. O most ingeniously imagined, dear sir! for by that means I shall have a just excuse to give her leave to see a relation, and bid her stay there till I call her.

Court. It grieves me much to leave you so soon, madam; but I shall comfort myself with the thoughts of the happiness you have made me hope for.

Lady Cock. I wish it were in my power eternally to oblige you, dear sir.

Court. Your humble servant, madam.

Lady Cock. Your humble servant, sweet sir.

[*Exit* COURTAL.

Sentry——why, Sentry——where are you?

Enter SENTRY.

Sent. Here, madam.

Lady Cock. What a strange thing this is! Will you never take warning, but still be leaving me alone in these suspicious occasions?

Sent. I was but in the next room, madam.

Lady Cock. What may Mr. Courtal think of my innocent intentions? I protest, if you serve me so again I shall be strangely angry. You should have more regard to your lady's honour.

Sent. If I stay in the room, she will not speak kindly to me in a week after; and if I go out, she always chides me thus. This is a strange infirmity she has, but I must bear with it; for, on my conscience, custom has made it so natural, she cannot help it.

Lady Cock. Are my cousins come home yet?

Sent. Not yet, madam.

Lady Cock. Dost thou know whither they went this evening?

Sent. I heard them say they would go take the air, madam.

Lady Cock. Well, I see it is impossible with virtuous counsel to reclaim them; truly, they are so careless of their own, I could wish Sir Joslin would remove 'em, for fear they should bring an unjust imputation on my honour.

Sent. Heavens forbid, madam!

Enter ARIANA *and* GATTY.

Lady Cock. Your servant, cousins.

Amb. Your servant, madam.

Lady Cock. How have you spent the cool of the evening?

Gat. As the custom is, madam, breathing the fresh air in the Park and Mulberry Garden.

Lady Cock. Without the company of a relation or some discreet body to justify your reputations to the world? You are young, and may be yet insensible of it, but this is a strange censorious age, I assure you.

[*Noise of music without.*

Aria. Hark! what music's this?

Gat. I'll lay my life my uncle's drunk, and hath picked us up a couple of worthy servants, and brought them home with him in triumph.

Enter the Music playing, SIR OLIVER *strutting and swaggering,* SIR JOSLIN *singing and dancing with* MR. COURTAL *and* MR. FREEMAN *on each hand.* GATTY *and* ARIANA, *seeing* COURTAL *and* FREEMAN, *shriek and exeunt.*

Sir Jos. Heyday! I told you they were a couple of skittish fillies, but I never knew 'em boggle at a man before. I'll fetch 'em again, I warrant you, boys.
[*Exit after them.*

Free. (*to* COURTAL). These are the very self-same gowns and petticoats.

Court. Their surprise confirms us it must be them.

Free. 'Slife, we have betrayed ourselves very pleasantly.

Court. Now am I undone to all intents and purposes, for they will innocently discover all to my lady, and she will have no mercy.

Sir Oliv. (*strutting*). Dan, dan, da ra, dan, &c. Avoid my presence! the very sight of that face makes me more impotent than an eunuch!

Lady Cock. Dear Sir Oliver!
[*Offering to embrace him.*

Sir Oliv. Forbear your conjugal clippings; I will have a wench; thou shalt fetch me a wench, Sentry!

Sent. Can you be so inhuman to my dear lady?

Sir Oliv. Peace, Envy, or I will have thee executed for petty treason; thy skin flayed off, stuffed, and hung up in my hall in the country, as a terror to my whole family.

Court. What crime can deserve this horrid punishment?

Sir Oliv. I'll tell thee, Ned. 'Twas my fortune t'other day to have an intrigue with a tinker's wife in the country, and this malicious slut betrayed the very ditch where we used to make our assignations to my lady.

Free. She deserves your anger, indeed, Sir Oliver; but be not so unkind to your virtuous lady.

Sir Oliv. Thou dost not know her, Frank; I have had a design to break her heart ever since the first month that I had her, and 'tis so tough that I have not yet cracked one string on't.

Court. You are too unmerciful, Sir Oliver.

Sir Oliv. Hang her, Ned; by wicked policy she would usurp my empire, and in her heart is a very Pharaoh; for every night she's a putting me upon making bricks without straw.

Court. I cannot see a virtuous lady so afflicted, without offering her some consolation. [*Aside to her.*] Dear madam, is it not as I told you?

Lady Cock. (*to* COURTAL, *aside*). The Fates could not have been more propitious, and I shall not be wanting to the furthering of our mutual happiness.

Enter SIR JOSLIN, *with* ARIANA *and* GATTY *on each hand, dancing and singing.*

CATCH.

This is sly and pretty,
And this is wild and witty;

*If either stay'd
Till she died a maid,
I'faith, 'twould be great pity.*

Sir Jos. Here they are, boys, i'faith, and now little Joslin's a man of his word. Heuk! sly girl and madcap, to 'em, to 'em, to 'em, boys, alou!
　　　　　　　[*Flings them to* COURTAL *and* FREEMAN,
　　　　　　　　　　　　　　　who kiss their hands.
What's yonder, your lady in tears, brother Cockwood? come, come, I'll make up all breaches.
　　　　　　　[*He sings, And we'll all be merry and frolic.*
Fie, fie, though man and wife are seldom in good-humour alone, there are few want the discretion to dissemble it in company.
　　　　　　　[SIR JOSLIN, SIR OLIVER, *and* LADY *stand
　　　　　　　　　　　　　　　talking together.*
Free. I knew we should surprise you, ladies.

Court. Faith, I thought this conjuring to be but a mere jest till now, and could not believe the astrological rascal had been so skilful.

Free. How exactly he described 'em, and how punctual he was in his directions to apprehend 'em!

Gat. Then you have been with a conjurer, gentlemen.

Court. You cannot blame us, ladies; the loss of our hearts was so considerable, that it may well excuse the indirect means we took to find out the pretty thieves that stole 'em.

Aria. Did not I tell you what men of business these were, sister?

Gat. I vow I innocently believed they had some

pre-engagement to a scrivener or a surgeon, and wished 'em so well, that I am sorry to find 'em so perfidious.

Free. Why, we have kept our oaths, ladies.

Aria. You are much beholding to providence.

Gat. But we are more, sister; for had we once been deluded into an opinion they had been faithful, who knows into what inconveniences that error might have drawn us?

Court. Why should you be so unreasonable, ladies, to expect that from us we should scarce have hoped for from you? Fie, fie, the keeping of one's word is a thing below the honour of a gentleman.

Free. A poor shift! fit only to uphold the reputation of a paltry citizen.

Sir Jos. Come, come, all will be well again, I warrant you, lady.

Lady Cock. These are insupportable injuries, but I will bear 'em with an invincible patience, and to-morrow make him dearly sensible how unworthy he has been.

Sir Jos. To-morrow my brother Cockwood will be another man.—So, boys, and how do you like the flesh and blood of the Jolleys?—Heuk, sly girl—and madcap, hey—Come, come, you have heard them exercise their tongues awhile; now you shall see them ply their feet a little. This is a clean-limbed wench, and has neither spavin, splinter, nor wind-gall; tune her a jig and play't roundly, you shall see her bounce it away like a nimble frigate before a fresh gale—hey, methinks I see her under sail already. [GATTY *dances a jig.*

Sir Jos. Hey, my little madcap—here's a girl of the true breed of the Jolleys, i'faith—but hark you, hark you, a consultation, gentlemen—bear up, brother Cockwood, a little. What think you if we pack these idle huswives to bed now, and retire into a room by ourselves, and have a merry catch, and a bottle or two of the best, and perfect the good work we have so unanimously carried on to-day?

Sir Oliv. A most admirable intrigue—Tan, dan, da, ra, dan, come, come, march to your several quarters: go, we have sent for a civil person or two, and are re-solved to fornicate in private.

Lady Cock. This is a barbarous return of all my kindness.

Free. and Court. Your humble servant, madam.

[*Exeunt* LADY COCKWOOD *and* SENTRY.

Court. Hark you! hark you, ladies! do not harbour too ill an opinion of us, for, faith, when you have had a little more experience of the world, you'll find we are no such abominable rascals.

Gat. We shall be so charitable to think no worse of you than we do of all mankind for your sakes, only that you are perjured, perfidious, inconstant, ungrateful.

Free. Nay, nay, that's enough, in all conscience, ladies; and now you are sensible what a shameful thing it is to break one's word, I hope you'll be more careful to keep yours to-morrow.

Gat. Invent an oath, and let it be so horrid——

Court. Nay, nay, it is too late for raillery, i'faith, ladies.

Gat. and Aria. Well, your servant, then.

Free. and *Court.* Your servant, ladies.

[*Exeunt Ladies.*

Sir Oliv. Now the enemy's marched out.——

Sir Jos. Then the castle's our own, boys——hey.

And here and there I had her,
And everywhere I had her,
Her toy was such, that every touch
Would make a lover madder.

Free. and *Court.* Hey, brave Sir Joslin!

Sir Oliv. Ah, my dear little witty Joslin, let me hug thee.

Sir Jos. Strike up, you obstreperous rascals, and march along before us. [*Exeunt singing and dancing.*

ACT III.

Scene I.—The New Exchange.

Mrs. Trinket *sitting in a shop: People passing by as in the Exchange.*

Trink.

WHAT d'ye buy? what d'ye lack, gentlemen? gloves, ribbons, and essences; ribbons, gloves, and essences?

Enter Mr. Courtal.

Mr. Courtal! I thought you had a quarrel to the Change, and were resolved we should never see you here again.

Court. Your unkindness indeed, Mrs. Trinket, had been enough to make a man banish himself for ever.

Enter Mrs. Gazette.

Trink. Look you, yonder comes fine Mrs. Gazette; thither you intend your visit, I am sure.

Gaz. Mr. Courtal! Your servant.

Court. Your servant, Mistress Gazette.

Gaz. This happiness was only meant to Mistress

Trinket; had it not been my good fortune to pass by by chance, I should have lost my share on't.

Court. This is too cruel, Mistress Gazette, when all the unkindness is on your side, to rally your servant thus.

Gaz. I vow this tedious absence of yours made me believe you intended to try an experiment on my poor heart, to discover that hidden secret, how long a despairing lover may languish without the sight of the party.

Court. You are always very pleasant on this subject, Mistress Gazette.

Gaz. And have not you reason to be so?

Court. Not that I know of.

Gaz. Yes, you hear the good news.

Court. What good news?

Gaz. How well this dissembling becomes you! But now I think better on't, it cannot concern you; you are more a gentleman than to have an amour last longer than an Easter term with a country lady; and yet there are some, I see, as well in the country as in the city, that have a pretty way of huswifing a lover, and can spin an intrigue out a great deal farther than others are willing to do.

Court. What pretty art have they, good Mistress Gazette?

Gaz. When tradesmen see themselves in an ill condition, and are afraid of breaking, can they do better than to take in a good substantial partner to help carry on their trading?

Court. Sure you have been at riddle me, riddle me, lately; you are so wondrous witty.

Gaz. And yet I believe my Lady Cockwood is so haughty, she had rather give over the vanity of an intrigue than take in a couple of young handsome kinswomen to help to maintain it.

Court. I knew it would out at last; indeed, it is the principle of most good women that love gaming, when they begin to grow a little out of play themselves, to make an interest in some young gamester or other, in hopes to rook a favour now and then. But you are quite out in your policy; my Lady Cockwood is none of these, I assure you. Hark you, Mistress Gazette, you must needs bestir yourself a little for me this morning, or else Heaven have mercy on a poor sinner.

Gaz. I hope this wicked woman has no design upon your body already. Alas! I pity your tender conscience.

Court. I have always made thee my confidante, and now I come to thee as to a faithful counsellor.

Gaz. State your case.

Court. Why, this ravenous kite is upon wing already, is fetching a little compass, and will be here within this half hour to swoop me away.

Gaz. And you would have me your scarecrow?

Court. Something of that there is in't; she is still your customer.

Gaz. I have furnished her and the young ladies with a few fashionable toys since they came to town, to keep 'em in countenance at a play or in the Park.

Court. I would have thee go immediately to the young ladies, and by some device or other entice 'em hither.

Gaz. I came just now from taking measure of 'em for a couple of handkerchiefs.

Court. How unlucky's this!

Gaz. They are calling for their hoods and scarves, and are coming hither to lay out a little money in ribbons and essences. I have recommended them to Mistress Trinket's shop here.

Court. This falls out more luckily than what I had contrived myself, or could have done; for here will they be busy just before the door where we have made our appointment. But if this long-winged devil should chance to truss me before they come——

Gaz. I will only step up and give some directions to my maid about a little business that is in haste, and come down again and watch her; if you are snapped, I'll be with you presently and rescue you, I warrant you, or at least stay you till more company come. She dares not force you away in my sight; she knows I am great with Sir Oliver, and as malicious a devil as the best of 'em. Your servant, sir. [*Exit* GAZETTE.

Enter FREEMAN.

Court. Freeman! 'tis well you are come.

Free. Well! what counterplot? what hopes of disappointing the old and of seeing the young ladies? I am ready to receive your orders.

Court. Faith, things are not so well contrived as I could have wished 'em, and yet I hope, by the help of Mistress Gazette, to keep my word, Frank.

Free. Nay, now I know what tool thou hast made choice of, I make no question but the business will go well forward; but I am afraid this last unlucky business has so distasted these young trouts, they will not be so easily tickled as they might have been.

Court. Never fear it; whatsoever women say, I am sure they seldom think the worse of a man for running at all; 'tis a sign of youth and high mettle, and makes them rather pique who shall tame him. That which troubles me most is, we lost the hopes of variety, and a single intrigue in love is as dull as a single plot in a play, and will tire a lover worse than t'other does an audience.

Free. We cannot be long without some under-plots in this town; let this be our main design, and if we are anything fortunate in our contrivance, we shall make it a pleasant comedy.

Court. Leave all things to me, and hope the best. Begone, for I expect their coming immediately; walk a turn or two above, or fool awhile with pretty Mistress Anvil, and scent your eyebrows and periwig with a little essence of oranges[1] or jessamine; and when you see us all together at Mistress Gazette's shop, put in as it were by chance. I protest yonder comes the old haggard;[2] to your post quickly! 'Sdeath, where's Gazette and these young ladies now? [*Exit* FREEMAN.

Enter LADY COCKWOOD *and* SENTRY.

O madam, I have waited here at least an hour, and

---

[1] A favourite perfume. Compare *The Virtuoso* (act iii.): "I have choice good gloves, amber, orangery." Steele, in the *Tatler* (No. 113), gives a list of the "effects" of a fop, to be sold by auction; amongst them we find "a quart of orange-flower water."

[2] Hawk: the word often signifies a loose woman.

time seems very tedious when it delays so great a happiness as you bring with you.

Lady Cock. I vow, sir, I did but stay to give Sir Oliver his due correction for those unseemly injuries he did me last night. Is your coach ready?

Court. Yes, madam; but how will you dispose of your maid?

Lady Cock. My maid! For heaven's sake, what do you mean, sir? Do I ever use to go abroad without her?

Court. 'Tis upon no design, madam, I speak it, I assure you; but my glass coach broke last night, and I was forced to bring my chariot, which can hold but two.

Lady Cock. O heaven! you must excuse me, dear sir; for I shall deny myself the sweetest recreations in the world, rather than yield to anything that may bring a blemish upon my spotless honour.

Enter GAZETTE.

Gaz. Your humble servant, madam. Your servant, Mr. Courtal.

Lady Cock. and Court. Your servant, Mistress Gazette.

Gaz. I am extreme glad to see your ladyship here. I intended to send my maid to your lodgings this afternoon, madam, to tell you I have a parcel of new lace come in, the prettiest patterns that ever were seen; for I am very desirous so good a customer as your ladyship should see 'em first, and have your choice.

Lady Cock. I am much beholding to you, Mistress Gazette; I was newly come into the Exchange, and intended to call at your shop before I went home.

Enter ARIANA *and* GATTY; GAZETTE *goes to them.*

Court. 'Sdeath, here are your cousins, too! Now there is no hope left for a poor unfortunate lover to comfort himself withal.

Aria. and Gat. Your servant, madam.

Lady Cock. I am newly come into the Exchange, and by chance met with Master Courtal here, who will needs give himself the trouble to play the gallant and wait upon me.

Gat. Does your ladyship come to buy?

Lady Cock. A few trifles. Mistress Gazette says she has a parcel of very fine new laces; shall we go look upon 'em?

Aria. We will only fancy a suit of knots or two at this shop, and buy a little essence, and wait upon your ladyship immediately.

Gat. Mistress Gazette, you are skilled in the fashion, pray let our choice have your approbation.

Gaz. Most gladly, madam.

[*All go to the shop to look upon ware except* COURTAL *and* LADY COCKWOOD.

Court. 'Sdeath, madam, if you had made no ceremony, but stept into the coach presently, we had escaped this mischief.

Lady Cock. My over-tenderness of my honour has blasted all my hopes of happiness.

Court. To be thus unluckily surprised in the height of all our expectation leaves me no patience.

Lady Cock. Moderate your passion a little, sir; I may yet find out a way.

Court. Oh! 'tis impossible, madam; never think on't now you have been seen with me; to leave 'em upon any pretence will be so suspicious, that my concern for your honour will make me so feverish and disordered, that I shall lose the taste of all the happiness you give me.

Lady Cock. Methinks you are too scrupulous, heroic sir.

Court. Besides the concerns I have for you, madam, you know the obligations I have to Sir Oliver, and what professions of friendship there are on both sides; and to be thought perfidious and ungrateful, what an affliction would that be to a generous spirit!

Lady Cock. Must we then unfortunately part thus?

Court. Now I have better thought on't, that is not absolutely necessary neither.

Lady Cock. These words revive my dying joys, dear sir; go on.

Court. I will by-and-by, when I see it most convenient, beg the favour of your ladyship and your young kinswomen to accept of a treat and a fiddle; you make some little difficulty at first, but upon earnest persuasion comply, and use your interest to make the young ladies do so too. Your company will secure their reputations, and their company take off from you all suspicion.

Lady Cock. The natural inclination they have to be jigging will make them very ready to comply. But what advantage can this be to our happiness, dear sir?

Court. Why, first, madam, if the young ladies or

Mistress Gazette have any doubts upon their surprising us together, our joining company will clear 'em all; next, we shall have some satisfaction in being an afternoon together, though we enjoy not that full freedom we so passionately desire.

Lady Cock. Very good, sir.

Court. But then, lastly, madam, we gain an opportunity to contrive another appointment to-morrow, which may restore us unto all those joys we have been so unfortunately disappointed of to-day.

Lady Cock. This is a very prevailing argument indeed; but since Sir Oliver believes I have conceived so desperate a sorrow, 'tis fit we should keep this from his knowledge.

Court. Are the young ladies secret?

Lady Cock. They have the good principles not to betray themselves, I assure you.

Court. Then 'tis but going to a house that is not haunted by the company, and we are secure; and now I think on't, the Bear in Drury Lane[1] is the fittest place for our purpose.

Lady Cock. I know your honour, dear sir, and submit to your discretion.——

[*To them* ARIANA, GATTY, *and* GAZETTE, *from the shop.*

---

[1] "An excellent ordinary, after the French manner," according to Pepys, Feb. 18th, 1668. He dined there four days afterwards, "with mighty pleasure, and excellent meat." Gay gives that quarter of the town a bad name:—

O may thy virtue guard thee through the roads
Of Drury's mazy courts and dark abodes.
Trivia, iii. 259-60.

Have you gratified your fancies, cousins?

Aria. We are ready to wait upon you, madam.

Gat. I never saw colours better mingled.

Gaz. How lively they set off one another, and how they add to the complexion!

Lady Cock. Mr. Courtal, your most humble servant.

Court. Pray, madam, let me have the honour to wait upon you and these young ladies, till I see you in your coach.

Lady Cock. Your friendship to Sir Oliver would engage you in an unnecessary trouble.

Aria. Let not an idle ceremony take you from your serious business, good sir.

Gat. I should rather have expected to have seen you, sir, walking in Westminster Hall, watching to make a match at tennis, or waiting to dine with a Parliament man, than to meet you in such an idle place as the Exchange is.

Court. Methinks, ladies, you are well acquainted with me upon the first visit.

Aria. We received your character before, you know, sir, in the Mulberry Garden, upon oath.

Court. (*aside*). 'Sdeath, what shall I do? Now out comes all my roguery.

Gat. Yet I am apt to believe, sister, that was some malicious fellow that wilfully perjured himself, on purpose to make us have an ill opinion of this worthy gentleman.

Court. Some rash men would be apt enough to inquire him out and cut his throat, ladies, but I heartily forgive him whosoever he was; for, on my conscience, 'twas not so much out of malice to me as out of love to you he did it.

Gaz. He might imagine Mr. Courtal was his rival.

Court. Very likely, Mistress Gazette.

Lady Cock. Whosoever he was, he was an unworthy fellow, I warrant him; Mr. Courtal is known to be a person of worth and honour.

Aria. We took him for an idle fellow, madam, and gave but very little credit to what he said.

Court. 'Twas very obliging, lady, to believe nothing to the disadvantage of a stranger.——What a couple of young devils are these!

Lady Cock. Since you are willing to give yourself this trouble.

Court. I ought to do my duty, madam.

[*Exeunt all but* ARIANA *and* GATTY.

Aria. How he blushed and hung down his head!

Gat. A little more had put him as much out of countenance as a country clown is when he ventures to compliment his attorney's daughter. [*They follow.*

SCENE II.—SIR OLIVER'S DINING-ROOM.

Enter SIR JOSLIN *and Servant severally.*

Sir Jos. How now, old boy! where's my brother Cockwood to-day?

Serv. He desires to be in private, sir.

Sir Jos. Why? what's the matter, man?

Serv. This is a day of humiliation, sir, with him, for last night's transgression.

Sir Jos. I have business of consequence to impart to him, and must and will speak with him.——So, ho! brother Cockwood?

Sir Oliv. (*without*). Who's that? my brother Jolley?

Sir Jos. The same, the same; come away, boy.

Sir Oliv. (*without*). For some secret reasons I desire to be in private, brother.

Sir Jos. I have such a design on foot as would draw Diogenes out of his tub to follow it; therefore I say, come away, come away.

SIR OLIVER *entering in a nightgown and slippers.*

Sir Oliv. There is such a strange temptation in thy voice, never stir.

Sir Jos. What, in thy gown and slippers yet! Why, brother, I have bespoke dinner, and engaged Master Rakehell, the little smart gentleman I have often promised thee to make thee acquainted withal, to bring a whole bevy of damsels in sky, and pink, and flame-coloured taffetas. Come, come, dress thee quickly; there's to be Madam Rampant, a girl that shines and will drink at such a rate, she's a mistress for Alexander, were he alive again.

Sir Oliv. How unluckily this falls out! Thomas, what clothes have I to put on?

Serv. None but your penitential suit, sir; all the rest are secured.

Sir Oliv. Oh, unspeakable misfortune! that I should be in disgrace with my lady now!

Sir Jos. Come, come, never talk of clothes; put on anything; thou hast a person and a mien will bear it out bravely.

Sir Oliv. Nay, I know my behaviour will show I am a gentleman; but yet the ladies will look scurvily upon me, brother.

Sir Jos. That's a jest, i'faith! He that has *terra firma* in the country may appear in anything before 'em.

> *For he that would have a wench kind,*
> *Ne'er smugs up himself like a ninny;*
> *But plainly tells her his mind,*
> *And tickles her first with a guinea.*

Ay, boy.——

Sir Oliv. I vow thou hast such a bewitching way with thee!

Sir Jos. How lovely will the ladies look when they have a beer-glass in their hands!

Sir Oliv. I now have a huge mind to venture; but if this should come to my lady's knowledge?

Sir Jos. I have bespoke dinner at the Bear, the privat'st place in town. There will be no spies to betray us, if Thomas be but secret, I dare warrant thee, brother Cockwood.

Sir Oliv. I have always found Thomas very faithful; but faith, 'tis too unkind, considering how tenderly my lady loves me.

Sir Jos. Fie, fie, a man, and kept so much under correction by a busk and a fan!

Sir Oliv. Nay, I am in my nature as valiant as any

man, when once I set out; but, i'faith, I cannot but think how my dear lady will be concerned when she comes home and misses me.

Sir Jos. A pox upon these qualms!

Sir Oliv. Well, thou hast seduced me; but I shall look so untowardly.

Sir Jos. Again art thou at it? In, in, and make all the haste that may be; Rakehell and the ladies will be there before us else.

Sir Oliv. Well, thou art an arrant devil——hey ——for the ladies, brother Jolley.

Sir Jos. Hey for the ladies, brother Cockwood.
[*Exeunt singing,* For he that would, *&c.*

SCENE III.—THE BEAR.

Without. Ho! Francis, Humphrey, show a room there.

Enter COURTAL, FREEMAN, LADY COCKWOOD, ARIANA, GATTY, *and* SENTRY.

Court. Pray, madam, be not so full of apprehension; there is no fear that this should come to Sir Oliver's knowledge.

Lady Cock. I were ruined if it should, sir! Dear, how I tremble! I never was in one of these houses before.

Sent. (*aside*). This is a bait for the young ladies to

swallow; she has been in most of the eating-houses about town, to my knowledge.

Court. Ho, Francis!

Enter Waiter.

Waiter. Your worship's welcome, sir; but I must needs desire you to walk into the next room, for this is bespoke.

Lady Cock. Mr. Courtal, did not you say this place was private?

Court. I warrant you, madam. What company dines here, Francis?

Waiter. A couple of country knights, Sir Joslin Jolley and Sir Oliver Cockwood, very honest gentlemen.

Lady Cock. Combination to undo me!

Court. Peace, madam, or you'll betray yourself to the waiter.

Lady Cock. I am distracted! Sentry, did not I command thee to secure all Sir Oliver's clothes, and leave nothing for him to put on but his penitential suit, that I might be sure he could not stir abroad to-day?

Sent. I obeyed you in everything, madam; but I have often told you this Sir Joslin is a wicked seducer.

Aria. If my uncle sees us, sister, what will he think of us?

Gat. We come but to wait upon her ladyship.

Free. You need not fear, you chickens are secure under the wings of that old hen.

Court. Is there to be nobody, Francis, but Sir Oliver and Sir Joslin?

Waiter. Faith, sir, I was enjoined secresy; but you have an absolute power over me. Coming lately out of the country where there is but little variety, they have a design to solace themselves with <u>a fresh girl or two, as I understand the business.</u> [*Exit Waiter.*

Lady Cock. Oh, Sentry! Sir Oliver disloyal! My misfortunes come too thick upon me.

Court. (*aside*). Now is she afraid of being disappointed on all hands.

Lady Cock. I know not what to do, Mr. Courtal; I would not be surprised here myself, and yet I would prevent Sir Oliver from prosecuting his wicked and perfidious intentions.

Aria. Now shall we have admirable sport, what with her fear and jealousy.

Gat. I lay my life she routs the wenches.

Enter Waiter.

Waiter. I must needs desire you to step into the next room; Sir Joslin and Sir Oliver are below already.

Lady Cock. I have not power to move a foot.

Free. We will consider what is to be done within, madam.

Court. Pray, madam, come; I have a design in my head which shall secure you, surprise Sir Oliver, and free you from all your fears.

Lady Cock. It cannot be, sir.

Court. Never fear it. Francis, you may own Mr. Freeman and I are in the house, if they ask for us;

but not a word of these ladies, as you tender the wearing of your ears. [*Exeunt.*

Enter SIR JOSLIN, SIR OLIVER, *and Waiter.*

Sir Jos. Come, brother Cockwood, prithee be brisk.

Sir Oliv. I shall disgrace myself for ever, brother.

Sir Jos. Pox upon care! never droop like a cock in moulting-time; thou art spark enough in all conscience.

Sir Oliv. But my heart begins to fail me when I think of my lady.

Sir Jos. What, more qualms yet?

Sir Oliv. Well, I will be courageous. But it is not necessary these strangers should know this is my penitential suit, brother.

Sir Jos. They shall not, they shall not. Hark you, old boy, is the meat provided? Is the wine and ice come? And are the melodious rascals at hand I spoke for?

Waiter. Everything will be in readiness, sir.

Sir Jos. If Master Rakehell, with a coachful or two of vizard-masks and silk petticoats, call at the door, usher 'em up to the place of execution.

Waiter. You shall be obeyed, sir. [*Exit Waiter.*

Enter RAKEHELL.

Sir Jos. Ho, here's my little Rakehell come! Brother Cockwood, let me commend this ingenious gentleman to your acquaintance; he is a knight of the industry, has many admirable qualities, I assure you.

Sir Oliv. I am very glad, sir, of this opportunity to know you.

Rake. I am happy, sir, if you esteem me your servant. Hark you, Sir Joslin, is this Sir Oliver Cockwood, in earnest?

Sir Jos. In very good earnest, I assure you; he is a little fantastical now and then, and dresses himself up in an old fashion. But that's all one among friends, my little Rakehell.

Sir Oliv. Where are the damsels you talked of, brother Jolley? I hope Master Rakehell has not forgot 'em.

Rake. They are arming for the *rencontre*.

Sir Jos. What, tricking and trimming?

Rake. Even so, and will be here immediately.

Sir Oliv. They need not make themselves so full of temptation; my brother Jolley and I can be wicked enough without it.

Sir Jos. The truth is, my little Rakehell, we are both mighty men-at-arms, and thou shalt see us charge anon to the terror of the ladies.

Rake. Methinks that dress, Sir Oliver, is a little too rustical for a man of your capacity.

Sir Oliv. I have an odd humour, sir, now and then; but I have wherewithal at home to be as spruce as any man.

Rake. Your periwig is too scandalous, Sir Oliver; your black cap and border is never wore but by a fiddler or a waiter.

Sir Jos. Prithee, my little Rakehell, do not put my brother Cockwood out of conceit of himself; methinks your *calotte*¹ is a pretty ornament, and makes a man look both polite and politic.

Rake. I will allow you 'tis a grave wear, and fit for men of business that are every moment bending of their brows and scratching of their heads,² [so that] every project would claw out another periwig; but a lover had better appear before his mistress with a bald pate: 'twill make the ladies apprehend a savour, stop their noses, and avoid you. 'Slife, Love in a Cap is more ridiculous than Love in a Tub,³ or Love in a Pipkin.

Sir Oliv. I must confess your whole head is now in fashion; but there was a time when your *calotte* was not so despicable.

Rake. Here's a perruque, sir.

Sir Oliv. A very good one.

Rake. A very good one! 'tis the best in England. Pray, Sir Joslin, take him in your hand, and draw a comb through him; there is not such another friz in Europe.

Sir Jos. 'Tis a very fine one, indeed.

Rake. Pray, Sir Oliver, do me the favour to grace it on your head a little.

Sir Oliv. To oblige you, sir.

Rake. You never wore anything became you half so well in all your life before.

Sir Jos. Why, you never saw him in your life before.

---

[1] A clerical cap.
[2] Some words must have fallen out: "so that" carries on the sense fairly well.
[3] The allusion is obvious. Was *Love in a Pipkin* the name of some play?

Rake. That's all one, sir; I know 'tis impossible. Here's a beaver,[1] Sir Oliver, feel him; for fineness, substance, and for fashion, the Court of France never saw a better; I have bred him but a fortnight, and have him at command already. Clap him on boldly; never hat took the fore-cock and the hind-cock at one motion so naturally.

Sir Oliv. I think you have a mind to make a spark of me before I see the ladies.

Rake. Now you have the mien of a true Cavalier, and with one look may make a lady kind and a Hector humble; and since I named a Hector, here's a sword, sir. Sa, sa, sa! try him, Sir Joslin, put him to't, cut through the staple, run him through the door, beat him to the hilts; if he breaks, you shall have liberty to break my pate, and pay me never a groat of the ten for't.

Sir Jos. 'Tis a very pretty weapon indeed, sir.

Rake. The hilt is true French-wrought, and *doré* by the best workman in France. This sword and this castor, with an embroidered button and loop which I have to vary him upon occasion, were sent me out of France for a token by my elder brother, that went over with a handsome equipage, to take the pleasure of this *campagne.*

Sir Oliv. Have you a mind to sell these things, sir?

Rake. That is below a gentleman; yet if a person of honour, or a particular friend, such as I esteem you,

---

[1] "The broker here his spacious beaver wears."—*Trivia*, ii. 277. Allusions, however, are frequent.

Sir Oliver, take at any time a fancy to a band, a cravat, a velvet coat, a vest, a ring, a flageolet, or any other little toy I have about me, I am good-natured, and may be easily persuaded to play the fool upon good terms.

Enter FREEMAN.

Sir Jos. Worthy Master Freeman!

Sir Oliv. Honest Frank, how cam'st thou to find us out, man?

Free. By mere chance, sir. Ned Courtal is without, writing a letter, and I came in to know whether you had any particular engagements, gentlemen.

Sir Oliv. We resolved to be in private; but you are men without exception.

Free. Methinks you intended to be in private indeed, Sir Oliver. 'Sdeath, what disguise have you got on? Are you grown grave since last night, and come to sin incognito?

Sir Oliv. Hark you in your ear, Frank; this is my habit of humiliation, which I always put on the next day after I have transgressed, the better to make my pacification with my incensed lady.

Free. Ha, ha, ha!——

Rake. Master Freeman, your most humble servant, sir.

Free. Oh, my little dapper officer! are you here?

Sir Jos. Ah! Master Freeman, we have bespoke all the jovial entertainment that a merry wag can wish for—good meat, good wine, and a wholesome wench or two for the digestion. We shall have Madam

Rampant, the glory of the town, the brightest she that shines, or else my little Rakehell is not a man of his word, sir.

Rake. I warrant you she comes, Sir Joslin.

Sir Joslin *sings.*

And if she comes she shall not 'scape,
If twenty pounds will win her;
Her very eye commits a rape,
'Tis such a tempting sinner.

Enter Courtal.

Court. Well said, Sir Joslin; I see you hold up still, and bate not an ace of your good-humour!

Sir Jos. Noble Master Courtal!

Court. Bless me, Sir Oliver! what, are you going to act a droll? How the people would throng about you if you were but mounted on a few deal boards in Covent Garden [1] now!

Sir Oliv. Hark you, Ned, this is the badge of my lady's indignation for my last night's offence; do not insult over a poor sober man in affliction.

Court. Come, come, send home for your clothes: I hear you are to have ladies, and you are not to learn at these years how absolutely necessary a rich vest and a perruque are to a man that aims at their favours.

---

[1] Explained by Pepys: "At Whitehall with the King, before whom the puppet-plays I saw this summer in Covent Garden are acted this night."—Mynors Bright's ed., ii. 55; cf. the *Diary*, May 9th and 23rd, 1662.

Sir Oliv. A pox on't, Ned! my lady's gone abroad in a damned jealous melancholy humour, and has commanded her woman to secure 'em.

Court. Under lock and key?

Sir Oliv. Ay, ay, man, 'tis usual in these cases: out of pure love, in hopes to reclaim me, and to keep me from doing myself an injury by drinking two days together.

Court. What a loving lady 'tis!

Sir Oliv. There are sots that would think themselves happy in such a lady, Ned; but to a true bred gentleman all lawful solace is abomination.

Rake. Mr. Courtal, your most humble servant, sir.

Court. Oh! my little knight of the industry, I am glad to see you in such good company.

Free. Courtal, hark you, are the masking-habits which you sent to borrow at the playhouse come yet?

Court. Yes, and the ladies are almost dressed. This design will add much to our mirth, and give us the benefit of their meat, wine, and music for our entertainment.

Free. 'Twas luckily thought of.

Sir Oliv. Hark, the music comes. [*Music.*

Sir Jos. Hey, boys!——let 'em enter, let 'em enter.

Enter Waiter.

Waiter. An't please your worships, there is a mask of ladies without that desire to have the freedom to come in and dance.

Sir Jos. Hey, boys!——

Sir Oliv. Did you bid 'em come in masquerade, Mr. Rakehell?

Rake. No; but Rampant is a mad wench; she was half-a-dozen times a-mumming in private company last Shrovetide, and I lay my life she has put 'em all upon this frolic.

Court. They are mettled girls, I warrant them, Sir Joslin, let 'em be what they will.

Sir Jos. Let 'em enter, let 'em enter, ha, boys!——

Enter Music, and the Ladies in an antic, and then they take out: my LADY COCKWOOD, SIR OLIVER; *the young Ladies,* COURTAL *and* FREEMAN; *and* SENTRY, SIR JOSLIN; *and dance a set dance.*

Sir Oliv. Oh, my little rogue! have I got thee? How I will turn, and wind, and feague thy body!

Sir Jos. Mettle on all sides, mettle on all sides, i'faith! How swimmingly would this pretty little ambling filly carry a man of my body!

Sings.

She's so bonny and brisk,
How she'd curvet and frisk,
If a man were once mounted upon her!
Let me have but a leap,
Where 'tis wholesome and cheap,
And a fig for your person of honour.

Sir Oliv. 'Tis true, little Joslin, i'faith.

Court. They have warmed us, Sir Oliver.

Sir Oliv. Now am I as rampant as a lion, Ned, and could love as vigorously as a seaman that is newly landed after an East India voyage.

Court. Take my advice, Sir Oliver; do not in your rage deprive yourself of your only hope of an accommodation with your lady.

Sir Oliv. I had rather have a perpetual civil war than purchase peace at such a dishonourable rate. A poor fiddler, after he has been three days persecuted at a country wedding, takes more delight in scraping upon his old squeaking fiddle than I do in fumbling on that domestic instrument of mine.

Court. Be not so bitter, Sir Oliver, on your own dear lady.

Sir Oliv. I was married to her when I was young, Ned, with a design to be baulked, as they tie whelps to the bellwether; where I have been so butted, 'twere enough to fright me, were I not pure mettle, from ever running at sheep again.

Court. That's no sure rule, Sir Oliver; for a wife's a dish of which if a man once surfeit he shall have a better stomach to all others ever after.

Sir Oliv. What a shape is here, Ned! so exact and tempting, 'twould persuade a man to be an implicit sinner, and take her face upon credit.

Sir Jos. Come, brother Cockwood, let us get 'em to lay aside these masking fopperies, and then we'll feague 'em in earnest. Give us a bottle, waiter.

Free. Not before dinner, good Sir Joslin.——

Sir Oliv. Lady, though I have out of drollery put myself into this contemptible dress at present, I am a gentleman and a man of courage, as you shall find anon by my brisk behaviour.

Rake. Sir Joslin! Sir Oliver! These are none of our ladies; they are just come to the door in a coach, and have sent for me down to wait upon 'em up to you.

Sir Jos. Hey, boys! more game, more game! Fetch 'em up, fetch 'em up.

Sir Oliv. Why, what a day of sport will here be, Ned! [*Exit* RAKEHELL.

Sir Jos. They shall all have fair play, boys.

Sir Oliv. And we will match ourselves, and make a prize on't—Ned Courtal and I against Frank Freeman and your brother Jolley; and Rakehell shall be judge for gloves and silk stockings, to be bestowed as the conqueror shall fancy.

Sir Jos. Agreed, agreed, agreed.

Court. and Free. A match, a match.

Sir Oliv. Hey—boys!

[LADY COCKWOOD *counterfeits a fit.*

Sent. (*pulling off her mask*). O heavens! my dear lady! Help, help!

Sir Oliv. What's here? Sentry and my lady! 'Sdeath, what a condition am I in now, Brother Jolley? You have brought me into this premunire.[1] For heaven's sake, run down quickly, and send the rogue and whores away. Help, help! Oh, help! Dear madam, sweet lady!

[*Exit* SIR JOSLIN; SIR OLIVER
kneels down by her.

---

[1] "I'm in such a fright! the strangest quandary and premunire."
—*The Double Dealer*, iv. 3.

Sent. Oh, she's gone, she's gone!

Free. Give her more air.

Court. Fetch a glass of cold water, Freeman.

Sir Oliv. Dear madam, speak; sweet madam, speak.

Sent. Out upon thee for a vile hypocrite! thou art the wicked author of all this: who but such a reprobate, such an obdurate sinner as thou art, could go about to abuse so sweet a lady?

Sir Oliv. Dear Sentry, do not stab me with thy words, but stab me with thy bodkin rather, that I may here die a sacrifice at her feet for all my disloyal actions.

Sent. No, live; live to be a reproach and shame to all rebellious husbands. Ah, that she had but my heart!—but thou hast bewitched her affections— thou shouldst then dearly smart for this abominable treason.

Gat. So, now she begins to come to herself.

Aria. Set her more upright and bend her a little forward.

Lady Cock. Unfortunate woman! let me go; why do you hold me? Would I had a dagger at my heart, to punish it for loving that ungrateful man.

Sir Oliv. Dear madam, were I but worthy of your pity and belief.

Lady Cock. Peace, peace, perfidious man; I am too tame and foolish——Were I every day at the plays, the Park, and Mulberry Garden, with a kind look secretly to indulge the unlawful passion of some young gallant; or did I associate myself with the gaming madams, and were every afternoon at my Lady

Briefs and my Lady Meanwell's at ombre[1] and quebas, pretending ill luck to borrow money of a friend, and then pretending good luck to excuse the plenty to a husband, my suspicious demeanour had deserved this; but I who, out of a scrupulous tenderness to my honour, and to comply with thy base jealousy, have denied myself all those blameless recreations which a virtuous lady might enjoy, to be thus inhumanly reviled in my own person, and thus unreasonably robbed and abused in thine too!

Court. Sure she will take up anon, or crack her mind, or else the devil's in't.

Lady Cock. Do not stay and torment me with thy sight; go, graceless wretch! follow thy treacherous resolutions, do, and waste that poor stock of comfort which I should have at home, upon those your ravenous cormorants below. I feel my passion begin to swell again. [*She has a little fit again.*

Court. Now will she get an absolute dominion over him, and all this will be my plague in the end.

Sir Oliv. (*running up and down*). Ned Courtal, Frank Freeman, Cousin Ariana, and dear Cousin Gatty, for heaven's sake! join all, and moderate her passion——Ah, Sentry! forbear thy unjust reproaches, take pity on thy master! thou hast a great influence over her, and I have always been mindful of thy favours.

Sent. You do not deserve the least compassion, nor would I speak a good word for you, but that I know

---

[1] Famous for ever in the third canto of the *Rape of the Lock*. Quebas is less immortal, *caret quia vate sacro.*

for all this 'twill be acceptable to my poor lady. Dear madam, do but look up a little; Sir Oliver lies at your feet, an humble penitent.

Aria. How bitterly he weeps! how sadly he sighs!

Gat. I dare say he counterfeited his sin, and is real in his repentance.

Court. Compose yourself a little, pray, madam; all this was mere raillery, a way of talk which Sir Oliver, being well-bred, has learned among the gay people of the town.

Free. If you did but know, madam, what an odious thing it is to be thought to love a wife in good company, you would easily forgive him.

Lady Cock. No, no, 'twas the mild correction which I gave him for his insolent behaviour last night that has encouraged him again thus to insult over my affections.

Court. Come, come, Sir Oliver, out with your bosom-secret, and clear all things to your lady; is it not as we have said?

Sir Oliv. Or may I never have the happiness to be in her good grace again; and as for the harlots, dear madam, here is Ned Courtal and Frank Freeman, that have often seen me in company of the wicked; let 'em speak, if they ever knew me tempted to a disloyal action in their lives.

Court. On my conscience, madam, I may more safely swear that Sir Oliver has been constant to your ladyship than that a girl of twelve years old has her maidenhead this warm and ripening age.

Enter SIR JOSLIN.

Sir Oliv. Here's my brother Jolley, too, can witness the loyalty of my heart, and that I did not intend any treasonable practice against your ladyship in the least.

Sir Jos. Unless feaguing 'em with a beer-glass be included in the statute. Come, Master Courtal, to satisfy my lady and put her in a little good-humour, let us sing the catch I taught you yesterday, that was made by a country vicar on my brother Cockwood and me.

They sing.

> *Love and wenching are toys,*
> *Fit to please beardless boys,*
> *They're sports we hate worse than a leaguer;*
> *When we visit a miss,*
> *We still brag how we kiss,*
> *But 'tis with a bottle we feague her.*

Sir Jos. Come, come, madam, let all things be forgot; dinner is ready, the cloth is laid in the next room. Let us in and be merry; there was no harm meant, as I am true little Joslin.

Lady Cock. Sir Oliver knows I can't be angry with him, though he plays the naughty man thus. But why, my dear, would y'expose yourself in this ridiculous habit to the censure of both our honours?

Sir Oliv. Indeed I was to blame to be over-persuaded; I intended dutifully to retire into the pantry, and there civilly to divert myself at backgammon with the butler.

Sir Jos. Faith, I must even own the fault was mine; I enticed him hither, lady.

Sir Oliv. How the devil, Ned, came they to find us out here?

Court. No bloodhound draws so sure as a jealous woman.

Sir Oliv. I am afraid Thomas has been unfaithful. Prithee, Ned, speak to my lady, that there may be a perfect understanding between us, and that Sentry may be sent home for my clothes, that I may no longer wear the marks of her displeasure.

Court. Let me alone, Sir Oliver.

[*He goes to my* LADY COCKWOOD. How do you find yourself, madam, after this violent passion?

Lady Cock. This has been a lucky adventure, Mr. Courtal; now am I absolute mistress of my own conduct for a time.

Court. Then shall I be a happy man, madam: I knew this would be the consequence of all, and yet could not I forbear the project.

Sir Oliv. (*to* SIR JOSLIN). How didst thou shuffle away Rakehell and the ladies, brother?

Sir Jos. I have appointed 'em to meet us at six o'clock at the New Spring Garden.

Sir Oliv. Then will we yet, in spite of the stars that have crossed us, be in conjunction with Madam Rampant, brother.

Court. Come, gentlemen, dinner is on the table.

Sir Jos. Ha! sly girl and madcap, I'll enter you, i'faith; since you have found the way to the Bear, I'll feague you.

Sings.

When we visit a miss,
We still brag how we kiss;
But 'tis with a bottle we feague her.

[*Exeunt, singing.*

ACT IV.

Scene I.—A Dining-Room.

Enter Lady Cockwood.

Lady Cockwood.

A LADY cannot be too jealous of her servant's love this faithless and inconstant age. His amorous carriage to that prating girl to-day, though he pretends it was to blind Sir Oliver, I fear will prove a certain sign of his revolted heart; the letters I have counterfeited in these girls' names will clear all; if he accept of that appointment and refuses mine, I need not any longer doubt.

Enter Sentry.

Sentry, have the letters and message been delivered as I directed?

Sent. Punctually, madam; I knew they were to be found at the latter end of a play. I sent a porter first with the letter to Mr. Courtal, who was at the King's House; he sent for him out by the doorkeeper, and delivered it into his own hands.

Lady Cock. Did you keep on your vizard, that the fellow might not know how to describe you?

Sent. I did, madam.

Lady Cock. And how did he receive it?

Sent. Like a traitor to all goodness, with all the signs of joy imaginable.

Lady Cock. Be not angry, Sentry; 'tis as my heart wished it. What did you do with the letter to Mr. Freeman? For I thought fit to deceive 'em both, to make my policy less suspicious to Courtal.

Sent. The porter found him at the Duke's House,[1] madam, and delivered it with like care.

Lady Cock. Very well.

Sent. After the letters were delivered, madam, I went myself to the playhouse, and sent in for Mr. Courtal, who came out to me immediately; I told him your ladyship presented your humble service to him, and that Sir Oliver was going into the City with Sir Joslin to visit his brother Cockwood, and that it would add much more to your ladyship's happiness if he would be pleased to meet you in Gray's Inn Walks[2] this lovely evening.

---

[1] Originally a tennis-court (cf. the epilogue to *Love for Love*); it was opened as a theatre in 1662 under Davenant's direction. In 1671 the company removed to Dorset Gardens, where the new house was inaugurated by a performance of Dryden's *Sir Martin Mar-all*, on November the 9th, the prologue for the occasion being written by Etheredge (see the *Poems*). The King's House, in Drury Lane, was under Killigrew's management. Built in 1663 and burnt down in 1672, it was reopened in 1674, with a prologue and epilogue by Dryden. In 1682 the rival companies united.

[2] A favourite promenade. Pepys sometimes strolled there after church; *e.g.*, on Sunday, June 23rd, 1661, when "a great store of gallants" were taking the air.

Lady Cock. And how did he entertain the motion?

Sent. Bless me! I tremble still to think upon it! I could not have imagined he had been so wicked: he counterfeited the greatest passion, railed at his fate, and swore a thousand horrid oaths, that since he came into the playhouse he had notice of a business that concerned both his honour and fortune, and that he was an undone man if he did not go about it presently; prayed me to desire your ladyship to excuse him this evening, and that to-morrow he would be wholly at your devotion.

Lady Cock. Ha, ha, ha! he little thinks how much he has obliged me.

Sent. I had much ado to forbear upbraiding him with his ingratitude to your ladyship.

Lady Cock. Poor Sentry! be not concerned for me; I have conquered my affection, and thou shalt find it is not jealousy has been my counsellor in this. Go, let our hoods and masks be ready, that I may surprise Courtal, and make the best advantage of this lucky opportunity.

Sent. I obey you, madam. [*Exit* SENTRY.

Lady Cock. How am I filled with indignation? To find my person and my passion both despised, and what is more, so much precious time fooled away in fruitless expectation. I would poison my face, so I might be revenged on this ungrateful villain.

Enter SIR OLIVER.

Sir Oliv. My dearest!

Lady Cock. My dearest dear! prithee do not go into the City to-night.

Sir Oliv. My brother Jolley is gone before, and I am to call him at Counsellor Trot's chamber in the Temple.

Lady Cock. Well, if you did but know the fear I have upon me when you are absent, you would not seek occasions to be from me thus.

Sir Oliv. Let me comfort thee with a kiss; what shouldst thou be afraid of?

Lady Cock. I cannot but believe that every woman that sees thee must be in love with thee, as I am. Do not blame my jealousy.

Sir Oliv. I protest I would refuse a countess rather than abuse thee, poor heart.

Lady Cock. And then you are so desperate upon the least occasion, I should have acquainted you else with something that concerns your honour.

Sir Oliv. My honour! you ought in duty to do it.

Lady Cock. Nay, I knew how passionate you would be presently; therefore you shall never know it.

Sir Oliv. Do not leave me in doubt; I shall suspect everyone I look upon; I will kill a common councilman or two before I come back, if you do not tell me.

Lady Cock. Dear, how I tremble! Will you promise me you will not quarrel then? If you tender my life and happiness, I am sure you will not.

Sir Oliv. I will bear anything rather than be an enemy to thy quiet, my dear.

Lady Cock. I could wish Mr. Courtal a man of

better principles, because I know you love him, my dear.

Sir Oliv. Why, what has he done?

Lady Cock. I always treated him with great respects, out of my regard to your friendship; but he, like an impudent man as he is, to-day, misconstruing my civility, in most unseemly language made a foul attempt upon my honour.

Sir Oliv. Death, and hell, and furies, I will have my pumps and long sword!

Lady Cock. Oh, I shall faint! Did not you promise me you would not be so rash?

Sir Oliv. Well, I will not kill him, for fear of murdering thee, my dear.

Lady Cock. You may decline your friendship, and by your coldness give him no encouragement to visit our family.

Sir Oliv. I think thy advice the best for this once, indeed; for it is not fit to publish such a business. But if he should be ever tempting or attempting, let me know it, prithee, my dear.

Lady Cock. If you moderate yourself according to my directions now, I shall never conceal anything from you that may increase your just opinion of my conjugal fidelity.

Sir Oliv. Was ever man blessed with such a virtuous lady! [*Aside.*] Yet cannot I forbear going a-ranging again. Now must I to the Spring Garden to meet my brother Jolley and Madam Rampant.

Lady Cock. Prithee be so good to think how melancholy I spend my time here; for I have joy in no company but thine, and let that bring thee home a little sooner.

Sir Oliv. Thou hast been so kind in this discovery that I am loth to leave thee.

Lady Cock. I wish you had not been engaged so far.

Sir Oliv. Ay, that's it. Farewell, my virtuous dear.
[*Exit* SIR OLIVER.

Lady Cock. Farewell, my dearest dear. I know he has not courage enough to question Courtal; but this will make him hate him, increase his confidence of me, and justify my banishing that false fellow our house: it is not fit a man that has abused my love should come hither and pry into my actions; besides, this will make his access more difficult to that wanton baggage.

Enter ARIANA *and* GATTY *with their hoods and masks.*
Whither are you going, cousins.

Gat. To take the air upon the water, madam.

Aria. And for variety, to walk a turn or two in the New Spring Garden.

Lady Cock. I heard you were gone abroad with Mr. Courtal and Mr. Freeman.

Gat. For heaven's sake, why should your ladyship have such an ill opinion of us?

Lady Cock. The truth is, before I saw you, I believed it merely the vanity of that prating man; Mr. Courtal told Mistress Gazette this morning that you were so well acquainted already that you would meet him and Mr. Freeman anywhere, and that you had promised 'em to receive and make appointment by letters.

Gat. Oh, impudent man!

Aria. Now you see the consequence, sister, of our rambling; they have raised this false story from our innocent fooling with 'em in the Mulberry Garden last night.

Gat. I could almost forswear ever speaking to a man again.

Lady Cock. Was Mr. Courtal in the Mulberry Garden last night?

Aria. Yes, madam.

Lady Cock. And did he speak to you?

Gat. There passed a little harmless raillery betwixt us; but you amaze me, madam.

Aria. I could not imagine any man could be thus unworthy.

Lady Cock. He has quite lost my good opinion too. In duty to Sir Oliver, I have hitherto showed him some countenance; but I shall hate him hereafter for your sakes. But I detain you from your recreations, cousins.

Gat. We are very much obliged to your ladyship for this timely notice.

Aria. and Gat. Your servant, madam.

[*Exeunt* ARIANA *and* GATTY.

Lady Cock. Your servant, cousins.——In the Mulberry Garden last night! when I sat languishing and vainly expecting him at home. This has incensed me so, that I could kill him. I am glad these girls are gone to the Spring Garden, it helps my design; the letters I have counterfeited have appointed Courtal and Freeman to meet them there, they will produce 'em, and confirm all I have said. I will daily poison these girls with such lies as shall make their quarrel to Courtal irreconcilable, and render Freeman only suspected; for I would not have him thought equally guilty. He secretly began to make an address to me at the Bear, and this breach shall give him an opportunity to pursue it.

Enter SENTRY.

Sent. Here are your things, madam.

Lady Cock. That's well. Oh, Sentry, I shall once more be happy; for now Mr. Courtal has given me an occasion that I may without ingratitude check his unlawful passion, and free myself from the trouble of an intrigue that gives me every day such fearful apprehensions of my honour.

[*Exeunt* LADY COCKWOOD *and* SENTRY.

SCENE II.—NEW SPRING GARDEN.

Enter SIR JOSLIN, RAKEHELL, *and Waiter*.

Waiter. Will you be pleased to walk into an arbour, gentlemen?

Sir Jos. By-and-by, good sir.

Rake. I wonder Sir Oliver is not come yet.

Sir Jos. Nay, he will not fail, I warrant thee, boy;

but what's the matter with thy nose, my little Rakehell?

Rake. A foolish accident; jesting at the Fleece this afternoon, I mistook my man a little; a dull rogue that could not understand raillery, made a sudden repartee with a quart pot, Sir Joslin.

Sir Jos. Why didst not thou stick him to the wall, my little Rakehell?

Rake. The truth is, Sir Joslin, he deserved it; but look you, in case of a doubtful wound, I am unwilling to give my friends too often the trouble to bail me; and if it should be mortal, you know a younger brother has not wherewithal to rebate the edge of a witness and mollify the hearts of a jury.

Sir Jos. This is very prudently considered indeed.

Rake. 'Tis time to be wise, sir; my courage has almost run me out of a considerable annuity. When I lived first about this town, I agreed with a surgeon for twenty pounds a quarter to cure me of all the knocks, bruises, and green wounds I should receive, and in one half-year the poor fellow begged me to be released of his bargain, and swore I would undo him else in lint and balsam.

Enter SIR OLIVER.

Sir Jos. Ho! here's my brother Cockwood come.

Sir Oliv. Ay, brother Jolley, I have kept my word, you see; but 'tis a barbarous thing to abuse my lady; I have had such a proof of her virtue, I will tell thee all anon. But where's Madam Rampant, and the rest of the ladies, Mr. Rakehell?

Rake. Faith, sir, being disappointed at noon, they were unwilling any more to set a certainty at hazard. 'Tis term time, and they have severally betook themselves, some to their chamber practice, and others to the places of public pleading.

Sir Oliv. Faith, brother Jolley, let us even go into an arbour, and then feague Mr. Rakehell.

Sir Jos. With all my heart; would we had Madam Rampant.

Sings.

> *She's as frolic and free*
> *As her lovers dare be,*
> *Never awed by a foolish punctilio;*
> *She'll not start from her place,*
> *Though thou nam'st a black ace,*
> *And will drink a beer-glass to Spudilio.*

Hey, boys! Come, come, come! let's in, and delay our sport no longer,

[*Exeunt singing,* She'll not start from her, *&c.*

Enter COURTAL *and* FREEMAN *severally.*

Court. Freeman!

Free. Courtal, what the devil's the matter with thee? I have observed thee prying up and down the walks like a citizen's wife that has dropped her holiday pocket-handkerchief.

Court. What unlucky devil has brought thee hither?

Free. I believe a better natured devil than yours,

Courtal, if a leveret be better meat than an old puss that has been coursed by most of the young fellows of her country. I am not working my brain for a counterplot; a disappointment is not my business.

Court. You are mistaken, Freeman. Prithee be gone and leave me the garden to myself, or I shall grow as testy as an old fowler that is put by his shoot after he has crept half a mile upon his belly.

Free. Prithee be thou gone, or I shall take it as unkindly as a chemist would, if thou shouldst kick down his limbec in the very minute that he looked for projection.

Court. Come, come, you must yield, Freeman; your business cannot be of such consequence as mine.

Free. If ever thou hadst a business of such consequence in thy life as mine is, I will condescend to be made incapable of affairs presently.

Court. Why, I have an appointment made me, man, without my seeking, by a woman for whom I would have mortgaged my whole estate to have had her abroad but to break a cheese-cake.

Free. And I have an appointment made me without my seeking too, by such a she, that I will break the whole ten commandments rather than disappoint her of her breaking one.

Court. Come, you do but jest, Freeman; a forsaken mistress could not be more malicious than thou art. Prithee be gone.

Free. Prithee do thou be gone.

Court. 'Sdeath! the sight of thee will scare my woman for ever.

Free. 'Sdeath! the sight of thee will make my woman believe me the falsest villain breathing.

Court. We shall stand fooling till we are both undone, and I know not how to help it.

Free. Let us proceed honestly like friends, discover the truth of things to one another, and if we cannot reconcile our business, we will draw cuts and part fairly.

Court. I do not like that way; for talk is only allowable at the latter end of an intrigue, and should never be used at the beginning of an amour, for fear of frighting a young lady from her good intentions—— Yet I care not, though I read the letter; but I will conceal the name.

Free. I have a letter too, and am content to do the same.

Court. (*reads*). *Sir, in sending you this letter, I proceed against the modesty of our sex*——

Free. 'Sdeath! this begins just like my letter.

Court. Do you read on then.

Free. (*reads*). *But let not the good opinion I have conceived of you, make you too severe in your censuring of me*——

Court. Word for word.

Free. Now do you read again.

Court. (*reads*). *If you give yourself the trouble to be walking in the New Spring Garden this evening, I will meet you there and tell you a secret, which I have reason to fear, because it comes to your knowledge by my means, will make you hate your humble servant.*

Free. Verbatim my letter, heyday!

Court. Prithee let's compare the hands.

[*They compare them.*

Free. 'Sdeath! the hand's the same.

Court. I hope the name is not the same too.

Free. If it be, we are finely jilted, faith.

Court. I long to be undeceived; prithee do thou show first, Freeman.

Free. No——but both together, if you will.

Court. Agreed.

Free. Ariana.

Court. Gatty——Ha, ha, ha!

Free. The little rogues are masculine in their proceedings, and have made one another confidantes in their love.

Court. But I do not like this altogether so well, Frank; I wish they had appointed us several places; for though 'tis evident they have trusted one another with the bargain, no woman ever seals before witness.

Free. Prithee, how didst thou escape the snares of the old devil this afternoon?

Court. With much ado: Sentry had set me; if her ladyship had got me into her clutches, there had been no getting off without a rescue, or paying down the money; for she always arrests upon execution.

Free. You made a handsome lie to her woman.

Court. For all this, I know she's angry; for she thinks nothing a just excuse in these cases, though it were to save the forfeit of a man's estate, or reprieve the life of her own natural brother.

Free. Faith, thou hast not done altogether like a gentleman with her; thou shouldst fast thyself up to a stomach now and then, to oblige her; if there were nothing in it but the hearty welcome, methinks 'twere enough to make thee bear sometimes with the homeliness of the fare.

Court. I know not what I might do in a camp, where there was no other woman; but I shall hardly in this town, where there is such plenty, forbear good meat, to get myself an appetite to horseflesh.

Free. This is rather an aversion in thee, than any real fault in the woman; if this lucky business had not fallen out, I intended with your good leave to have outbid you for her ladyship's favour.

Court. I should never have consented to that, Frank; though I am a little restiff at present, I am not such a jade but I should strain if another rode against me; I have e'er now liked nothing in a woman that I have loved at last in spite only because another had a mind to her.

Free. Yonder are a couple of vizards tripping towards us.

Court. 'Tis they, i'faith.

Free. We need not divide, since they come together.

Court. I was a little afraid, when we compared letters, they had put a trick upon us; but now I am confirmed they are mighty honest.

Enter ARIANA *and* GATTY.

Aria. We cannot avoid 'em.

Gat. Let us dissemble our knowledge of their business a little, and then take 'em down in the height of their assurance.

Court. and *Free.* Your servant, ladies.

Aria. I perceive it is as impossible, gentlemen, to walk without you as without our shadows: never were poor women so haunted by the ghosts of their self-murdered lovers.

Gat. If it should be our good fortunes to have you in love with us, we will take care you shall not grow desperate and leave the world in an ill-humour.

Aria. If you should, certainly your ghosts would be very malicious.

Court. 'Twere pity you should have your curtains drawn in the dead of the night, and your pleasing slumbers interrupted by anything but flesh and blood, ladies.

Free. Shall we walk a turn?

Aria. By yourselves, if you please.

Gat. Our company may put a constraint upon you; for I find you daily hover about these gardens, as a kite does about a backside, watching an opportunity to catch up the poultry.

Aria. Woe be to the daughter or wife of some merchant tailor or poor feltmaker now! for you seldom row to Foxhall[1] without some such plot against the City.

---

[1] *i.e.* Vauxhall, famed for its gardens, which were called the "New Spring Gardens." They were laid out in 1661, or thereabout. Allusions to them in Pepys (who complained of their being dear) and the dramatists are endless. Sir Roger and Mr. Spectator went there by water; the former deplored the comparative scarcity of nightingales in the grounds.—*Spectator*, No.

Free. You wrong us, ladies; our business has happily succeeded, since we have the honour to wait upon you.

Gat. You could not expect to see us here.

Court. Your true lover, madam, when he misses his mistress, is as restless as a spaniel that has lost his master; he ranges up and down the plays, the Park, and all the gardens, and never stays long but where he has the happiness to see her.

Gat. I suppose your mistress, Mr. Courtal, is always the last woman you are acquainted with.

Court. Do not think, madam, I have that false measure of my acquaintance which poets have of their verses, always to think the last best—though I esteem you so, in justice to your merit.

Gat. Or if you do not love her best, you always love to talk of her most; as a barren coxcomb that wants discourse is ever entertaining company out of the last book he read in.

Court. Now you accuse me most unjustly, madam; who the devil that has common sense will go a-birding with a clack in his cap?

Aria. Nay, we do not blame you, gentlemen; every one in their way: a huntsman talks of his dogs, a falconer of his hawks, a jockey of his horse, and a gallant of his mistress.

Gat. Without the allowance of this vanity, an amour would soon grow as dull as matrimony.

383. After 1702 the fame of the gardens declined; in 1732 they were reopened with great success, and continued popular down to the days of Becky Sharp.

Court. Whatsoever you say, ladies, I cannot believe you think us men of such abominable principles.

Free. For my part, I have ever held it as ungrateful to boast of the favours of a mistress as to deny the courtesies of a friend.

Court. A friend that bravely ventures his life in the field to serve me, deserves but equally with a mistress that kindly exposes her honour to oblige me, especially when she does it as generously too, and with as little ceremony.

Free. And I would no more betray the honour of such a woman, than I would the life of a man that should rob on purpose to supply me.

Gat. We believe you men of honour, and know it is below you to talk of any woman that deserves it.

Aria. You are so generous, you seldom insult after a victory.

Gat. And so vain, that you always triumph before it.

Court. 'Sdeath! what's the meaning of all this?

Gat. Though you find us so kind, Mr. Courtal, pray do not tell Mistress Gazette to-morrow that we came hither on purpose this evening to meet you.

Court. I would as soon print it, and fee a fellow to post it up with the playbills.

Gat. You have reposed a great deal of confidence in her, for all you pretend this ill opinion of her secresy now.

Court. I never trusted her with the name of a mistress that I should be jealous of if I saw her receive fruit and go out of the playhouse with a stranger.

Gat. For aught as I see, we are infinitely obliged to you, sir.

Court. 'Tis impossible to be insensible of so much goodness, madam?

Gat. What goodness, pray, sir?

Court. Come, come, give over this raillery.

Gat. You are so ridiculously unworthy, that 'twere a folly to reprove you with a serious look.

Court. On my conscience, your heart begins to fail you, now we are coming to the point, as a young fellow's that was never in the field before.

Gat. You begin to amaze me.

Court. Since you yourself sent the challenge, you must not in honour fly off now.

Gat. Challenge! Oh, heavens! this confirms all. Were I a man, I would kill thee for the injuries thou hast already done me.

Free. (*to* ARIANA). Let not your suspicion of my unkindness make you thus scrupulous; was ever city ill treated that surrendered without assault or summons?

Aria. Dear sister, what ill spirit brought us hither? I never met with so much impudence in my life.

Court. (*aside*). Hey, jilts! they are as good at it already as the old one, i'faith.

Free. Come, ladies, you have exercised your wit enough; you would not venture letters of such consequence for a jest only.

Gat. Letters! Bless me, what will this come to?

Court. To that none of us shall have cause to repent, I hope, madam.

Aria. Let us fly 'em, sister; they are devils, and not men; they could never be so malicious else.

Enter LADY COCKWOOD *and* SENTRY.

Lady Cock. Your servant, cousins.

Court. (*starting*). Ho, my Lady Cockwood! My ears are grown an inch already.

Aria. My lady! She'll think this an appointment, sister.

Free. This is Madam Macchiavel, I suspect, Courtal.

Court. Nay, 'tis her plot doubtless. Now am I as much out of countenance as I should be if Sir Oliver should take me making bold with her ladyship

Lady Cock. Do not let me discompose you; I can walk alone, cousins.

Gat. Are you so uncharitable, madam, to think we have any business with 'em?

Aria. It has been our ill fortune to meet 'em here, and nothing could be so lucky as your coming, madam, to free us from 'em.

Gat. They have abused us in the grossest manner.

Aria. Counterfeited letters under our hands.

Lady Cock. Never trouble yourselves, cousins; I have heard this is a common practice with such unworthy men. Did they not threaten to divulge them, and defame you to the world?

Gat. We cannot believe they intend anything less, madam.

Lady Cock. Doubtless they had such a mean opinion

of your wit and honour, that they thought to fright you to a base compliance with their wicked purposes.

Aria. I hate the very sight of 'em.

Gat. I could almost wish myself a disease, to breathe infection upon 'em.

Court. Very pretty! we have carried on our designs very luckily against these young ladies.

Free. We have lost their good opinion for ever.

Lady Cock. I know not whether their folly or their impudence be greater; they are not worth your anger, they are only fit to be laughed at and despised.

Court. A very fine old devil this!

Lady Cock. Mr. Freeman, this is not like a gentleman, to affront a couple of young ladies thus; but I cannot blame you so much, you are in a manner a stranger to our family. But I wonder how that base man can look me in the face, considering how civilly he has been treated at our house.

Court. The truth is, madam, I am a rascal; but I fear you have contributed to the making me so. Be not as unmerciful as the devil is to a poor sinner.

Sent. Did you ever see the like? Never trust me, if he has not the confidence to make my virtuous lady accessory to his wickedness.

Lady Cock. Ay, Sentry! 'tis a miracle if my honour escapes, considering the access which his greatness with Sir Oliver has given him daily to me.

Free. Faith, ladies, we did not counterfeit these letters; we are abused as well as you.

Court. I received mine from a porter at the King's

Playhouse, and I will show it you, that you may see if you know the hand.

Lady Cock. Sentry, are you sure they never saw any of your writing?

Court. 'Sdeath! I am so discomposed, I know not where I have put it.

Sent. Oh, madam! now I remember myself, Mistress Gatty helped me once to indite a letter to my sweetheart.

Lady Cock. Forgetful wench! then I am undone.

Court. Oh! here it is——Hey, who's here?

[*As he has the letter in his hand, enter* SIR JOSLIN, SIR OLIVER, *and* RAKEHELL, *all drunk, with music.*

They sing.
She's no mistress of mine
That drinks not her wine,
Or frowns at my friend's drinking motions;
If my heart thou wouldst gain,
Drink thy bottle of champagne.
'Twill serve thee for paint and love-potions.

Sir Oliv. Who's here? Courtal, in my lady's company! I'll despatch him presently; help me, brother Jolley. [*He draws.*

Lady Cock. For heaven's sake, Sir Oliver!

Court. (*drawing*). What do you mean, sir?

Sir Oliv. I'll teach you more manners than to make your attempts on my lady, sir.

P

Lady Cock. and Sent. Oh! murder, murder!

[*They shriek.*

Lady Cock. Save my dear Sir Oliver! Oh, my dear Sir Oliver!

[*The young ladies shriek and run out; they all draw to part them; they fight off the stage;* LADY COCKWOOD *shrieks and runs out.*

ACT V.

SCENE I.—SIR OLIVER'S DINING-ROOM.

Enter LADY COCKWOOD. *Table and carpet.*

Lady Cockwood.

I DID not think he had been so desperate in his drink; if they had killed one another, I had then been revenged and freed from all my fears.

Enter SENTRY.

Sentry, your carelessness and forgetfulness some time or other will undo me. Had not Sir Oliver and Sir Joslin come so luckily into the garden, the letters had been discovered, and my honour left to the mercy of a false man and two young fleering girls. Did you speak to Mr. Freeman unperceived in the hurry?

Sent. I did, madam, and he promised me to disengage himself as soon as possibly he could, and wait upon your ladyship with all secresy.

Lady Cock. I have some reason to believe him a man of honour.

Sent. Methinks indeed his very look, madam, speaks him to be much more a gentleman than Mr. Courtal;

but I was unwilling before now to let your ladyship know my opinion, for fear of offending your inclinations.

Lady Cock. I hope by his means to get these letters into my own hands, and so prevent the inconveniences they may bring upon my honour.

Sent. I wonder, madam, what should be Sir Oliver's quarrel to Mr. Courtal.

Lady Cock. You know how apt he is to be suspicious in his drink; 'tis very likely he thought Mr. Courtal betrayed him at the Bear to-day.

Sent. Pray heaven he be not jealous of your ladyship, finding you abroad so unexpectedly; if he be, we shall have a sad hand of him when he comes home, madam.

Lady Cock. I should have apprehended it much myself, Sentry, if his drunkenness had not unadvisedly engaged him in his quarrel; as soon as he grows a little sober, I am sure his fear will bring him home, and make him apply himself to me with all humility and kindness; for he is ever underhand fain to use my interest and discretion to make friends to compound these businesses, or to get an order for the securing his person and his honour.

Sent. I believe verily Mr. Courtal would have been so rude to have killed him, if Mr. Freeman and the rest had not civilly interposed their weapons.

Lady Cock. Heavens forbid! though he be a wicked man, I am obliged in duty to love him. Whither did my cousins go after we came home, Sentry?

Sent. They are at the next door, madam, laughing

and playing at lanterloo¹ with my old Lady Loveyouth and her daughters.

Lady Cock. I hope they will not come home then to interrupt my affairs with Mr. Freeman.

[*Knocking without.*

Hark! somebody knocks, it may be him; run down quickly.

Sent. I fly, madam. [*Exit* SENTRY.

Lady Cock. Now if he has a real inclination for my person, I'll give him a handsome opportunity to reveal it.

Enter SENTRY *and* FREEMAN.

Free. Your servant, madam.

Lady Cock. Oh, Mr. Freeman! this unlucky accident has robbed me of all my quiet; I am almost distracted with thinking of the danger Sir Oliver's dear life is in.

Free. You need not fear, madam, all things will be reconciled again to-morrow.

Sent. You would not blame my lady's apprehensions, did you but know the tenderness of her affections.

Lady Cock. Mr. Courtal is a false and merciless man.

Free. He has always owned a great respect for your ladyship, and I never heard him mention you with the least dishonour.

Lady Cock. He cannot without injuring the truth;

---

¹ Or lantrillou; also lanctre loo. From the French *lanturelu?* The game is often referred to.

heaven knows my innocence. I hope you did not let him know, sir, of your coming hither.

Free. I should never merit the happiness to wait upon you again, had I so abused this extraordinary favour, madam.

Lady Cock. If I have done anything unbeseeming my honour, I hope you will be just, sir, and impute it to my fear. I know no man so proper to compose this unfortunate difference as yourself, and if a lady's tears and prayers have power to move you to compassion, I know you will employ your utmost endeavour to preserve me my dear Sir Oliver.

Free. Do not, madam, afflict yourself so much; I dare engage my life, his life and honour shall be both secure.

Lady Cock. You are truly noble, sir; I was so distracted with my fears that I cannot well remember how we parted at the Spring Garden.

Free. We all divided, madam; after your ladyship and the young ladies were gone together, Sir Oliver, Sir Joslin, and the company with them, took one boat, and Mr. Courtal and I another.

Lady Cock. Then I need not apprehend their meeting again to-night.

Free. You need not, madam; I left Mr. Courtal in his chamber wondering what should make Sir Oliver draw upon him, and fretting and fuming about the trick that was put upon us with the letters to-day.

Lady Cock. Oh! I had almost forgot myself; I assure you, sir, those letters were sent by one that has no inclination to be any enemy of yours.

[*Knocking below.*

Somebody knocks. [*Exit* SENTRY.
If it be Sir Oliver, I am undone; he will hate me mortally if he does but suspect I use any secret means to hinder him from justifying his reputation honourably to the world.

Enter SENTRY.

Sent. Oh, madam! here is Mr. Courtal below in the entry, discharging a coachman; I told him your ladyship was busy, but he would not hear me, and I find, do what I can, he will come up.

Lady Cock. I would not willingly suspect you, sir.

Free. I have deceived him, madam, in my coming hither, and am as unwilling he should find me here as you can be.

Lady Cock. He will not believe my innocent business with you, but will raise a new scandal on my honour, and publish it to the whole town.

Sent. Let him step into the closet, madam.

Lady Cock. Quick, sir, quick, I beseech you; I will send him away again immediately. [*Exit* SENTRY.

Enter COURTAL.

Lady Cock. Mr. Courtal! Have you no sense of honour nor modesty left? After so many injuries, to come into our house, and without my approbation rudely press upon my retirement thus?

Court. Pray, madam, hear my business.

Lady Cock. Thy business is maliciously to pursue my ruin; thou com'st with a base design to have Sir

Oliver catch thee here and destroy the only happiness I have.

Court. I come, madam, to beg your pardon for the fault I did unwillingly commit, and to know of you the reason of Sir Oliver's quarrel to me.

Lady Cock. Thy guilty conscience is able to tell thee that, vain and ungrateful man!

Court. I am innocent, madam, of all things that may offend him; and I am sure, if you would but hear me, I should remove the justice of your quarrel too.

Lady Cock. You are mistaken, sir, if you think I am concerned for your going to the Spring Garden this evening; my quarrel is the same with Sir Oliver, and is so just, that thou deserv'st to be poisoned for what thou hast done.

Court. Pray, madam, let me know my fault.

Lady Cock. I blush to think upon't. Sir Oliver since we came from the Bear has heard something thou hast said concerning me; but what it is I could not get him to discover. He told me 'twas enough for me to know he was satisfied of my innocence.

Court. This is mere passion, madam.

Lady Cock. This is the usual revenge of such base men as thou art, when they cannot compass their ends, with their venomous tongues to blast the honour of a lady.

Court. This is a sudden alteration, madam; within these few hours you had a kinder opinion of me.

Lady Cock. 'Tis no wonder you brag of favours behind my back, that have the impudence to upbraid me with kindness to my face. Dost thou think I could ever have a good thought of thee, whom I have always found so treacherous in thy friendship to Sir Oliver? [*Knock at the door.*

Enter SENTRY.

Sent. Oh, madam! here is Sir Oliver come home.

Lady Cock. Oh, heavens! I shall be believed guilty now, and he will kill us both. [*He draws.*

Court. I warrant you, madam, I'll defend your life.

Lady Cock. Oh! there will be murder, murder; for heaven's sake, sir, hide yourself in some corner or other.

Court. I'll step into that closet, madam.

Sent. Hold, hold, sir, by no means; his pipes and his tobacco-box lie there, and he always goes in to fetch 'em.

Lady Cock. Your malice will soon be at an end: heaven knows what will be the fatal consequence of your being found here.

Sent. Madam, let him creep under the table, the carpet is long enough to hide him.

Lady Cock. Have you good-nature enough to save the life and reputation of a lady?

Court. Anything to oblige you, madam.

[*He goes under the table.*

Lady Cock. (*running to the closet*). Be sure you do not stir, sir, whatsoever happens.

Court. Not unless he pulls me out by the ears.

Sent. Good! he thinks my lady speaks to him.

Enter SIR OLIVER.

Lady Cock. My dear Sir Oliver.——

Sir Oliv. I am unworthy of this kindness, madam.

Lady Cock. Nay, I intend to chide you for your naughtiness anon; but I cannot choose but hug thee and kiss thee a little first; I was afraid I should never have had thee alive within these arms again.

Sir Oliv. Your goodness does so increase my shame, I know not what to say, madam.

Lady Cock. Well, I am glad I have thee safe at home. I will lock thee up above in my chamber, and will not so much as trust thee downstairs till there be an end of this quarrel.

Sir Oliv. I was so little myself, I knew not what I did, else I had not exposed my person to so much danger before thy face.

Sent. 'Twas cruelly done, sir, knowing the killing concerns my lady has for you.

Lady Cock. If Mr. Courtal had killed thee I was resolved not to survive thee; but before I had died I would have dearly revenged thy murder.

Sir Oliv. As soon as I had recollected myself a little, I could not rest till I came home to give thee this satisfaction, that I will do nothing without thy advice and approbation, my dear. I know thy love makes thy life depend upon mine, and it is unreasonable I should upon my own rash head hazard that, though it be for the justification of thy honour. Uds me! I have let fall a China orange[1] that was recom-

---

[1] "A great rarity," says Pepys, "none to be had."—March 6th, 1666.

mended to me for one of the best that came over this year. 'Slife, light the candle, Sentry; 'tis run under the table. [*Knocking.*

Lady Cock. Oh, I am not well!

Sent. Oh, heaven! who's that that knocks so hastily?

[SENTRY *takes up the candle; there is a great knocking at the door; she runs away with the candle.*

Sir Oliv. Why, Sentry! bring back the candle. Are you mad to leave us in the dark, and your lady not well? How is it, my dear!

Lady Cock. For heaven's sake run after her, Sir Oliver, snatch the candle out of her hand, and teach her more manners.

Sir Oliv. I will, my dear. [*Exit* SIR OLIVER.

Lady Cock. What shall I do? Was ever woman so unfortunate in the management of affairs!

Court. What will become of me now?

Lady Cock. It must be so; I had better trust my honour to the mercy of them two than be betrayed to my husband. Mr. Courtal, give me your hand quickly, I beseech you.

Court. Here, here, madam; what's to be done now?

Lady Cock. I will put you into the closet, sir.

Court. He'll be coming in for his tobacco-box and pipes.

Lady Cock. Never fear that, sir.

Free. (*out of the closet door*). Now shall I be discovered; pox on your honourable intrigue, would I were safe at Gifford's!

Lady Cock. Here, here, sir, this is the door; whatsoever you feel, be not frighted; for should you make the least disturbance, you will destroy the life, and, what is more, the honour of an unfortunate lady.

Court. So, so, if you have occasion to remove again, make no ceremony, madam.

Enter SIR OLIVER, SENTRY, ARIANA, *and* GATTY.

Sir Oliv. Here is the candle; how dost thou, my dear?

Lady Cock. I could not imagine, Sentry, you had been so ill-bred to run away and leave your master and me in the dark.

Sent. I thought there had been another candle upon the table, madam.

Lady Cock. Good! you thought! you are always excusing of your carelessness; such another misdemeanour——

Sir Oliv. Prithee, my dear, forgive her.

Lady Cock. The truth is, I ought not to be very angry with her at present, 'tis a good-natured creature; she was so frighted, for fear of thy being mischiefed in the Spring Garden, that I verily believe she scarce knows what she does yet.

Sir Oliv. Light the candle, Sentry, that I may look for my orange.

Lady Cock. You have been at my Lady Loveyouth's, cousins, I hear.

Aria. We have, madam.

Gat. She charged us to remember her service to you.

Sir Oliv. So, here it is, my dear; I brought it home on purpose for thee.

Lady Cock. 'Tis a lovely orange, indeed! Thank you, my dear; I am so discomposed with the fright I have had, that I would fain be at rest.

Sir Oliv. Get a candle, Sentry. Will you go to bed, my dear?

Lady Cock. With all my heart, Sir Oliver. 'Tis late, cousins, you had best retire to your chamber, too.

Gat. We shall not stay long here, madam.

Sir Oliv. Come, my dear.

Lady Cock. Good night, cousins.

Gat. and Aria. Your servant, madam.

[*Exeunt* SIR OLIVER, LADY COCKWOOD, *and* SENTRY.

Aria. I cannot but think of those letters, sister.

Gat. That is, you cannot but think of Mr. Freeman, sister; I perceive he runs in thy head as much as a new gown uses to do in the country the night before 'tis expected from London.

Aria. You need not talk, for I am sure the losses of an unlucky gamester are not more his meditation than Mr. Courtal is yours.

Gat. He has made some slight impression on my memory, I confess; but I hope a night will wear him out again, as it does the noise of a fiddle after dancing.

Aria. Love, like some stains, will wear out of itself, I know, but not in such a little time as you talk of, sister.

Gat. It cannot last longer than the stain of a mulberry at most; the next season out that goes, and my heart cannot be long unfruitful, sure.

Aria. Well, I cannot believe they forged these letters. What should be their end?

Gat. That you may easily guess at; but methinks they took a very improper way to compass it.

Aria. It looks more like the malice or jealousy of a woman than the design of two witty men.

Gat. If this should prove a fetch of her ladyship's, now, that is a-playing the loving hypocrite above with her dear Sir Oliver.

Aria. How unluckily we were interrupted when they were going to show us the hand!

Gat. That might have discovered all: I have a small suspicion that there has been a little familiarity between her ladyship and Mr. Courtal.

Aria. Our finding of 'em together in the Exchange, and several passages I observed at the Bear, have almost made me of the same opinion.

Gat. Yet I would fain believe the continuance of it is more her desire than his inclination. That which makes me mistrust him most is her knowing we made 'em an appointment.

Aria. If she were jealous of Mr. Courtal she would not be jealous of Mr. Freeman too; they both pretend to have received letters.

Gat. There is something in it more than we are able to imagine; time will make it out, I hope, to the advantage of the gentlemen.

Aria. I would gladly have it so; for I believe, should they give us a just cause, we should find it a hard task to hate them.

Gat. How I love the song I learnt t'other day, since I saw them in the Mulberry Garden!

She sings.

To little or no purpose I spent many days
In ranging the Park, th' Exchange, and the plays;
For ne'er in my rambles, till now, did I prove
So lucky to meet with the man I could love.
Oh! how I am pleased when I think on this man,
That I find I must love, let me do what I can!

How long I shall love him I can no more tell
Than, had I a fever, when I should be well.
My passion shall kill me before I will show it,
And yet I would give all the world he did know it:
But oh! how I sigh when I think, should he woo me,
I cannot deny what I know would undo me!

Aria. Fie, sister! thou art so wanton.

Gat. I hate to dissemble when I need not; 'twould look as affected in us to be reserved now we're alone, as for a player to maintain the character she acts in the tiring-room.

Aria. Prithee sing a good song.

Gat. Now art thou for a melancholy madrigal, composed by some amorous coxcomb who swears in all companies he loves his mistress so well, that he would not do her the injury were she willing to grant him the favour, and it may be is sot enough to believe he would oblige her in keeping his oath, too.

Aria. Well, I will reach thee thy guitar out of the closet, to take thee off of this subject.

Gat. I'd rather be a nun than a lover at thy rate: devotion is not able to make me half so serious as love has made thee already.

[ARIANA *opens the closet,* COURTAL *and* FREEMAN *come out.*

Court. Ha, Freeman! Is this your business with a lawyer? Here's a new discovery, i'faith!

[*The ladies shriek and run out.*

Free. Peace, man, I will satisfy your jealousy hereafter; since we have made this lucky discovery, let us mind the present businesses.

[COURTAL *and* FREEMAN *catch the ladies and bring them back.*

Court. Nay, ladies, now we have caught you, there is no escaping till we're come to a right understanding.

Enter[1] LADY COCKWOOD, SIR OLIVER, *and* SENTRY.

Free. Come, never blush, we are as loving as you can be for your hearts, I assure you.

Court. Had it not been our good-fortunes to have been concealed here, you would have had ill-nature enough to dissemble with us at least a fortnight longer.

Lady Cock. What's the matter with you here? Are you mad, cousins? Bless me, Mr. Courtal and Mr. Freeman! in our house at these unseasonable hours!

Sir Oliv. Fetch me down my long sword, Sentry; I lay my life Courtal has been tempting the honour of the young ladies.

Lady Cock. Oh, my dear! [*She holds him.*

---

[1] Obviously they are not immediately seen by the characters already on the stage.

Gat. We are almost scared out of our wits; my sister went to reach my guitar out of the closet, and found 'em both shut up there.

Lady Cock. Come, come, this will not serve your turn; I am afraid you had a design secretly to convey 'em into your chamber. Well, I will have no more of these doings in my family, my dear; Sir Joslin shall remove these girls to-morrow.

Free. You injure the young ladies, madam; their surprise shows their innocence.

Court. If anybody be to blame, it is Mistress Sentry.

Sent. What mean you, sir? Heaven knows, I know no more of their being here——

Court. Nay, nay, Mistress Sentry, you need not be ashamed to own the doing of a couple of young gentlemen such a good office.

Sent. Do not think to put your tricks upon me, sir.

Court. Understanding by Mistress Sentry, madam, that these young ladies would very likely sit and talk in the dining-room an hour before they went to bed of the accidents of the day, and being impatient to know whether that unlucky business which happened in the Spring Garden about the letters had quite destroyed our hopes of gaining their esteem; for a small sum of money Mr. Freeman and I obtained the favour of her to shut us up where we might overhear 'em.

Lady Cock. Is this the truth, Sentry?

Sent. I humbly beg your pardon, madam.

Lady Cock. A lady's honour is not safe that keeps

a servant so subject to corruption; I will turn her out of my service for this.

Sir Oliv. Good! I was suspicious their businesses had been with my lady at first.

Lady Cock. (*aside*). Now will I be in charity with him again, for putting this off so handsomely.

Sir Oliv. Hark you, my dear, shall I forbid Mr. Courtal my house?

Lady Cock. Oh! by no means, my dear; I had forgot to tell thee, since I acquainted thee with that business, I have been discoursing with my Lady Loveyouth, and she blamed me infinitely for letting thee know it, and laughed exceedingly at me, believing Mr. Courtal intended thee no injury, and told me 'twas only a harmless gallantry which his French breeding has used him to.

Sir Oliv. Faith, I am apt enough to believe it; for, on my conscience, he is a very honest fellow. Ned Courtal! How the devil came it about that thee and I fell to sa, sa, in the Spring Garden?

Court. You are best able to resolve yourself that, Sir Oliver.

Sir Oliv. Well, the devil take me, if I had the least unkindness for thee. Prithee, let us embrace and kiss, and be as good friends as ever we were, dear rogue.

Court. I am so reasonable, Sir Oliver, that I will ask no other satisfaction for the injury you have done me.

Free. Here's the letter, madam.

Aria. Sister, look here, do you know this hand?

Gat. 'Tis Sentry's.

Lady Cock. Oh, heavens! I shall be ruined yet.

Gat. She has been the contriver of all this mischief.

Court. Nay, now you lay too much to her charge in this; she was but my lady's secretary, I assure you; she has discovered the whole plot to us.

Sent. What does he mean?

Lady Cock. Will he betray me at last?

Court. My lady being in her nature severely virtuous, is, it seems, offended at the innocent freedom you take in rambling up and down by yourselves; which made her, out of a tenderness to your reputations, counterfeit these letters, in hopes to fright you to that reservedness which she approves of.

Lady Cock. (*aside*). This has almost redeemed my opinion of his honour. Cousins, the little regard you had to the good counsel I gave you, puts me upon this business.

Gat. Pray, madam, what was it Mistress Gazette told you concerning us?

Lady Cock. Nothing, nothing, cousins. What I told you of Mr. Courtal was mere invention, the better to carry on my design for your good.

Court. Freeman! Pray, what brought you hither?

Free. A kind summons from her ladyship.

Court. Why did you conceal it from me?

Free. I was afraid thy peevish jealousy might have destroyed the design I had of getting an opportunity to clear ourselves to the young ladies.

Court. Fortune has been our friend in that beyond

expectation. [*To the Ladies.*] I hope, ladies, you are satisfied of our innocence now.

Gat. Well, had you been found guilty of the letters, we were resolved to have counterfeited two contracts under your hands, and have suborned witnesses to swear 'em.

Aria. That had been a full revenge; for I know you would think it as great a scandal to be thought to have an inclination for marriage, as we should to be believed willing to take our freedom without it.

Court. The more probable thing, ladies, had been only to pretend a promise; we have now and then courage enough to venture so far for a valuable consideration.

Gat. The truth is, such experienced gentlemen as you are seldom mortgage your persons without it be to redeem your estates.

Court. 'Tis a mercy we have 'scaped the mischief so long and are like to do penance only for our own sins; most families are a wedding behindhand in the world, which makes so many young men fooled into wives, to pay their fathers' debts. All the happiness a gentleman can desire is, to live at liberty till he be forced that way to pay his own.

Free. Ladies, you know we are not ignorant of the good intentions you have towards us; pray let us treat a little.

Gat. I hope you are not in so desperate a condition as to have a good opinion of marriage, are you?

Aria. 'Tis to as little purpose to treat with us of anything under that, as it is for those kind ladies that have obliged you with a valuable consideration to challenge the performance of your promise.

Sir Oliv. Well, and how, and how, my dear Ned, goes the business between you and these ladies? Are you like to drive a bargain?

Court. Faith, Sir Oliver, we are about it.

Sir Oliv. And cannot agree, I warrant you; they are for having you take a lease for life, and you are for being tenants at will, Ned; is it not so?

Gat. These gentlemen have found it so convenient lying in lodgings, they'll hardly venture on the trouble of taking a house of their own.

Court. A pretty country seat, madam, with a handsome parcel of land, and other necessaries belonging to't, may tempt us; but for a town tenement that has but one poor conveniency, we are resolved we'll never deal. [*A noise of music without.*

Sir Oliv. Hark! my brother Jolley's come home.

Aria. Now, gentlemen, you had best look to yourselves, and come to an agreement with us quickly; for I'll lay my life my uncle has brought home a couple of fresh chapmen that will outbid you.

Enter SIR JOSLIN, *with music.*

Sir Jos. Hey, boys! [*Dance.*

Sings.

A catch and a glass,
A fiddle and a lass,
What more would an honest man have?

> *Hang your temperate sot,*
> *Who would seem what he's not;*
> *'Tis I am wise, he's but grave.*

Sir Jos. What's here? Mr. Courtal and Mr. Freeman!

Sir Oliv. Oh, man! here has been the prettiest, the luckiest discovery on all sides! We are all good friends again.

Sir Jos. Hark you, brother Cockwood, I have got Madam Rampant; Rakehell and she are without.

Sir Oliv. Oh, heavens! Dear brother Jolley, send her away immediately; my lady has such an aversion to a naughty woman that she will swoon if she does but see her.

Sir Jos. Faith, I was hard put to't; I wanted a lover, and rather than I would break my old wont I dressed up Rampant in a suit I bought of Rakehell; but since this good company's here,

Enter RAKEHELL.

I'll send her away. My little Rakehell, come hither; you see here are two powerful rivals; therefore, for fear of kicking, or a worse disaster, take Rampant with you, and be going quickly.

Rake. Your humble servant, sir.

[*Exit* RAKEHELL.

Court. You may hereafter spare yourself this labour, Sir Joslin; Mr. Freeman and I have vowed ourselves humble servants to these ladies.

Free. I hope we shall have your approbation, sir.

Sir Jos. Nay, if you have a mind to commit matrimony, I'll send for a canonical sir shall despatch you presently.

Free. You cannot do better.

Court. What think you of taking us in the humour? Consideration may be your foe, ladies.

Aria. Come, gentlemen, I'll make you a fair proposition; since you have made a discovery of our inclinations, my sister and I will be content to admit you in the quality of servants.

Gat. And if, after a month's experience of your good behaviour, upon serious thoughts, you have courage enough to engage further, we will accept of the challenge and believe you men of honour.

Sir Jos. Well spoke, i'faith, girls; and is it a match, boys?

Court. If the heart of man be not very deceitful, 'tis very likely it may be so.

Free. A month is a tedious time, and will be a dangerous trial of our resolutions; but I hope we shall not repent before marriage, whate'er we do after.

Sir Jos. How stand matters between you and your lady, brother Cockwood? Is there peace on all sides?

Sir Oliv. Perfect concord, man; I will tell thee all that has happened since I parted from thee when we are alone; 'twill make thee laugh heartily. Never man was so happy in a virtuous and a loving lady!

Sir Jos. Though I have led Sir Oliver astray this

day or two, I hope you will not exclude me the Act of Oblivion,[1] madam.

Lady Cock. The nigh relation I have to you, and the respect I know Sir Oliver has for you, makes me forget all that has passed, sir; but pray be not the occasion of any new transgressions.

Sent. I hope, Mr. Courtal, since my endeavours to serve you have ruined me in the opinion of my lady, you will intercede for a reconciliation.

Court. Most willingly, Mistress Sentry——Faith, madam, since things have fallen out so luckily, you must needs receive your woman into favour again.

Lady Cock. Her crime is unpardonable, sir.

Sent. Upon some solemn protestations, madam, that the gentlemen's intentions were honourable, and having reason to believe the young ladies had no aversion to their inclinations, I was of opinion I should have been ill-natured if I had not assisted 'em in the removing those difficulties that delayed their happiness.

Sir Oliv. Come, come, girl, confess how many guineas prevail upon your easy nature.

Sent. Ten, an't please you, sir.

Sir Oliv. 'Slife, a sum able to corrupt an honest man in office! Faith, you must forgive her, my dear.

Lady Cock. If it be your pleasure, Sir Oliver, I cannot but be obedient.

Sent. If Sir Oliver, madam, should ask me to see this gold, all may be discovered yet.

---

[1] A covert reference, perhaps, to the Act of Indemnity passed at the Restoration.

Lady Cock. If he does, I will give thee ten guineas out of my cabinet.

Sent. (aside). I shall take care to put him upon't; 'tis fit that I who have borne all the blame should have some reasonable reward for't.

Court. I hope, madam, you will not envy me the happiness I am to enjoy with your fair relation.

Lady Cock. Your ingenuity and goodness, sir, have made a perfect atonement for you.

Court. Pray, madam, what was your business with Mr. Freeman?

Lady Cock. Only to oblige him to endeavour a reconciliation between you and Sir Oliver; for though I was resolved never to see your face again, it was death to me to think your life was in danger.

Sent. What a miraculous come off is this, madam!

Lady Cock. It has made me so truly sensible of those dangers to which an aspiring lady must daily expose her honour, that I am resolved to give over the great business of this town and hereafter modestly confine myself to the humble affairs of my own family.

Court. 'Tis a very pious resolution, madam, and the better to confirm you in it, pray entertain an able chaplain.

Lady Cock. Certainly fortune was never before so unkind to the ambition of a lady.

Sir Jos. Come, boys, faith, we will have a dance before we go to bed——Sly girl and madcap, give me your hands that I may give 'em to these gentlemen; a parson shall join you ere long, and then you will have authority to dance to some purpose. Brother Cockwood, take out your lady, I am for Mistress Sentry.

We'll foot it, and side it, my pretty little miss,
And when we are weary, we'll lie down and kiss.

Play away, boys. [*They dance.*

Court. (*to* GATTY). Now shall I sleep as little without you as I should do with you. Madam, expectation makes me almost as restless as jealousy.

Free. Faith, let us despatch this business. Yet I never could find the pleasure of waiting for a dish of meat when a man was heartily hungry.

Gat. Marrying in this heat would look as ill as fighting in your drink.

Aria. And be no more a proof of love than 'tother is of valour.

Sir Jos. Never trouble your heads further; since I perceive you are all agreed on the matter, let me alone to hasten the ceremony. Come, gentlemen, lead 'em to their chambers; brother Cockwood, do you show the way with your lady. Ha, Mistress Sentry!

Sings.

I gave my love a green gown
I'th' merry month of May,
And down she fell as wantonly
As a tumbler does at play.

Hey, boys! lead away, boys!

Sir Oliv. Give me thy hand, my virtuous, my dear:
Henceforwards may our mutual loves increase,
And when we are a-bed, we'll sign the peace.
                              [*Exeunt omnes.*

THE MAN OF MODE;

OR,

SIR FOPLING FLUTTER.

A COMEDY.

ACTED AT THE DUKE'S THEATRE.

TO HER ROYAL HIGHNESS
THE DUCHESS.

Madam,

POETS, however they may be modest otherwise, have always too good an opinion of what they write. The world, when it sees this play dedicated to your Royal Highness, will conclude I have more than my share of that vanity. But I hope the honour I have of belonging to you will excuse my presumption. 'Tis the first thing I have produced in your service, and my duty obliges me to what my choice durst not else have aspired.

I am very sensible, madam, how much it is beholding to your indulgence for the success it had in the acting, and your protection will be no less fortunate to it in the printing; for all are so ambitious of making their court to you, that none can be severe to what you are pleased to favour.

This universal submission and respect is due to the greatness of your rank and birth; but you have other illustrious qualities which are much more engaging. Those would but dazzle, did not these really charm the eyes and understandings of all who have the happiness to approach you.

Authors, on these occasions, are never wanting to publish a particular of their patron's virtues and perfections; but your Royal Highness's are so eminently known, that, did I follow their examples, I should but paint those wonders here of which everyone already has the idea in his mind. Besides, I do not think it proper to aim at that in prose which is so glorious a subject for verse; in which hereafter if I show more zeal than skill, it will not grieve me much, since I less passionately desire to be esteemed a poet, than to be thought,

 Madam,
  Your Royal Highness's
   most humble, most obedient,
    and most faithful servant,
     GEORGE ETHEREDGE.

PROLOGUE.

By Sir Car Scroope, Baronet.

LIKE dancers on the ropes poor poets fare,
  Most perish young, the rest in danger are;
This, one would think, should make our authors wary,
But, gamester like, the giddy fools miscarry.
A lucky hand or two so tempts 'em on,
They cannot leave off play till they're undone.
With modest fears a muse does first begin,
Like a young wench newly enticed to sin;
But tickled once with praise, by her good will,
The wanton fool would never more lie still.
'Tis an old mistress you'll meet here to-night,
Whose charms you once have look'd on with delight;
But now of late such dirty drabs have known ye,
A muse o'th' better sort's ashamed to own ye.
Nature well drawn, and wit, must now give place
To gaudy nonsense and to dull grimace:
Nor is it strange that you should like so much
That kind of wit, for most of yours is such.
But I'm afraid that while to France we go,
To bring you home fine dresses, dance, and show,
The stage, like you, will but more foppish grow.

THE PROLOGUE.

foreign wares why should we fetch the scum
hen we can be so richly served at home?
r, heaven be thank'd, 'tis not so wise an age
t your own follies may supply the stage.
ough often plough'd, there's no great fear the soil
uld barren grow by the too frequent toil,
hile at your doors are to be daily found
h loads of dunghill to manure the ground.
s by your follies that we players thrive,
 the physicians by diseases live;
d as each year some new distemper reigns,
hose friendly poison helps t'increase their gains,
among you there starts up every day
ne new unheard-of fool for us to play.
en for your own sakes be not too severe,
r what you all admire at home, damn here:
ce each is fond of his own ugly face,
hy should you, when we hold it, break the glass?

DRAMATIS PERSONÆ.

MR. DORIMANT,
MR. MEDLEY,
OLD BELLAIR, } *Gentlemen.*
YOUNG BELLAIR,
SIR FOPLING FLUTTER.

LADY TOWNLEY,
EMILIA,
MRS. LOVEIT, } *Gentlewomen.*
BELINDA,
LADY WOODVIL,
HARRIET, *her daughter.*

PERT *and* BUSY, *waiting-women.*
A *Shoemaker.*
An Orange-Woman.
Three Slovenly Bullies.
Two Chairmen.
MR. SMIRK, *a parson.*
HANDY, *a valet-de-chambre.*

Pages, Footmen, &c.

Scene: LONDON.

THE MAN OF MODE;
OR,
SIR FOPLING FLUTTER.

ACT I.

SCENE I.—A DRESSING-ROOM. *A table covered with a toilet; clothes laid ready.*

Enter DORIMANT *in his gown and slippers, with a note in his hand made up, repeating verses.*

Dorimant.

NOW for some ages had the pride of Spain
Made the sun shine on half the world in vain.

[*Then looking on the note.*
For Mrs. Loveit.

What a dull insipid thing is a *billet-doux* written in cold blood, after the heat of the business is over! It is a tax upon good-nature which I have here been labouring to pay, and have done it, but with as much regret as ever fanatic paid the Royal Aid or Church Duties. 'Twill have the same fate, I know, that all my notes to her have had of late, 'twill not be thought kind enough. Faith, women are i' the right when they jealously examine our letters, for in them we always first discover our decay of passion.——Hey! Who waits?

Enter HANDY.

Handy. Sir——

Dor. Call a footman.

Handy. None of 'em are come yet.

Dor. Dogs! Will they ever lie snoring a-bed till noon?

Handy. 'Tis all one, sir: if they're up, you indulge 'em so they're ever poaching after whores all the morning.

Dor. Take notice henceforward, who's wanting in his duty, the next clap he gets, he shall rot for an example. What vermin are those chattering without?

Handy. Foggy Nan the orange-woman and swearing Tom the shoemaker.

Dor. Go; call in that overgrown jade with the flasket of guts before her; fruit is refreshing in a morning. [*Exit* HANDY.

It is not that I love you less
Than when before your feet I lay.

Enter Orange-Woman with HANDY.

How now, Double Tripe! what news do you bring?

Or. Wom. News! Here's the best fruit has come to town t'year; gad, I was up before four o'clock this morning, and bought all the choice i' the market.

Dor. The nasty refuse of your shop.

Or. Wom. You need not make mouths at it; I assure you 'tis all culled ware.

Dor. The citizens buy better on a holiday in their walk to Totnam.[1]

Or. Wom. Good or bad, 'tis all one; I never knew you commend anything. Lord! would the ladies had heard you talk of 'em as I have done. Here, bid your man give me an angel. [*Sets down the fruit.*

Dor. Give the bawd her fruit again.

Or. Wom. Well, on my conscience, there never was the like of you. God's my life, I had almost forgot to tell you there is a young gentlewoman lately come to town with her mother, that is so taken with you.

Dor. Is she handsome?

Or. Wom. Nay, gad, there are few finer women, I tell you but so, and a hugeous fortune, they say. Here, eat this peach, it comes from the stone; 'tis better than any Newington y'have tasted.

Dor. This fine woman, I'll lay my life,

[*Taking the peach.*

is some awkward, ill-fashioned, country toad, who, not having above four dozen of black hairs on her head, has adorned her baldness with a large white fruz, that she may look sparkishly in the forefront of the King's box at an old play.

Or. Wom. Gad, you'd change your note quickly if you did but see her.

Dor. How came she to know me?

---

[1] Cf. *The Virtuoso* (v.): "The suburb fools trudge to Lamb's Conduit or Totnam." Later on the walk became more modish:

    When the sweet breathing spring unfolds the buds
    . . . .
    Then Totenham fields with roving beauty swarms.
                     Gay, *Epistle to Pulteney.*

Or. Wom. She saw you yesterday at the Change; she told me you came and fooled with the woman at the next shop.

Dor. I remember there was a mask observed me indeed. Fooled, did she say?

Or. Wom. Ay, I vow she told me twenty things you said too; and acted with her head and with her body so you——

Enter MEDLEY.

Med. Dorimant, my life, my joy, my darling sin, how dost thou?

Or. Wom. Lord! what a filthy trick these men have got of kissing one another! [*She spits.*

Med. Why do you suffer this cartload of scandal to come near you and make your neighbours think you so improvident to need a bawd?

Or. Wom. Good, now we shall have it! you did but want him to help you; come, pay me for my fruit.

Med. Make us thankful for it, huswife; bawds are as much out of fashion as gentlemen-ushers: none but old formal ladies use the one, and none but foppish old strangers employ the other—go, you are an insignificant brandy bottle.

Dor. Nay, there you wrong her, three quarts of canary is her business.

Or. Wom. What you please, gentlemen.

Dor. To him! give him as good as he brings.

Or. Wom. Hang him, there is not such another heathen in the town again, except it be the shoemaker without.

Med. I shall see you hold up your hand at the bar next sessions for murder, huswife; that shoemaker can take his oath you are in fee with the doctors to sell green fruit to the gentry, that the crudities may breed diseases.

Or. Wom. Pray give me my money.

Dor. Not a penny; when you bring the gentlewoman hither you spoke of, you shall be paid.

Or. Wom. The gentlewoman! the gentlewoman may be as honest as your sister, for aught as I know. Pray pay me, Mr. Dorimant, and do not abuse me so; I have an honester way of living, you know it.

Med. Was there ever such a restiff bawd?

Dor. Some jade's tricks she has, but she makes amends when she's in good-humour. Come, tell me the lady's name, and Handy shall pay you.

Or. Wom. I must not, she forbid me.

Dor. That's a sure sign she would have you.

Med. Where does she live?

Or. Wom. They lodge at my house.

Med. Nay, then she's in a hopeful way.

Or. Wom. Good Mr. Medley, say your pleasure of me, but take heed how you affront my house. God's my life, in a hopeful way!

Dor. Prithee, peace! what kind of woman's the mother?

Or. Wom. A goodly grave gentlewoman. Lord! how she talks against the wild young men o' the town! As for your part, she thinks you an arrant devil; should she see you, on my conscience she would look if you had not a cloven foot.

Dor. Does she know me?

Or. Wom. Only by hearsay; a thousand horrid stories have been told her of you, and she believes 'em all.

Med. By the character, this should be the famous Lady Woodvil and her daughter Harriet.

Or. Wom. The devil's in him for guessing, I think.

Dor. Do you know 'em?

Med. Both very well; the mother's a great admirer of the forms and civility of the last age.

Dor. An antiquated beauty may be allowed to be out of humour at the freedoms of the present. This is a good account of the mother; pray, what is the daughter?

Med. Why, first she's an heiress, vastly rich.

Dor. And handsome?

Med. What alteration a twelvemonth may have bred in her I know not, but a year ago she was the beautifullest creature I ever saw; a fine, easy, clean shape; light brown hair in abundance; her features regular; her complexion clear and lively; large wanton eyes; but above all, a mouth that has made me kiss it a thousand times in imagination, teeth white and even, and pretty pouting lips, with a little moisture ever hanging on them, that look like the Provence rose fresh on the bush, ere the morning sun has quite drawn up the dew.

Dor. Rapture, mere rapture!

Or. Wom. Nay, gad, he tells you true; she's a delicate creature.

Dor. Has she wit?

Med. More than is usual in her sex, and as much malice. Then she's as wild as you would wish her, and has a demureness in her looks that makes it so surprising.

Dor. Flesh and blood cannot hear this, and not long to know her.

Med. I wonder what makes her mother bring her up to town; an old doting keeper cannot be more jealous of his mistress.

Or. Wom. She made me laugh yesterday; there was a judge came to visit 'em, and the old man, she told me, did so stare upon her, and when he saluted her smacked so heartily; who would think it of 'em?

Med. God a mercy, a judge![1]

Dor. Do 'em right, the gentlemen of the long robe have not been wanting by their good examples to countenance the crying sin o' the nation.

Med. Come, on with your trappings; 'tis later than you imagine.

Dor. Call in the shoemaker, Handy.

Or. Wom. Good Mr. Dorimant, pay me; gad, I had rather give you my fruit than stay to be abused by that foul-mouthed rogue; what you gentlemen say, it matters not much, but such a dirty fellow does one more disgrace.

Dor. Give her ten shillings, and be sure you tell the young gentlewoman I must be acquainted with her.

Or. Wom. Now do you long to be tempting this pretty creature. Well, heavens mend you!

Med. Farewell.

[*Exeunt Orange-Woman and* HANDY.

[1] The first edition (1676) has "God-a-mercy, Judge": the correction seems to me necessary.

Dorimant, when did you see your *pis-aller*, as you call her, Mrs. Loveit?

Dor. Not these two days.

Med. And how stand affairs between you?

Dor. There has been great patching of late, much ado; we make a shift to hang together.

Med. I wonder how her mighty spirit bears it.

Dor. Ill enough, on all conscience; I never knew so violent a creature.

Med. She's the most passionate in her love, and the most extravagant in her jealousy, of any woman I ever heard of. What note is that?

Dor. An excuse I am going to send her for the neglect I am guilty of.

Med. Prithee read it.

Dor. No, but if you will take the pains you may.

Med. (reads). I never was a lover of business, but now I have a just reason to hate it, since it has kept me these two days from seeing you. I intend to wait upon you in the afternoon, and in the pleasure of your conversation forget all I have suffered during this tedious absence. This business of yours, Dorimant, has been with a vizard at the playhouse; I have had an eye on you. If some malicious body should betray you, this kind note would hardly make your peace with her.

Dor. I desire no better.

Med. Why, would her knowledge of it oblige you?

Dor. Most infinitely; next to the coming to a good understanding with a new mistress, I love a quarrel with an old one; but the devil's in't, there has been such a calm in my affairs of late, I have not had the pleasure of making a woman so much as break her fan, to be sullen, or forswear herself these three days.

Med. A very great misfortune. Let me see, I love mischief well enough to forward this business myself; I'll about it presently, and though I know the truth of what you've done will set her a-raving, I'll heighten it a little with invention, leave her in a fit o' the mother, and be here again before you're ready.

Dor. Pray stay; you may spare yourself the labour; the business is undertaken already by one who will manage it with as much address, and I think with a little more malice than you can.

Med. Who i' the devil's name can this be?

Dor. Why the vizard—that very vizard you saw me with.

Med. Does she love mischief so well as to betray herself to spite another?

Dor. Not so neither, Medley. I will make you comprehend the mystery: this mask, for a farther confirmation of what I have been these two days swearing to her, made me yesterday at the playhouse make her a promise before her face utterly to break off with Loveit; and because she tenders my reputation, and would not have me do a barbarous thing, has contrived a way to give me a handsome occasion.

Med. Very good.

Dor. She intends, about an hour before me, this afternoon to make Loveit a visit, and (having the privilege, by reason of a professed friendship between 'em) to talk of her concerns.

Med. Is she a friend?

Dor. Oh, an intimate friend!

Med. Better and better; pray proceed.

Dor. She means insensibly to insinuate a discourse of me, and artificially raise her jealousy to such a height, that transported with the first motions of her passion, she shall fly upon me with all the fury imaginable as soon as ever I enter; the quarrel being thus happily begun, I am to play my part, confess and justify all my roguery, swear her impertinence and ill-humour makes her intolerable, tax her with the next fop that comes into my head, and in a huff march away; slight her, and leave her to be taken by whosoever thinks it worth his time to lie down before her.

Med. This vizard is a spark, and has a genius that makes her worthy of yourself, Dorimant.

Enter HANDY, *Shoemaker, and Footman.*

Dor. You rogue there, who sneak like a dog that has flung down a dish, if you do not mend your waiting I'll uncase you, and turn you loose to the wheel of fortune. Handy, seal this, and let him run with it presently. [*Exeunt* HANDY[1] *and Footman.*

Med. Since you're resolved on a quarrel, why do you send her this kind note?

Dor. To keep her at home in order to the business. [*To the Shoemaker.*] How-now, you drunken sot?

Shoem. 'Zbud, you have no reason to talk; I have not had a bottle of sack of yours in my belly this fortnight.

---

[1] Who presently returns, though the entry is not marked.

Med. The orange-woman says your neighbours take notice what a heathen you are, and design to inform the bishop and have you burned for an atheist.

Shoem. Damn her, dunghill! if her husband does not remove her, she stinks so the parish intend to indict him for a nuisance.

Med. I advise you like a friend, reform your life; you have brought the envy of the world upon you by living above yourself. Whoring and swearing are vices too genteel for a shoemaker.

Shoem. 'Zbud, I think you men of quality will grow as unreasonable as the women; you would engross the sins o' the nation; poor folks can no sooner be wicked, but they're railed at by their betters.

Dor. Sirrah, I'll have you stand i' the pillory for this libel.

Shoem. Some of you deserve it, I'm sure; there are so many of 'em, that our journeymen now-a-days, instead of harmless ballads, sing nothing but your damned lampoons.

Dor. Our lampoons, you rogue?

Shoem. Nay, good master, why should not you write your own commentaries as well as Cæsar?

Med. The rascal's read, I perceive.

Shoem. You know the old proverb—ale and history.

Dor. Draw on my shoes, sirrah.

Shoem. Here's a shoe!

Dor. Sits with more wrinkles than there are in an angry bully's forehead.

Shoem. 'Zbud, as smooth as your mistress's skin

does upon her; so, strike your foot in home. 'Zbud, if e'er a *monsieur* of 'em all make more fashionable wear, I'll be content to have my ears whipped off with my own paring-knife.

Med. And served up in a *ragoût* instead of coxcombs to a company of French shoemakers for a collation.

Shoem. Hold, hold! damn 'em, caterpillars! let 'em feed upon cabbage. Come, master, your health this morning next my heart now.

Dor. Go, get you home, and govern your family better; do not let your wife follow you to the alehouse, beat your whore, and lead you home in triumph.

Shoem. 'Zbud, there's never a man i' the town lives more like a gentleman with his wife than I do. I never mind her motions, she never inquires into mine; we speak to one another civilly, hate one another heartily, and because 'tis vulgar to lie and soak together, we have each of us our several settle-bed.

Dor. Give him half-a-crown.

Med. Not without he will promise to be bloody drunk.

Shoem. Tope's the word i' the eye of the world, for my master's honour, Robin.

Dor. Do not debauch my servants, sirrah.

Shoem. I only tip him the wink; he knows an alehouse from a hovel. [*Exit Shoemaker.*

Dor. My clothes, quickly.

Med. Where shall we dine to-day?

Enter BELLAIR.

Dor. Where you will; here comes a good third man.

Bell. Your servant, gentlemen.

Med. Gentle sir, how will you answer this visit to your honourable mistress? 'Tis not her interest you should keep company with men of sense, who will be talking reason.

Bell. I do not fear her pardon, do you but grant me yours for my neglect of late.

Med. Though you've made us miserable by the want of your good company, to show you I am free from all resentment, may the beautiful cause of our misfortune give you all the joys happy lovers have shared ever since the world began.

Bell. You wish me in heaven, but you believe me on my journey to hell.

Med. You have a good strong faith, and that may contribute much towards your salvation. I confess I am but of an untoward constitution, apt to have doubts and scruples, and in love they are no less distracting than in religion; were I so near marriage, I should cry out by fits as I ride in my coach, *Cuckold*, *Cuckold*, with no less fury than the mad fanatic does *Glory* in Bedlam.

Bell. Because religion makes some run mad, must I live an atheist?

Med. Is it not great indiscretion for a man of credit, who may have money enough on his word, to go and deal with Jews, who for little sums make men enter into bonds and give judgments?

Bell. Preach no more on this text, I am determined, and there is no hope of my conversion.

Dor. (*to* HANDY, *who is fiddling about him*). Leave your unnecessary fiddling; a wasp that's buzzing about a man's nose at dinner is not more troublesome than thou art.

Handy. You love to have your clothes hang just, sir.

Dor. I love to be well dressed, sir; and think it no scandal to my understanding.

Handy. Will you use the essence, or orange-flower water?

Dor. I will smell as I do to-day, no offence to the ladies' noses.

Handy. Your pleasure, sir.

Dor. That a man's excellency should lie in neatly tying of a ribbon or a cravat! How careful's nature in furnishing the world with necessary coxcombs?

Bell. That's a mighty pretty suit of yours, Dorimant.

Dor. I am glad 't has your approbation.

Bell. No man in town has a better fancy in his clothes than you have.

Dor. You will make me have an opinion of my genius.

Med. There is a great critic, I hear, in these matters lately arrived piping hot from Paris.

Bell. Sir Fopling Flutter, you mean.

Med. The same.

Bell. He thinks himself the pattern of modern gallantry.

Dor. He is indeed the pattern of modern foppery.

Med. He was yesterday at the play, with a pair of gloves up to his elbows and a periwig more exactly curled than a lady's head newly dressed for a ball.

Bell. What a pretty lisp he has!

Dor. Ho! that he affects in imitation of the people of quality in France.

Med. His head stands for the most part on one side, and his looks are more languishing than a lady's when she lolls at stretch in her coach or leans her head carelessly against the side of a box i' the play-house.

Dor. He is a person indeed of great acquired follies.

Med. He is like many others, beholding to his education for making him so eminent a coxcomb; many a fool had been lost to the world had their indulgent parents wisely bestowed neither learning nor good breeding on 'em.

Bell. He has been, as the sparkish word is, brisk upon the ladies already; he was yesterday at my Aunt Townley's, and gave Mrs. Loveit a catalogue of his good qualities under the character of a complete gentleman, who, according to Sir Fopling, ought to dress well, dance well, fence well, have a genius for love-letters, an agreeable voice for a chamber, be very amorous, something discreet, but not over-constant.

Med. Pretty ingredients to make an accomplished person.

Dor. I am glad he pitched upon Loveit.

Bell. How so?

Dor. I wanted a fop to lay to her charge, and this is as pat as may be.

Bell. I am confident she loves no man but you.

Dor. The good fortune were enough to make me vain, but that I am in my nature modest.

Bell. Hark you, Dorimant; with your leave, Mr. Medley, 'tis only a secret concerning a fair lady.

Med. Your good breeding, sir, gives you too much trouble; you might have whispered without all this ceremony.

Bell. (*to* DORIMANT). How stand your affairs with Belinda of late?

Dor. She's a little jilting baggage.

Bell. Nay, I believe her false enough, but she's ne'er the worse for your purpose; she was with you yesterday in a disguise at the play.

Dor. There we fell out, and resolved never to speak to one another more.

Bell. The occasion?

Dor. Want of courage to meet me at the place appointed. These young women apprehend loving as much as the young men do fighting at first; but once entered, like them too, they all turn bullies straight.

Enter HANDY.[1]

Handy (*to* BELLAIR). Sir, your man without desires to speak with you.

Bell. Gentlemen, I'll return immediately.

[*Exit* BELLAIR.

Med. A very pretty fellow this.

[1] Whose previous exit had not been noticed.

Dor. He's handsome, well-bred, and by much the most tolerable of all the young men that do not abound in wit.

Med. Ever well-dressed, always complaisant, and seldom impertinent; you and he are grown very intimate, I see.

Dor. It is our mutual interest to be so: it makes the women think the better of his understanding and judge more favourably of my reputation; it makes him pass upon some for a man of very good sense and I upon others for a very civil person.

Med. What was that whisper?

Dor. A thing which he would fain have known, but I did not think it fit to tell him; it might have frighted him from his honourable intentions of marrying.

Med. Emilia, give her her due, has the best reputation of any young woman about the town who has beauty enough to provoke detraction; her carriage is unaffected, her discourse modest, not at all censorious nor pretending, like the counterfeits of the age.

Dor. She's a discreet maid, and I believe nothing can corrupt her but a husband.

Med. A husband?

Dor. Yes, a husband; I have known many women make a difficulty of losing a maidenhead who have afterwards made none of a cuckold.

Med. This prudent consideration, I am apt to think, has made you confirm poor Bellair in the desperate resolution he has taken.

Dor. Indeed, the little hope I found there was of her, in the state she was in, has made him by my advice contribute something towards the changing of her condition.

Enter BELLAIR.

Dear Bellair, by heavens I thought we had lost thee; men in love are never to be reckoned on when we would form a company.

Bell. Dorimant, I am undone; my man has brought the most surprising news i' the world.

Dor. Some strange misfortune is befallen your love.

Bell. My father came to town last night, and lodges i' the very house where Emilia lies.

Med. Does he know it is with her you are in love?

Bell. He knows I love, but knows not whom, without some officious sot has betrayed me.

Dor. Your Aunt Townley is your confidante and favours the business.

Bell. I do not apprehend any ill office from her; I have received a letter, in which I am commanded by my father to meet him at my aunt's this afternoon; he tells me farther he has made a match for me, and bids me resolve to be obedient to his will or expect to be disinherited.

Med. Now's your time, Bellair; never had lover such an opportunity of giving a generous proof of his passion.

Bell. As how, I pray?

Med. Why, hang an estate, marry Emilia out of hand, and provoke your father to do what he threatens; 'tis but despising a coach, humbling yourself to a pair of goloshes, being out of countenance when you meet your friends, pointed at and pitied wherever you go by all the amorous fops that know you, and your fame will be immortal.

Bell. I could find in my heart to resolve not to marry at all.

Dor. Fie, fie! that would spoil a good jest and disappoint the well-natured town of an occasion of laughing at you.

Bell. The storm I have so long expected hangs o'er my head and begins to pour down upon me; I am on the rack, and can have no rest till I'm satisfied in what I fear; where do you dine?

Dor. At Long's or Locket's.[1]

Med. At Long's let it be.

Bell. I'll run and see Emilia, and inform myself how matters stand; if my misfortunes are not so great as to make me unfit for company, I'll be with you.

[*Exit* BELLAIR.

Enter a Footman with a letter.

Foot. (*to* DORIMANT). Here's a letter, sir.

Dor. The superscription's right: *For Mr. Dorimant.*

Med. Let's see: the very scrawl and spelling of a true-bred whore.

Dor. I know the hand; the style is admirable, I assure you.

Med. Prithee read it.

---

[1] Famous ordinaries; the former in the Haymarket, the latter near Charing Cross. "I'll marry a drawer," says Lady Wishfort in *The Way of the World*, iii. 1, "to have him poisoned in his wine. I'll send for Robin from Locket's immediately." Compare, too, *Love for Love*, iii. 3.

Dor. (reads). *I told a you you dud not love me, if you dud, you would have seen me again e'er now; I have no mony, and am very mallicolly;˙pray send me a guynie to see the operies. Your servant to command, Molly.*

Med. Pray let the whore have a favourable answer, that she may spark it in a box and do honour to her profession.

Dor. She shall, and perk up i' the face of quality. Is the coach at door?

Handy. You did not bid me send for it.

Dor. Eternal blockhead! [HANDY *offers to go out.* Hey, sot.——

Handy. Did you call me, sir?

Dor. I hope you have no just exception to the name, sir?

Handy. I have sense, sir.

Dor. Not so much as a fly in winter.——How did you come, Medley?

Med. In a chair.

Footman. You may have a hackney coach if you please, sir.

Dor. I may ride the elephant if I please, sir; call another chair, and let my coach follow to Long's.

[*Exeunt singing, Be calm, ye great parents, &c.*

ACT II.

Scene I.

Enter my LADY TOWNLEY *and* EMILIA.

Lady Townley.

I WAS afraid, Emilia, all had been discovered.

Emil. I tremble with the apprehension still.

Lady Town. That my brother should take lodgings i' the very house where you lie!

Emil. 'Twas lucky we had timely notice to warn the people to be secret; he seems to be a mighty good-humoured old man.

Lady Town. He ever had a notable smirking way with him.

Emil. He calls me rogue, tells me he can't abide me, and does so bepat me.

Lady Town. On my word you are much in his favour then.

Emil. He has been very inquisitive, I am told, about my family, my reputation, and my fortune.

Lady Town. I am confident he does not i' the least suspect you are the woman his son's in love with.

Emil. What should make him then inform himself so particularly of me?

Lady Town. He was always of a very loving temper

himself; it may be he has a doting fit upon him; who knows?

Emil. It cannot be.

Enter YOUNG BELLAIR.

Lady Town. Here comes my nephew. Where did you leave your father?

Y. Bell. Writing a note within. Emilia, this early visit looks as if some kind jealousy would not let you rest at home.

Emil. The knowledge I have of my rival gives me a little cause to fear your constancy.

Y. Bell. My constancy! I vow——

Emil. Do not vow——Our love is frail as is our life, and full as little in our power; and are you sure you shall outlive this day?

Y. Bell. I am not, but when we are in perfect health 'twere an idle thing to fright ourselves with the thoughts of sudden death.

Lady Town. Pray what has passed between you and your father i' the garden?

Y. Bell. He's firm in his resolution, tells me I must marry Mrs. Harriet, or swears he'll marry himself and disinherit me; when I saw I could not prevail with him to be more indulgent, I dissembled an obedience to his will which has composed his passion, and will give us time, and I hope opportunity, to deceive him.

Enter OLD BELLAIR *with a note in his hand.*

Lady Town. Peace, here he comes.

O. Bell. Harry, take this, and let your man carry

it for me to Mr. Fourbes's chamber, my lawyer, i' the Temple. [*Exit* YOUNG BELLAIR.

[*To* EMILIA.] Neighbour, adod, I am glad to see thee here; make much of her, sister, she's one of the best of your acquaintance; I like her countenance and her behaviour well, she has a modesty that is not common i' this age, adod, she has.

Lady Town. I know her value, brother, and esteem her accordingly.

O. Bell. Advise her to wear a little more mirth in her face, adod, she's too serious.

Lady Town. The fault is very excusable in a young woman.

O. Bell. Nay, adod, I like her ne'er the worse, a melancholy beauty has her charms; I love a pretty sadness in a face which varies now and then, like changeable colours, into a smile.

Lady Town. Methinks you speak very feelingly, brother.

O. Bell. I am but five-and-fifty, sister, you know, an age not altogether insensible! [*To* EMILIA.] Cheer up, sweetheart, I have a secret to tell thee may chance to make thee merry; we three will make collation together anon; i' the meantime mum, I can't abide you; go, I can't abide you.

Enter YOUNG BELLAIR.

Harry, come, you must along with me to my Lady Woodvil's. I am going to slip the boy at a mistress.

Y. Bell. At a wife, sir, you would say.

O. Bell. You need not look so grum, sir; a wife is no curse when she brings the blessing of a good estate with her; but an idle town flirt, with a painted face, a rotten reputation, and a crazy fortune, adod, is the devil and all; and such a one I hear you are in league with.

Y. Bell. I cannot help detraction, sir.

O. Bell. Out, a pise o' their breeches, there are keeping fools enough for such flaunting baggages, and they are e'en too good for 'em. [*To* EMILIA.] Remember night, go, you're a rogue, you're a rogue; fare you well, fare you well; come, come, come along, sir.

[*Exeunt* OLD *and* YOUNG BELLAIR.

Lady Town. On my word the old man comes on apace; I'll lay my life he's smitten.

Emil. This is nothing but the pleasantness of his humour.

Lady Town. I know him better than you; let it work, it may prove lucky.

Enter a Page.

Page. Madam, Mr. Medley has sent to know whether a visit will not be troublesome this afternoon?

Lady Town. Send him word his visits never are so.

[*Exit Page.*

Emil. He's a very pleasant man.

Lady Town. He's a very necessary man among us women; he's not scandalous i' the least, perpetually contriving to bring good company together, and always ready to stop up a gap at ombre; then he knows all the little news o' the town.

Emil. I love to hear him talk o' the intrigues; let 'em be never so dull in themselves, he'll make 'em pleasant i' the relation.

Lady Town. But he improves things so much one can take no measure of the truth from him. Mr. Dorimant swears a flea or a maggot is not made more monstrous by a magnifying glass than a story is by his telling it.

Emil. Hold, here he comes.

Enter MEDLEY.

Lady Town. Mr. Medley.

Med. Your servant, madam.

Lady Town. You have made yourself a stranger of late.

Emil. I believe you took a surfeit of ombre last time you were here.

Med. Indeed I had my bellyful of that termagant lady-dealer; there never was so insatiable a carder, an old gleeker never loved to sit to't like her; I have played with her now at least a dozen times till she's worn out all her fine complexion, and her tour [1] would keep in curl no longer.

Lady Town. Blame her not, poor woman; she loves nothing so well as a black ace.

Med. The pleasure I have seen her in when she has had hope in drawing for a matadore! [2]

Emil. 'Tis as pretty sport to her as persuading masks off is to you to make discoveries.

Lady Town. Pray, where's your friend Mr. Dorimant?

Med. Soliciting his affairs; he's a man of great employment, has more mistresses now depending than the most eminent lawyer in England has causes.

[1] Headdress.   [2] A game at cards.

Emil. Here has been Mrs. Loveit, so uneasy and out of humour these two days.

Lady Town. How strangely love and jealousy rage in that poor woman!

Med. She could not have picked out a devil upon earth so proper to torment her; he has made her break a dozen or two of fans already, tear half a score points in pieces, and destroy hoods and knots without number.

Lady Town. We heard of a pleasant serenade he gave her t'other night.

Med. A Danish serenade, with kettledrums and trumpets.

Emil. Oh, barbarous!

Med. What, you are of the number of the ladies whose ears are grown so delicate since our operas,[1] you can be charmed with nothing but *flûtes douces*[2] and French hautboys.

Emil. Leave your raillery, and tell us is there any new wit come forth, songs or novels?

Med. A very pretty piece of gallantry by an eminent author, called *The Diversions of Brussels;*[3] very

---

[1] "I saw an Italian opera in music, the first that had been in England of the kind."—Evelyn, Jan. 5, 1674.

[2] Here, and later on (iv. 1), variously spelt *flute doux* and *flutes deux*. It has been suggested to me (*Notes and Queries*, 7th S. v. 135) that *flûtes douces* is the right reading, and I have adopted it. The *flûte douce* may have been something like the *flûte d'amour*, or *Liebesflöte*, "an old form of flute with a narrow bore, supposed to have a smooth and fascinating quality."

[3] Possibly one of the romances which Pepys read surreptitiously. I have not been able to trace the book: was it by any

necessary to be read by all old ladies who are desirous to improve themselves at questions and commands, blindman's buff, and the like fashionable recreations.

Emil. Oh, ridiculous!

Med. Then there is *The Art of Affectation*, written by a late beauty of quality, teaching you how to draw up your breasts, stretch up your neck, to thrust out your breech, to play with your head, to toss up your nose, to bite your lips, to turn up your eyes, to speak in a silly soft tone of a voice, and use all the foolish French words that will infallibly make your person and conversation charming, with a short apology at the latter end, in the behalf of young ladies who notoriously wash and paint, though they have naturally good complexions.

Emil. What a deal of stuff you tell us?

Med. Such as the town affords, madam. The Russians hearing the great respect we have for foreign dancing have lately sent over some of their best balladines, who are now practising a famous ballet, which will be suddenly danced at the Bear Garden.

Lady Town. Pray forbear your idle stories, and give us an account of the state of love as it now stands.

Med. Truly there has been some revolutions in those affairs, great chopping and changing among the old, and some new lovers, whom malice, indiscretion, and misfortune have luckily brought into play.

chance the basis of D'Urfey's play, *The Campaigners, or Pleasant Adventures at Brussels*, 1698, in which, by the way, we have a footman called Mascarillo?

Lady Town. What think you of walking into the next room, and sitting down before you engage in this business?

Med. I wait upon you, and I hope (though women are commonly unreasonable) by the plenty of scandal I shall discover to give you very good content, ladies.

[*Exeunt.*

Scene II.

Enter Mrs. Loveit *and* Pert. Mrs. Loveit *putting up a letter, then pulling out her pocket-glass, and looking in it.*

Lov. Pert.

Pert. Madam.

Lov. I hate myself, I look so ill to-day.

Pert. Hate the wicked cause on't, that base man Mr. Dorimant, who makes you torment and vex yourself continually.

Lov. He is to blame, indeed.

Pert. To blame to be two days without sending, writing, or coming near you, contrary to his oath and covenant! 'twas to much purpose to make him swear: I'll lay my life there's not an article but he has broken —talked to the vizards i' the pit; waited upon the ladies from the boxes to their coaches; gone behind the scenes and fawned upon those little insignificant creatures the players; 'tis impossible for a man of his inconstant temper to forbear, I'm sure.

Lov. I know he is a devil, but he has something of the angel yet undefaced in him, which makes him so charming and agreeable that I must love him be he never so wicked.

Pert. I little thought, madam, to see your spirit tamed to this degree, who banished poor Mr. Lackwit but for taking up another lady's fan in your presence.

Lov. My knowing of such odious fools contributes to the making of me love Dorimant the better.

Pert. Your knowing of Mr. Dorimant, in my mind, should rather make you hate all mankind.

Lov. So it does, besides himself.

Pert. Pray, what excuse does he make in his letter?

Lov. He has had business.

Pert. Business in general terms would not have been a current excuse for another; a modish man is always very busy when he is in pursuit of a new mistress.

Lov. Some fop has bribed you to rail at him; he had business, I will believe it, and will forgive him.

Pert. You may forgive him anything, but I shall never forgive him his turning me into ridicule, as I hear he does.

Lov. I perceive you are of the number of those fools his wit has made his enemies.

Pert. I am of the number of those he's pleased to rally, madam; and if we may believe Mr. Wagfan and Mr. Caperwell, he sometimes makes merry with yourself too among his laughing companions.

Lov. Blockheads are as malicious to witty men as ugly women are to the handsome; 'tis their interest, and they make it their business to defame 'em.

Pert. I wish Mr. Dorimant would not make it his business to defame you.

Lov. Should he, I had rather be made infamous by him than owe my reputation to the dull discretion of those fops you talk of.

Enter BELINDA.

Belinda! [*Running to her.*

Bel. My dear.

Lov. You have been unkind of late.

Bel. Do not say unkind, say unhappy!

Lov. I could chide you; where have you been these two days?

Bel. Pity me rather, my dear, where I have been so tired with two or three country gentlewomen, whose conversation has been more insufferable than a country fiddle.

Lov. Are they relations?

Bel. No, Welsh acquaintance I made when I was last year at St. Winifred's; they have asked me a thousand questions of the modes and intrigues of the town, and I have told 'em almost as many things for news that hardly were so when their gowns were in fashion.

Lov. Provoking creatures, how could you endure 'em?

Bel. (*aside*). Now to carry on my plot; nothing but love could make me capable of so much falsehood;

'tis time to begin, lest Dorimant should come before her jealousy has stung her.

[*Laughs, and then speaks on.* I was yesterday at a play with 'em, where I was fain to show 'em the living, as the man at Westminster does the dead; that is Mrs. Such-a-one, admired for her beauty; this is Mr. Such-a-one, cried up for a wit; that is sparkish Mr. Such-a-one, who keeps reverend Mrs. Such-a-one, and there sits fine Mrs. Such-a-one, who was lately cast off by my Lord Such-a-one.

Lov. Did you see Dorimant there?

Bel. I did, and imagine you were there with him and have no mind to own it.

Lov. What should make you think so?

Bel. A lady masked in a pretty *déshabillé*, whom Dorimant entertained with more respect than the gallants do a common vizard.

Lov. (*aside*). Dorimant at the play entertaining a mask, oh heavens!

Bel. (*aside*). Good.

Lov. Did he stay all the while?

Bel. Till the play was done, and then led her out, which confirms me it was you.

Lov. Traitor!

Pert. Now you may believe he had business, and you may forgive him too.

Lov. Ungrateful, perjured man!

Bel. You seem so much concerned, my dear, I fear I have told you unawares what I had better have concealed for your quiet.

Lov. What manner of shape had she?

T

Bel. Tall and slender, her motions very genteel; certainly she must be some person of condition.

Lov. Shame and confusion be ever in her face when she shows it!

Bel. I should blame your discretion for loving that wild man, my dear; but they say he has a way so bewitching that few can defend their hearts who know him.

Lov. I will tear him from mine, or die i' the attempt.

Bel. Be more moderate.

Lov. Would I had daggers, darts, or poisoned arrows in my breast, so I could but remove the thoughts of him from thence!

Bel. Fie, fie! your transports are too violent, my dear. This may be but an accidental gallantry, and 'tis likely ended at her coach.

Pert. Should it proceed farther, let your comfort be, the conduct Mr. Dorimant affects will quickly make you know your rival, ten to one let you see her ruined, her reputation exposed to the town; a happiness none will envy her but yourself, madam.

Lov. Whoe'er she be, all the harm I wish her is, may she love him as well as I do, and may he give her as much cause to hate him!

Pert. Never doubt the latter end of your curse, madam.

Lov. May all the passions that are raised by neglected love, jealousy, indignation, spite, and thirst of revenge, eternally rage in her soul as they do now in mine! [*Walks up and down with a distracted air.*

Enter a Page.

Page. Madam, Mr. Dorimant.

Lov. I will not see him.

Page. I told him you were within, madam.

Lov. Say you lied, say I'm busy, shut the door; say anything.

Page. He's here, madam.

Enter DORIMANT.

Dor. They taste of death who do at Heaven arrive,
But we this paradise approach alive.

[*To* LOVEIT.] What, dancing the galloping nag without a fiddle? [*Offers to catch her by the hand; she flings away and walks on.*] I fear this restlessness of the body, madam, [*Pursuing her.*] proceeds from an unquietness of the mind. What unlucky accident puts you out of humour; a point ill washed, knots spoiled i' the making up, hair shaded awry, or some other little mistake in setting you in order?

Pert. A trifle, in my opinion, sir, more inconsiderable than any you mention.

Dor. Oh, Mrs. Pert, I never knew you sullen enough to be silent; come, let me know the business.

Pert. The business, sir, is the business that has taken you up these two days; how have I seen you laugh at men of business, and now to become a man of business yourself!

Dor. We are not masters of our own affections, our inclinations daily alter; now we love pleasure, and anon we shall dote on business: human frailty will have it so, and who can help it?

Lov. Faithless, inhuman, barbarous man!——

Dor. Good, now the alarm strikes.——

Lov. Without sense of love, of honour, or of gratitude, tell me—for I will know—what devil, masked she were you with at the play yesterday?

Dor. Faith, I resolved as much as you, but the devil was obstinate and would not tell me.

Lov. False in this as in your vows to me! you do know.

Dor. The truth is, I did all I could to know.

Lov. And dare you own it to my face? Hell and furies! [*Tears her fan in pieces.*

Dor. Spare your fan, madam; you are growing hot, and will want it to cool you.

Lov. Horror and distraction seize you, sorrow and remorse gnaw your soul, and punish all your perjuries to me!—— [*Weeps.*

Dor. *So thunder breaks the cloud in twain,*
And makes a passage for the rain.

[*Turning to* BELINDA.

Belinda, you are the devil that have raised this storm; you were at the play yesterday, and have been making discoveries to your dear.

Bel. You're the most mistaken man i' the world.

Dor. It must be so, and here I vow revenge; resolve to pursue and persecute you more impertinently than ever any loving fop did his mistress, hunt you i' the

Park, trace you i' the Mall, dog you in every visit you make, haunt you at the plays and i' the Drawing-room, hang my nose in your neck, and talk to you whether you will or no, and ever look upon you with such dying eyes, till your friends grow jealous of me, send you out of town, and make the world suspect your reputation. [*In a lower voice.*
At my Lady Townley's when we go from hence.
[*He looks kindly on* BELINDA.

Bel. I'll meet you there.

Dor. Enough.

Lov. Stand off, you shall not stare upon her so.
[*Pushing* DORIMANT *away.*

Dor. Good! There's one made jealous already.

Lov. Is this the constancy you vowed?

Dor. Constancy at my years! 'tis not a virtue in season; you might as well expect the fruit the autumn ripens i' the spring.

Lov. Monstrous principle!

Dor. Youth has a long journey to go, madam: should I have set up my rest at the first inn I lodged at, I should never have arrived at the happiness I now enjoy.

Lov. Dissembler, damned dissembler!

Dor. I am so, I confess; good nature and good manners corrupt me. I am honest in my inclinations, and would not, were't not to avoid offence, make a lady a little in years believe I think her young, wilfully mistake art for nature, and seem as fond of a thing I am weary of as when I doted on't in earnest.

Lov. False man!

Dor. True woman!

Lov. Now you begin to show yourself!

Dor. Love gilds us over and makes us show fine things to one another for a time, but soon the gold wears off, and then again the native brass appears.

Lov. Think on your oaths, your vows and protestations, perjured man.

Dor. I made 'em when I was in love.

Lov. And therefore ought they not to bind? Oh, impious!

Dor. What we swear at such a time may be a certain proof of a present passion; but, to say truth, in love there is no security to be given for the future.

Lov. Horrid and ungrateful, begone, and never see me more.

Dor. I am not one of those troublesome coxcombs, who because they were once well received take the privilege to plague a woman with their love ever after; I shall obey you, madam, though I do myself some violence. [*He offers to go, and* LOVEIT *pulls him back.*

Lov. Come back, you shall not go. Could you have the ill-nature to offer it?

Dor. When love grows diseased, the best thing we can do is to put it to a violent death; I cannot endure the torture of a lingering and consumptive passion.

Lov. Can you think mine sickly?

Dor. Oh, 'tis desperately ill! What worse symptoms

are there than your being always uneasy when I visit you, your picking quarrels with me on slight occasions, and in my absence kindly listening to the impertinencies of every fashionable fool that talks to you?

Lov. What fashionable fool can you lay to my charge?

Dor. Why, the very cock-fool of all those fools, Sir Fopling Flutter.

Lov. I never saw him in my life but once.

Dor. The worse woman you, at first sight to put on all your charms, to entertain him with that softness in your voice and all that wanton kindness in your eyes you so notoriously affect when you design a conquest.

Lov. So damned a lie did never malice yet invent. Who told you this?

Dor. No matter; that ever I should love a woman that can dote on a senseless caper, a tawdry French ribbon, and a formal cravat.

Lov. You make me mad.

Dor. A guilty conscience may do much; go on, be the game-mistress o' the town, and enter all our young fops as fast as they come from travel.

Lov. Base and scurrilous!

Dor. A fine mortifying reputation 'twill be for a woman of your pride, wit, and quality!

Lov. This jealousy's a mere pretence, a cursed trick of your own devising; I know you.

Dor. Believe it, and all the ill of me you can: I would not have a woman have the least good thought of me that can think well of Fopling; farewell; fall to, and much good may [it] do you with your coxcomb.

Lov. Stay, oh! stay, and I will tell you all.

Dor. I have been told too much already.

[*Exit* DORIMANT.

Lov. Call him again.

Pert. E'en let him go, a fair riddance.

Lov. Run, I say; call him again—I will have him called.

Pert. The devil should carry him away first, were it my concern. [*Exit* PERT.

Bel. He's frighted me from the very thoughts of loving men; for heaven's sake, my dear, do not discover what I told you; I dread his tongue as much as you ought to have done his friendship.

Enter PERT.

Pert. He's gone, madam.

Lov. Lightning blast him!

Pert. When I told him you desired him to come back, he smiled, made a mouth at me, flung into his coach, and said——

Lov. What did he say?

Pert. "*Drive away;*" and then repeated verses.

Lov. Would I had made a contract to be a witch, when first I entertained this great devil, monster, barbarian; I could tear myself in pieces. Revenge, nothing but revenge can ease me: plague, war, famine, fire, all that can bring universal ruin and misery on mankind; with joy I'd perish to have you in my power but this moment. [*Exit* LOVEIT.

Pert. Follow, madam; leave her not in this outrageous passion. [PERT *gathers up the things*.

Bel. He's given me the proof which I desired of his love:
But 'tis a proof of his ill-nature too;
I wish I had not seen him use her so.
I sigh to think that Dorimant may be
One day as faithless and unkind to me. [*Exeunt.*

ACT III.

Scene I.—Lady Woodvil's Lodgings.

Enter Harriet *and* Busy *her woman.*

Busy.

Dear madam! Let me set that curl in order.

Har. Let me alone, I will shake 'em all out of order.

Busy. Will you never leave this wildness?

Har. Torment me not.

Busy. Look! there's a knot falling off.

Har. Let it drop.

Busy. But one pin, dear madam.

Har. How do I daily suffer under thy officious fingers!

Busy. Ah, the difference that is between you and my Lady Dapper! How uneasy she is if the least thing be amiss about her!

Har. She is indeed most exact; nothing is ever wanting to make her ugliness remarkable.

Busy. Jeering people say so.

Har. Her powdering, painting, and her patching never fail in public to draw the tongues and eyes of all the men upon her.

Busy. She is indeed a little **too** pretending.

Har. That women should set up for beauty as much in spite of nature as some men have done for wit!

Busy. I hope, without offence, one may endeavour to make oneself agreeable.

Har. Not when 'tis impossible. Women then ought to be no more fond of dressing than fools should be talking. Hoods and modesty, masks and silence, things that shadow and conceal: they should think of nothing else.

Busy. Jesu! madam, what will your mother think is become of you? For heaven's sake, go in again.

Har. I won't.

Busy. This is the extravagant'st thing that ever you did in your life, to leave her and a gentleman who is to be your husband.

Har. My husband! Hast thou so little wit to think I spoke what I meant when I overjoyed her in the country with a low curtsey and *What you please, madam, I shall ever be obedient?*

Busy. Nay, I know not, you have so many fetches.

Har. And this was one to get her up to London; nothing else, I assure thee.

Busy. Well, the man, in my mind, is a fine man.

Har. The man indeed wears his clothes fashionably, and has a pretty negligent way with him, very courtly and much affected; he bows, and talks, and smiles so agreeably as he thinks.

Busy. I never saw anything so genteel.

Har. Varnished over with good breeding many a blockhead makes a tolerable show.

Busy. I wonder you do not like him.

Har. I think I might be brought to endure him, and that is all a reasonable woman should expect in a husband; but there is duty i' the case—and like the haughty Merab,

I find much aversion in my stubborn mind,
Which is bred by being promised and design'd.

Busy. I wish you do not design your own ruin! I partly guess your inclinations, madam,——that Mr. Dorimant——

Har. Leave your prating, and sing some foolish song or other.

Busy. I will; the song you love so well ever since you saw Mr. Dorimant.

SONG.

When first Amintas charm'd my heart,
My heedless sheep began to stray;
The wolves soon stole the greatest part,
And all will now be made a prey.

Ah! let not love your thoughts possess,
'Tis fatal to a shepherdess;
The dangerous passion you must shun,
Or else, like me, be quite undone.

Har. Shall I be paid down by a covetous parent for a purchase? I need no land; no, I'll lay myself out all in love. It is decreed——

Enter YOUNG BELLAIR.

Y. Bell. What generous resolution are you making, madam?

Har. Only to be disobedient, sir.

Y. Bell. Let me join hands with you in that.

Har. With all my heart; I never thought I should have given you mine so willingly. Here I, Harriet——

Y. Bell. And I, Harry——

Har. Do solemnly protest——

Y. Bell. And vow——

Har. That I with you——

Y. Bell. And I with you——

Both. Will never marry.——

Har. A match!

Y. Bell. And no match! How do you like this indifference now?

Har. You expect I should take it ill, I see.

Y. Bell. 'Tis not unnatural for you women to be a little angry [if] you miss a conquest, though you would slight the poor man were he in your power.

Har. There are some, it may be, have an eye like Bartholomew, big enough for the whole fair, but I am not of the number, and you may keep your gingerbread; 'twill be more acceptable to the lady whose dear image it wears, sir.

Y. Bell. I must confess, madam, you came a day after the fair.

Har. You own then you are in love.

Y. Bell. I do.

Har. The confidence is generous, and in return I

could almost find in my heart to let you know my inclinations.

Y. Bell. Are you in love?

Har. Yes, with this dear town, to that degree I can scarce endure the country in landscapes and in hangings.

Y. Bell. What a dreadful thing 'twould be to be hurried back to Hampshire?

Har. Ah! name it not!

Y. Bell. As for us, I find we shall agree well enough! Would we could do something to deceive the grave people!

Har. Could we delay their proceeding, 'twere well; a reprieve is a good step towards the getting of a pardon.

Y. Bell. If we give over the game we are undone; what think you of playing it on booty?

Har. What do you mean?

Y. Bell. Pretend to be in love with one another; 'twill make some dilatory excuses we may feign pass the better.

Har. Let us do't, if it be but for the dear pleasure of dissembling.

Y. Bell. Can you play your part?

Har. I know not what 'tis to love, but I have made pretty remarks by being now and then where lovers meet. Where did you leave their gravities?

Y. Bell. I' th' next room; your mother was censuring our modern gallant.

Enter OLD BELLAIR *and* LADY WOODVIL.

Har. Peace! Here they come, I will lean against

this wall and look bashfully down upon my fan, while you like an amorous spark modishly entertain me.

Lady Wood. Never go about to excuse 'em; come, come, it was not so when I was a young woman.

O. Bell. Adod, they're something disrespectful.

Lady Wood. Quality was then considered, and not rallied by every fleering fellow.

O. Bell. Youth will have its jest, adod it will.

Lady Wood. 'Tis good breeding now to be civil to none but players and Exchange women; they are treated by 'em as much above their condition as others are below theirs.

O. Bell. Out, a pise on 'em! talk no more; the rogues ha' got an ill habit of preferring beauty, no matter where they find it.

Lady Wood. See your son and my daughter, they have improved their acquaintance since they were within.

O. Bell. Adod, methinks they have; let's keep back and observe.

Y. Bell. Now for a look and gestures that may persuade 'em I am saying all the passionate things imaginable.

Har. Your head a little more on one side, ease yourself on your left leg, and play with your right hand.

Y. Bell. Thus, is it not?

Har. Now set your right leg firm on the ground, adjust your belt, then look about you.

Y. Bell. A little exercising will make me perfect.

Har. Smile, and turn to me again very sparkish.

Y. Bell. Will you take your turn and be instructed?

Har. With all my heart.

Y. Bell. At one motion play your fan, roll your eyes, and then settle a kind look upon me.

Har. So.

Y. Bell. Now spread your fan, look down upon it, and tell the sticks with a finger.

Har. Very modish!

Y. Bell. Clap your hand up to your bosom, hold down your gown; shrug a little, draw up your breasts, and let 'em fall again gently, with a sigh or two, &c.

Har. By the good instructions you give, I suspect you for one of those malicious observers who watch people's eyes and from innocent looks make scandalous conclusions.

Y. Bell. I know some, indeed, who, out of mere love to mischief, are as vigilant as jealousy itself, and will give you an account of every glance that passes at a play and i' th' circle.[1]

Har. 'Twill not be amiss now to seem a little pleasant.

Y. Bell. Clap your fan then in both your hands, snatch it to your mouth, smile, and with a lively motion fling your body a little forwards. So,——now spread it; fall back on the sudden, cover your face with it, and break out into a loud laughter——take up! look grave, and fall a-fanning of yourself—— admirably well acted.

Har. I think I am pretty apt at these matters.

O. Bell. Adod, I like this well.

Lady Wood. This promises something.

---

[1] In Hyde Park.

O. Bell. Come! there is love i' th' case, adod there is, or will be; what say you, young lady?

Har. All in good time, sir; you expect we should fall to and love, as gamecocks fight, as soon as we are set together; adod, you're unreasonable!

O. Bell. Adod, sirrah, I like thy wit well.

Enter a Servant.

Serv. The coach is at the door, madam.

O. Bell. Go, get you and take the air together.

Lady. Wood. Will not you go with us?

O. Bell. Out a pise. Adod, I ha' business and cannot. We shall meet at night at my sister Townley's.

Y. Bell. (*aside*). He's going to Emilia. I overheard him talk of a collation. [*Exeunt.*

SCENE II.

Enter LADY TOWNLEY, EMILIA, *and* MR. MEDLEY.

Lady Town. I pity the young lovers we last talked of; though, to say truth, their conduct has been so indiscreet they deserve to be unfortunate.

Med. You've had an exact account, from the great lady i' th' box down to the little orange-wench.

Emil. You're a living libel, a breathing lampoon; I wonder you are not torn in pieces.

Med. What think you of setting up an office of

intelligence for these matters? The project may get money.

Lady Town. You would have great dealings with country ladies.

Med. More than Muddiman[1] has with their husbands.

Enter BELINDA.

Lady Town. Belinda, what has been become of you? we have not seen you here of late with your friend Mrs. Loveit.

Bel. Dear creature, I left [her] but now so sadly afflicted.

Lady Town. With her old distemper, jealousy?

Med. Dorimant has played her some new prank.

Bel. Well, that Dorimant is certainly the worst man breathing.

Emil. I once thought so.

Bel. And do you not think so still?

Emil. No, indeed!

Bel. Oh, Jesu!

Emil. The town does him a great deal of injury, and I will never believe what it says of a man I do not know again, for his sake.

Bel. You make me wonder!

Lady Town. He's a very well-bred man.

Bel. But strangely ill-natured.

Emil. Then he's a very witty man.

Bel. But a man of no principles.

---

[1] Was this the gentleman whom Pepys found "a good scholar, an arch rogue"?—*Diary*, January 10th, 1660. Mentioned also in the *Letterbook*, January 23rd, 1688.

Med. Your man of principles is a very fine thing indeed!

Bel. To be preferred to men of parts by women who have regard to their reputation and quiet. Well, were I minded to play the fool, he should be the last man I'd think of.

Med. He has been the first in many lady's favours, though you are so severe, madam.

Lady Town. What he may be for a lover I know not, but he's a very pleasant acquaintance, I am sure.

Bel. Had you seen him use Mrs. Loveit as I have done, you would never endure him more.

Emil. What, he has quarrelled with her again?

Bel. Upon the slightest occasion; he's jealous of Sir Fopling.

Lady Town. She never saw him in her life but yesterday, and that was here.

Emil. On my conscience, he's the only man in town that's her aversion; how horribly out of humour she was all the while he talked to her!

Bel. And somebody has wickedly told him——

Emil. Here he comes.

Enter DORIMANT.

Med. Dorimant! you are luckily come to justify yourself——here's a lady——

Bel. Has a word or two to say to you from a disconsolate person.

Dor. You tender your reputation too much, I know, madam, to whisper with me before this good company.

Bel. To serve Mrs. Loveit, I'll make a bold venture.

Dor. Here's Medley, the very spirit of scandal.

Bel. No matter!

Emil. 'Tis something you are unwilling to hear, Mr. Dorimant.

Lady Town. Tell him, Belinda, whether he will or no.

Bel. (*aloud*). Mrs. Loveit——

Dor. Softly, these are laughers, you do not know 'em.

Bel. (*to* Dorimant, *apart*). In a word, you've made me hate you, which I thought you never could have done.

Dor. In obeying your commands.

Bel. 'Twas a cruel part you played! how could you act it?

Dor. Nothing is cruel to a man who could kill himself to please you; remember, five o'clock to-morrow morning.

Bel. I tremble when you name it.

Dor. Be sure you come.

Bel. I shall not.

Dor. Swear you will.

Bel. I dare not.

Dor. Swear, I say.

Bel. By my life! by all the happiness I hope for——

Dor. You will.

Bel. I will.

Dor. Kind.

Bel. I am glad I've sworn, I vow I think I should ha' failed you else!

Dor. Surprisingly kind! In what temper did you leave Loveit?

Bel. Her raving was prettily over, and she began to be in a brave way of defying you and all your works. Where have you been since you went from thence?

Dor. I looked in at the play.

Bel. I have promised, and must return to her again.

Dor. Persuade her to walk in the Mall[1] this evening.

Bel. She hates the place, and will not come.

Dor. Do all you can to prevail with her.

Bel. For what purpose?

Dor. Sir Fopling will be here anon; I'll prepare him to set upon her there before me.

Bel. You persecute her too much; but I'll do all you'll ha' me.

Dor. (*aloud*). Tell her plainly, 'tis grown so dull a business I can drudge on no longer.

Emil. There are afflictions in love, Mr. Dorimant.

Dor. You women make 'em, who are commonly as unreasonable in that as you are at play; without the advantage be on your side a man can never quietly give over when he's weary.

Med. If you would play without being obliged to complaisance, Dorimant, you should play in public places.

Dor. Ordinaries were a very good thing for that,

---

[1] *i.e.* Pall Mall, which roused the enthusiasm of even the fastidious Gay:

O bear me to the paths of fair Pell Mell.
Trivia, ii. 257.

but gentlemen do not of late frequent 'em; the deep play is now in private houses.

[BELINDA *offering to steal away.*

Lady Town. Belinda, are you leaving us so soon?

Bel. I am to go to the Park with Mrs. Loveit, madam. [*Exit* BELINDA.

Lady Town. This *confidence* will go nigh to spoil this young creature.

Med. 'Twill do her good, madam. Young men who are brought up under practising lawyers prove the abler counsel when they come to be called to the Bar themselves.

Dor. The town has been very favourable to you this afternoon, my Lady Townley; you use to have an *embarras* of chairs and coaches at your door, an uproar of footmen in your hall, and a noise of fools above here.

Lady Town. Indeed my house is the general *rendezvous*, and, next to the playhouse, is the common refuge of all the young idle people.

Emil. Company is a very good thing, madam, but I wonder you do not love it a little more chosen.

Lady Town. 'Tis good to have an universal taste; we should love wit, but for variety be able to divert ourselves with the extravagancies of those who want it.

Med. Fools will make you laugh.

Emil. For once or twice; but the repetition of their folly after a visit or two grows tedious and unsufferable.

Lady Town. You are a little too delicate, Emilia.

Enter a Page.

Page. Sir Fopling Flutter, madam, desires to know if you are to be seen.

Lady Town. Here's the freshest fool in town, and one who has not cloyed you yet. Page!

Page. Madam! [*Exit Page.*

Lady Town. Desire him to walk up.

Dor. Do not you fall on him, Medley, and snub him. Sooth him up in his extravagance; he will show the better.

Med. You know I have a natural indulgence for fools, and need not this caution, sir.

Enter SIR FOPLING FLUTTER, *with his Page after him.*

Sir Fop. Page, wait without. Madam, [*To* LADY TOWNLEY.] I kiss your hands. I see yesterday was nothing of chance; the *belles assemblées* form themselves here every day. Lady, [*To* EMILIA.] your servant. Dorimant, let me embrace thee; without lying, I have not met with any of my acquaintance who retain so much of Paris as thou dost—the very air thou hadst when the marquis mistook thee i' th' Tuileries, and cried, *Hé! Chevalier!* and then begged thy pardon.

Dor. I would fain wear in fashion as long as I can, sir; 'tis a thing to be valued in men as well as baubles.

Sir Fop. Thou art a man of wit, and understandest the town; prithee let thee and I be intimate, there is no living without making some good man the confidant of our pleasures.

Dor. 'Tis true! but there is no man so improper for such a business as I am.

Sir Fop. Prithee, why hast thou so modest an opinion of thyself?

Dor. Why, first, I could never keep a secret in my life, and then there is no charm so infallibly makes me fall in love with a woman as my knowing a friend loves her. I deal honestly with you.

Sir Fop. Thy humour's very gallant, or let me perish; I knew a French count so like thee.

Lady Town. Wit, I perceive, has more power over you than beauty, Sir Fopling, else you would not have let this lady stand so long neglected.

Sir Fop. (*to* EMILIA). A thousand pardons, madam; some civilities due, of course, upon the meeting a long absent friend. The *éclat* of so much beauty, I confess, ought to have charmed me sooner.

Emil. The *brilliant* of so much good language, sir, has much more power than the little beauty I can boast.

Sir Fop. I never saw anything prettier than this high work on your *point d'Espagne.*——

Emil. 'Tis not so rich as *point de Venise.*——

Sir Fop. Not altogether, but looks cooler, and is more proper for the season. Dorimant, is not that Medley?

Dor. The same, sir.

Sir Fop. Forgive me, sir; in this *embarras* of civilities I could not come to have you in my arms sooner. You understand an equipage the best of any man in town, I hear.

Med. By my own you would not guess it.

Sir Fop. There are critics who do not write, sir.

Med. Our peevish poets will scarce allow it.

Sir Fop. Damn 'em, they'll allow no man wit who does not play the fool like themselves, and show it! Have you taken notice of the *calèche* I brought over?

Med. Oh, yes! It has quite another air than the English makes.

Sir Fop. 'Tis as easily known from an English tumbril as an Inns of Court man is from one of us.

Dor. Truly, there is a *bel-air* in *calèches* as well as men.

Med. But there are few so delicate to observe it.

Sir Fop. The world is generally very *grossier* here, indeed.

Lady Town. He's very fine.

Emil. Extreme proper.

Sir Fop. A slight suit I made to appear in at my first arrival, not worthy your consideration, ladies.

Dor. The pantaloon is very well mounted.

Sir Fop. The tassels are new and pretty.

Med. I never saw a coat better cut.

Sir Fop. It makes me show long-waisted, and, I think, slender.

Dor. That's the shape our ladies dote on.

Med. Your breech, though, is a handful too high in my eye, Sir Fopling.

Sir Fop. Peace, Medley; I have wished it lower a thousand times, but a pox on't, 'twill not be.

Lady Town. His gloves are well fringed, large and graceful.

Sir Fop. I was always eminent for being *bien-ganté*.

Emil. He wears nothing but what are originals of the most famous hands in Paris.

Sir Fop. You are in the right, madam.
Lady Town. The suit?
Sir Fop. Barroy.[1]
Emil. The garniture?
Sir Fop. Le Gras.
Med. The shoes?
Sir Fop. Piccat.
Dor. The periwig?
Sir Fop. Chedreux.[2]
Lady Town. and Emil. The gloves?
Sir Fop. Orangerie: you know the smell, ladies. Dorimant, I could find in my heart for an amusement to have a gallantry with some of our English ladies.

Dor. 'Tis a thing no less necessary to confirm the reputation of your wit than a duel will be to satisfy the town of your courage.

Sir Fop. Here was a woman yesterday——
Dor. Mistress Loveit.
Sir Fop. You have named her.
Dor. You cannot pitch on a better for your purpose.
Sir Fop. Prithee, what is she?
Dor. A person of quality, and one who has a rest of reputation enough to make the conquest considerable. Besides, I hear she likes you too.

---

[1] Perhaps this should be *Barri*. The "drap du Barri" was later on extremely fashionable.

[2] A species of perruque, so called from the name of its inventor. Dryden wore a chedreux and a sword when he ate tarts with Mrs. Reeve at the Mulberry Garden, and Oldham, in his imitation of the Third Satire of Juvenal, has:

Their tawdry clothes, pulvilios, essences;
Their chedreux perruques and their vanities.

Sir Fop. Methought she seemed, though, very reserved and uneasy all the time I entertained her.

Dor. Grimace and affection. You will see her i' th' Mall to-night.

Sir Fop. Prithee let thee and I take the air together.

Dor. I am engaged to Medley, but I'll meet you at St. James's and give you some information upon the which you may regulate your proceedings.

Sir Fop. All the world will be in the Park to-night: ladies, 'twere pity to keep so much beauty longer within doors and rob the Ring of all those charms that should adorn it.——Hey, page!

Enter Page, and goes out again.

See that all my people be ready. Dorimant, *au revoir!* [*Exit* SIR FOPLING.

Med. A fine mettled coxcomb.

Dor. Brisk and insipid.

Med. Pert and dull.

Emil. However you despise him, gentlemen, I'll lay my life he passes for a wit with many.

Dor. That may very well be; nature has her cheats, stums a brain, and puts sophisticate dulness often on the tasteless multitude for true wit and good-humour. Medley, come.

Med. I must go a little way, I will meet you i' the Mall.

Dor. I'll walk through the garden thither. [*To the Women.*] We shall meet anon and bow.

Lady Town. Not to-night; we are engaged about a

business the knowledge of which may make you laugh hereafter.

Med. Your servant, ladies.

Dor. Au revoir! as Sir Fopling says.

[*Exeunt* MEDLEY *and* DORIMANT.

Lady Town. The old man will be here immediately.

Emil. Let's expect him i' th' garden.

Lady Town. Go, you are a rogue.

Emil. I can't abide you. [*Exeunt.*

SCENE III.—THE MALL.

Enter HARRIET *and* YOUNG BELLAIR, *she pulling him.*

Har. Come along.

Y. Bell. And leave your mother?

Har. Busy will be sent with a hue and cry after us; but that's no matter.

Y. Bell. 'Twill look strangely in me.

Har. She'll believe it a freak of mine and never blame your manners.

Y. Bell. What reverend acquaintance is that she has met?

Har. A fellow-beauty of the last King's time, though by the ruins you would hardly guess it.

[*Exeunt.*

Enter DORIMANT, *who crosses the stage.*

Enter YOUNG BELLAIR *and* HARRIET.

Y. Bell. By this time your mother is in a fine taking.

Har. If your friend Mr. Dorimant were but here now, that she might find me talking with him.

Y. Bell. She does not know him, but dreads him, I hear, of all mankind.

Har. She concludes if he does but speak to a woman she's undone; is on her knees every day to pray heaven defend me from him.

Y. Bell. You do not apprehend him so much as she does.

Har. I never saw anything in him that was frightful.

Y. Bell. On the contrary, have you not observed something extreme delightful in his wit and person?

Har. He's agreeable and pleasant I must own, but he does so much affect being so, he displeases me.

Y. Bell. Lord, madam, all he does and says is so easy and so natural.

Har. Some men's verses seem so to the unskilful, but labour i' the one and affectation in the other to the judicious plainly appear.

Y. Bell. I never heard him accused of affectation before.

Enter DORIMANT, *who stares upon her.*

Har. It passes on the easy town, who are favourably pleased in him to call it humour.

[*Exeunt* YOUNG BELLAIR *and* HARRIET.

Dor. 'Tis she! it must be she, that lovely hair, that easy shape, those wanton eyes, and all those melting charms about her mouth which Medley spoke of; I'll follow the lottery, and put in for a prize with my friend Bellair. [*Exit* DORIMANT *repeating*—

In love the victors from the vanquish'd fly ;
They fly that wound, and they pursue that die.

Enter YOUNG BELLAIR *and* HARRIET, *and after them* DORIMANT, *standing at a distance.*

Y. Bell. Most people prefer High Park[1] to this place.

Har. It has the better reputation, I confess; but I abominate the dull diversions there, the formal bows, the affected smiles, the silly by-words, and amorous tweers in passing; here one meets with a little conversation now and then.

Y. Bell. These conversations have been fatal to some of your sex, madam.

Har. It may be so; because some who want temper have been undone by gaming, must others who have it wholly deny themselves the pleasure of play?

Dor. Trust me, it were unreasonable, madam.
[*Coming up gently, and bowing to her.*
Har. Lord! who's this?
[*She starts, and looks grave.*
Y. Bell. Dorimant.

Dor. Is this the woman your father would have you marry?

Y. Bell. It is.

Dor. Her name?

Y. Bell. Harriet.

---

[1] *i.e.* Hyde Park, *the* park *par excellence;* references to it are endless. The great resort there was the so-called Ring. The name *High* Park seems unusual.

Dor. I am not mistaken, she's handsome.

Y. Bell. Talk to her, her wit is better than her face; we were wishing for you but now.

Dor. (*to* HARRIET). Overcast with seriousness o' the sudden! A thousand smiles were shining in that face but now; I never saw so quick a change of weather.

Har. (*aside*). I feel as great a change within; but he shall never know it.

Dor. You were talking of play, madam; pray what may be your stint?

Har. A little harmless discourse in public walks, or at most an appointment in a box barefaced at the playhouse; you are for masks and private meetings where women engage for all they are worth, I hear.

Dor. I have been used to deep play, but I can make one at small game when I like my gamester well.

Har. And be so unconcerned you'll ha' no pleasure in it.

Dor. Where there is a considerable sum to be won the hope of drawing people in makes every trifle considerable.

Har. The sordidness of men's natures, I know, makes 'em willing to flatter and comply with the rich, though they are sure never to be the better for 'em.

Dor. 'Tis in their power to do us good, and we despair not but at some time or other they may be willing.

Har. To men who have fared on this town like you, 'twould be a great mortification to live on hope; could you keep a Lent for a mistress?

Dor. In expectation of a happy Easter, and though time be very precious, think forty days well lost to gain your favour.

Har. Mr. Bellair! let us walk, 'tis time to leave him; men grow dull when they begin to be particular.

Dor. You're mistaken, flattery will not ensue, though I know you're greedy of the praises of the whole Mall.

Har. You do me wrong.

Dor. I do not; as I followed you I observed how you were pleased when the fops cried, *She's handsome, very handsome, By God she is,* and whispered aloud your name, the thousand several forms you put your face into; then, to make yourself more agreeable, how wantonly you played with your head, flung back your locks, and looked smilingly over your shoulder at 'em.

Har. I do not go begging the men's, as you do the ladies' good liking, with a sly softness in your looks and a gentle slowness in your bows as you pass by 'em——as thus, sir;—— [*Acts him.* Is not this like you?

Enter LADY WOODVIL *and* BUSY.

Y. Bell. Your mother, madam.
        [*Pulls* HARRIET; *she composes herself.*

Lady Wood. Ah, my dear child Harriet!

Busy. Now is she so pleased with finding her again she cannot chide her.

Lady Wood. Come away!

Dor. 'Tis now but high Mall, madam, the most entertaining time of all the evening.

Har. I would fain see that Dorimant, mother, you so cry out for a monster; he's in the Mall, I hear.

Lady Wood. Come away then! the plague is here, and you should dread the infection.

Y. Bell. You may be misinformed of the gentleman.

Lady Wood. Oh, no! I hope you do not know him! He is the prince of all the devils in the town, delights in nothing but in rapes and riots.

Dor. If you did but hear him speak, madam!

Lady Wood. Oh! he has a tongue, they say, would tempt the angels to a second fall.

Enter SIR FOPLING *with his Equipage, six Footmen and a Page.*

Sir Fop. Hey, Champagne, Norman, La Rose, La Fleur, La Tour, La Verdue. Dorimant!——

Lady Wood. Here, here he is among this rout, he names him; come away, Harriet, come away.

[*Exeunt* LADY WOODVIL, HARRIET, BUSY, *and* YOUNG BELLAIR.

Dor. This fool's coming has spoiled all; she's gone, but she has left a pleasing image of herself behind that wanders in my soul——It must not settle there.

Sir Fop. What reverie is this? Speak, man.

Dor. *Snatch'd from myself, how far behind*
    Already I behold the shore!

Enter MEDLEY.

Med. Dorimant, a discovery! I met with Bellair.

Dor. You can tell me no news, sir; I know all.

x

Med. How do you like the daughter?

Dor. You never came so near truth in your life as you did in her description.

Med. What think you of the mother?

Dor. Whatever I think of her, she thinks very well of me, I find.

Med. Did she know you?

Dor. She did not; whether she does now or no, I know not. Here was a pleasant scene towards, when in came Sir Fopling, mustering up his equipage, and at the latter end named me and frighted her away.

Med. Loveit and Belinda are not far off, I saw 'em alight at St. James's.

Dor. (*whispers*). Sir Fopling, hark you, a word or two. Look you do not want assurance.

Sir Fop. I never do on these occasions.

Dor. Walk on, we must not be seen together, make your advantage of what I have told you; the next turn you will meet the lady.

Sir Fop. Hey——Follow me all.

[*Exeunt* SIR FOPLING *and his Equipage.*

Dor. Medley, you shall see good sport anon between Loveit and this Fopling.

Med. I thought there was something toward by that whisper.

Dor. You know a worthy principle of hers?

Med. Not to be so much as civil to a man who speaks to her in the presence of him she professes to love.

Dor. I have encouraged Fopling to talk to her to-night.

Med. Now you are here she will go nigh to beat him.

Dor. In the humour she's in, her love will make her do some very extravagant thing, doubtless.

Med. What was Belinda's business with you at my Lady Townley's?

Dor. To get me to meet Loveit here in order to an *éclaircissement.* I made some difficulty of it, and have prepared this *rencontre* to make good my jealousy.

Med. Here they come!

Enter LOVEIT, BELINDA, *and* PERT.

Dor. I'll meet her and provoke her with a deal of dumb civility in passing by, then turn short and be behind her when Sir Fopling sets upon her——

See how unregarded now
That piece of beauty passes.

[*Exeunt* DORIMANT *and* MEDLEY.

Bel. How wonderful respectfully he bowed!

Pert. He's always over-mannerly when he has done a mischief.

Bel. Methought indeed at the same time he had a strange despising countenance.

Pert. The unlucky look, he thinks, becomes him.

Bel. I was afraid you would have spoke to him, my dear.

Lov. I would have died first; he shall no more find me the loving fool he has done.

Bel. You love him still!

Lov. No.

Pert. I wish you did not.

Lov. I do not, and I will have you think so. What made you hale me to this odious place, Belinda?

Bel. I hate to be hulched up in a coach; walking is much better.

Lov. Would we could meet Sir Fopling now!

Bel. Lord! would you not avoid him?

Lov. I would make him all the advances that may be.

Bel. That would confirm Dorimant's suspicion, my dear.

Lov. He is not jealous, but I will make him so, and be revenged a way he little thinks on.

Bel. (*aside*). If she should make him jealous, that may make him fond of her again: I must dissuade her from it. Lord! my dear, this will certainly make him hate you.

Lov. 'Twill make him uneasy, though he does not care for me; I know the effects of jealousy on men of his proud temper.

Bel. 'Tis a fantastic remedy, its operations are dangerous and uncertain.

Lov. 'Tis the strongest cordial we can give to dying love, it often brings it back when there's no sign of life remaining. But I design not so much the reviving his, as my revenge.

Enter Sir Fopling *and his Equipage.*

Sir Fop. Hey! bid the coachman send home four of his horses, and bring the coach to Whitehall; I'll walk over the Park——Madam, the honour of kissing your fair hands is a happiness I missed this afternoon at my Lady Townley's.

Lov. You were very obliging, Sir Fopling, the last time I saw you there.

Sir Fop. The preference was due to your wit and beauty. Madam, your servant; there never was so sweet an evening.

Bel. 'T has drawn all the rabble of the town hither.

Sir Fop. 'Tis pity there's not an order made that none but the *beau monde* should walk here.

Lov. 'Twould add much to the beauty of the place. See what a sort of nasty fellows are coming.

Enter three ill-fashioned Fellows, singing,

'Tis not for kisses alone, &c.

Lov. Fo! Their periwigs are scented with tobacco so strong——

Sir Fop. It overcomes our pulvilio[1]——Methinks I smell the coffee-house they came from.

1 *Man*. Dorimant's convenient, Madam Loveit.

2 *Man*. I like the oily buttock with her.

3 *Man*. What spruce prig is that?

1 *Man*. A caravan lately come from Paris.

2 *Man*. Peace, they smoke.[2]

There's something else to be done, &c.

[*All of them coughing; exeunt, singing.*

---

[1] A favourite essence.

> The patch, the powder-box, pulville-perfumes.
> Gay, *The Fan*, i. 129.

"Have you pulvilled the coachman?"—*The Way of the World*, iv. 1.

[2] *i.e.* suspect that we are talking about them.

Enter DORIMANT *and* MEDLEY.

Dor. They're engaged.

Med. She entertains him as if she liked him.

Dor. Let us go forward; seem earnest in discourse, and show ourselves. Then you shall see how she'll use him.

Bel. Yonder's Dorimant, my dear.

Lov. (*aside*). I see him, he comes insulting; but I will disappoint him in his expectation. [*To* SIR FOPLING.] I like this pretty nice humour of yours, Sir Fopling. With what a loathing eye he looked upon those fellows!

Sir Fop. I sat near one of 'em at a play to-day, and was almost poisoned with a pair of cordovan gloves he wears.

Lov. Oh! filthy cordovan, how I hate the smell!
[*Laughs in a loud affected way.*

Sir Fop. Did you observe, madam, how their cravats hung loose an inch from their neck, and what a frightful air it gave 'em?

Lov. Oh! I took particular notice of one that is always spruced up with a deal of dirty sky-coloured ribbon.

Bel. That's one of the walking flageolets who haunt the Mall o' nights.

Lov. Oh! I remember him; he's a hollow tooth enough to spoil the sweetness of an evening.

Sir Fop. I have seen the tallest walk the streets with a dainty pair of boxes neatly buckled on.

Lov. And a little footboy at his heels pocket-high, with a flat cap——a dirty face.

Sir Fop. And a snotty nose.

Lov. Oh——odious! there's many of my own sex with that Holborn equipage trip to Gray's Inn Walks, and now and then travel hither on a Sunday.

Med. She takes no notice of you.

Dor. Damn her! I am jealous of a counterplot!

Lov. Your liveries are the finest, Sir Fopling.—— Oh, that page! that page is the prettily'st dressed—— They are all Frenchmen?

Sir Fop. There's one damned English blockhead among 'em, you may know him by his mien.

Lov. Oh! that's he, that's he! what do you call him?

Sir Fop. Hey——I know not what to call him.——

Lov. What's your name?

Footman. John Trott, madam!

Sir Fop. Oh, unsufferable! Trott, Trott, Trott! there's nothing so barbarous as the names of our English servants. What countryman are you, sirrah?

Footman. Hampshire, sir.

Sir Fop. Then Hampshire be your name. Hey, Hampshire!

Lov. Oh, that sound! that sound becomes the mouth of a man of quality!

Med. Dorimant, you look a little bashful on the matter.

Dor. She dissembles better than I thought she could have done.

Med. You have tempted her with too luscious a bait: she bites at the coxcomb.

Dor. She cannot fall from loving me to that?

Med. You begin to be jealous in earnest.

Dor. Of one I do not love?

Med. You did love her.

Dor. The fit has long been over.

Med. But I have known men fall into dangerous relapses when they have found a woman inclining to another.

Dor. (to himself). He guesses the secret of my heart! I am concerned, but dare not show it lest Belinda should mistrust all I have done to gain her.

Bel. (aside). I have watched his look, and find no alteration there: did he love her, some signs of jealousy would have appeared.

Dor. I hope this happy evening, madam, has reconciled you to the scandalous Mall; we shall have you now hankering here again.

Lov. Sir Fopling, will you walk?

Sir Fop. I am all obedience, madam.

Lov. Come along then, and let's agree to be malicious on all the ill-fashioned things we meet.

Sir Fop. We'll make a *critique* on the whole Mall, madam.

Lov. Belinda, you shall engage——

Bel. To the reserve of our friends, my dear.

Lov. No, no exceptions——

Sir Fop. We'll sacrifice all to our diversion.

Lov. All——all——

Sir Fop. All.

Bel. All? Then let it be.

[*Exeunt* Sir Fopling, Loveit, Belinda, *and* Pert, *laughing.*

Med. Would you had brought some more of your friends, Dorimant, to have been witnesses of Sir Fopling's disgrace and your triumph.

Dor. 'Twere unreasonable to desire you not to laugh at me; but pray do not expose me to the town this day or two.

Med. By that time you hope to have regained your credit?

Dor. I know she hates Fopling, and only makes use of him in hope to work me on again; had it not been for some powerful considerations which will be removed to-morrow morning, I had made her pluck off this mask and show the passion that lies panting under.

Enter a Footman.

Med. Here comes a man from Bellair, with news of your last adventure.

Dor. I am glad he sent him. I long to know the consequence of our parting.

Footman. Sir, my master desires you to come to my Lady Townley's presently, and bring Mr. Medley with you. My Lady Woodvil and her daughter are there.

Med. Then all's well, Dorimant.

Footman. They have sent for the fiddles and mean to dance! He bid me tell you, sir, the old lady does not know you, and would have you own yourself to be Mr. Courtage. They are all prepared to receive you by that name.

Dor. That foppish admirer of quality who flatters

the very meat at honourable tables, and never offers love to a woman below a lady-grandmother.

Med. You know the character you are to act, I see.

Dor. This is Harriet's contrivance——wild, witty, lovesome, beautiful and young——come along, Medley.

Med. This new woman would well supply the loss of Loveit.

Dor. That business must not end so; before to-morrow's sun is set I will revenge and clear it:
And you and Loveit to her cost shall find,
I fathom all the depths of womankind. [*Exeunt.*

ACT IV.

SCENE I.—*The scene opens with the fiddles playing a country dance.*

Enter DORIMANT, LADY WOODVIL, YOUNG BELLAIR, *and* MRS. HARRIET, OLD BELLAIR *and* EMILIA, MR. MEDLEY *and* LADY TOWNLEY, *as having just ended the dance.*

Old Bellair.

SO, so, so, a smart bout, a very smart bout, adod!

Lady Town. How do you like Emilia's dancing, brother?

O. Bell. Not at all, not at all.

Lady Town. You speak not what you think, I am sure.

O. Bell. No matter for that; go, bid her dance no more, it don't become her, it don't become her, tell her I say so. [*Aside.*] Adod, I love her.

Dor. (*to* LADY WOODVIL). All people mingle now-a-days, madam, and in public places women of quality have the least respect showed 'em.

Lady Wood. I protest you say the truth, Mr. Courtage.

Dor. Forms and ceremonies, the only things that uphold quality and greatness, are now shamefully laid aside and neglected.

Lady Wood. Well! this is not the women's age, let 'em think what they will; lewdness is the business now, love was the business in my time.

Dor. The women indeed are little beholding to the young men of this age; they're generally only dull admirers of themselves, and make their court to nothing but their periwigs and their cravats, and would be more concerned for the disordering of 'em, though on a good occasion, than a young maid would be for the tumbling of her head or handkerchief.

Lady Wood. I protest you hit 'em.

Dor. They are very assiduous to show themselves at Court well dressed to the women of quality, but their business is with the stale mistresses of the town, who are prepared to receive their lazy addresses by industrious old lovers who have cast 'em off and made 'em easy.

Har. He fits my mother's humour so well, a little more and she'll dance a kissing dance with him anon.

Med. Dutifully observed, madam.

Dor. They pretend to be great critics in beauty; by their talk you would think they liked no face, and yet can dote on an ill one if it belong to a laundress or a tailor's daughter; they cry a woman's past her prime at twenty, decayed at four-and-twenty, old and unsufferable at thirty.

Lady Wood. Unsufferable at thirty! That they are in the wrong, Mr. Courtage, at five-and-thirty there are living proofs enough to convince 'em.

Dor. Ay, madam, there's Mrs. Setlooks, Mrs. Droplip, and my Lady Lowd; show me among all our opening buds a face that promises so much beauty as the remains of theirs.

Lady Wood. The depraved appetite of this vicious age tastes nothing but green fruit, and loathes it when 'tis kindly ripened.

Dor. Else so many deserving women, madam, would not be so untimely neglected.

Lady Wood. I protest, Mr. Courtage, a dozen such good men as you would be enough to atone for that wicked Dorimant and all the under-debauchees of the town. [HARRIET, EMILIA, YOUNG BELLAIR, MEDLEY, *and* LADY TOWNLEY *break out into laughter.* What's the matter there?

Med. A pleasant mistake, madam, that a lady has made, occasions a little laughter.

O. Bell. Come, come, you keep 'em idle, they are impatient till the fiddles play again.

Dor. You are not weary, madam?

Lady Wood. One dance more; I cannot refuse you, Mr. Courtage. [*They dance.*

Emil. You are very active, sir.

[*After the dance* OLD BELLAIR *singing and dancing up to* EMILIA.

O. Bell. Adod, sirrah, when I was a young fellow I could ha' capered up to my woman's gorget.

Dor. You are willing to rest yourself, madam?

Lady Town. We'll walk into my chamber and sit down.

Med. Leave us Mr. Courtage, he's a dancer, and the young ladies are not weary yet.

Lady Wood. We'll send him out again.

Har. If you do not quickly, I know where to send for Mr. Dorimant.

Lady Wood. This girl's head, Mr. Courtage, is ever running on that wild fellow.

Dor. 'Tis well you have got her a good husband, madam; that will settle it.

[*Exeunt* LADY TOWNLEY, LADY WOODVIL, *and* DORIMANT.

O. Bell. (*to* EMILIA). Adod, sweetheart, be advised, and do not throw thyself away on a young idle fellow.

Emil. I have no such intention, sir.

O. Bell. Have a little patience, thou shalt have the man I spake of. Adod, he loves thee, and will make a good husband, but no words.

Emil. But, sir.——

O. Bell. No answer——out a pise! peace! and think on't.

Enter DORIMANT.

Dor. Your company is desired within, sir.

O. Bell. I go, I go, good Mr. Courtage—— [*To* EMILIA.] Fare you well; go, I'll see you no more.

Emil. What have I done, sir?

O. Bell. You are ugly, you are ugly; is she not, Mr. Courtage?

Emil. Better words, or I shan't abide you.

O. Bell. Out a pise——adod, what does she say? Hit her a pat for me there. [*Exit* OLD BELLAIR.

Med. You have charms for the whole family.

Dor. You'll spoil all with some unseasonable jest, Medley.

Med. You see I confine my tongue and am content to be a bare spectator, much contrary to my nature.

Emil. Methinks, Mr. Dorimant, my Lady Woodvil is a little fond of you.

Dor. Would her daughter were!

Med. It may be you may find her so; try her, you have an opportunity.

Dor. And I will not lose it. Bellair, here's a lady has something to say to you.

Y. Bell. I wait upon her. Mr. Medley, we have both business with you.

Dor. Get you all together then. [*To* HARRIET.] That demure curtsey is not amiss in jest, but do not think in earnest it becomes you.

Har. Affectation is catching, I find; from your grave bow I got it.

Dor. Where had you all that scorn and coldness in your look?

Har. From nature, sir; pardon my want of art: I have not learnt those softnesses and languishings which now in faces are so much in fashion.

Dor. You need 'em not; you have a sweetness of your own, if you would but calm your frowns and let it settle.

Har. My eyes are wild and wandering like my passions, and cannot yet be tied to rules of charming.

Dor. Women, indeed, have commonly a method of managing those messengers of love; now they will look as if they would kill, and anon they will look as if they were dying. They point and rebate[1] their glances the better to invite us.

Har. I like this variety well enough, but hate the set face that always looks as it would say, *Come, love me*—a woman who at plays makes the *doux yeux* to a whole audience and at home cannot forbear 'em to her monkey.

Dor. Put on a gentle smile, and let me see how well it will become you.

Har. I am sorry my face does not please you as it is, but I shall not be complaisant and change it.

Dor. Though you are obstinate, I know 'tis capable of improvement, and shall do you justice, madam, if I chance to be at Court when the critics of the circle pass their judgment; for thither you must come.

Har. And expect to be taken in pieces, have all my features examined, every motion censured, and on the whole be condemned to be but pretty, or a beauty of the lowest rate. What think you?

Dor. The women, nay, the very lovers who belong to the Drawing-room, will maliciously allow you more than that; they always grant what is apparent that they may the better be believed when they name concealed faults they cannot easily be disproved in.

Har. Beauty runs as great a risk exposed at Court as wit does on the stage, where the ugly and the foolish all are free to censure.

Dor. (aside). I love her, and dare not let her know ti; I fear she has an ascendant o'er me, and may revenge

---

[1] A fencing term.

he wrongs I have done her sex. [*To her.*] Think of making a party, madam, love will engage.

Har. You make me start! I did not think to have heard of love from you.

Dor. I never knew what 'twas to have a settled ague yet, but now and then have had irregular fits.

Har. Take heed! sickness after long health is commonly more violent and dangerous.

Dor. (*aside*). I have took the infection from her, and feel the disease now spreading in me—— [*To her.*] Is the name of love so frightful that you dare not stand it?

Har. 'Twill do little execution out of your mouth on me, I am sure.

Dor. It has been fatal——

Har. To some easy women, but we are not all born to one destiny; I was informed you use to laugh at love, and not make it.

Dor. The time has been, but now I must speak——

Har. If it be on that idle subject, I will put on my serious look, turn my head carelessly from you, drop my lip, let my eyelids' fall and hang half o'er my eyes—thus—while you buzz a speech of an hour long in my ear, and I answer never a word; why do you not begin?

Dor. That the company may take notice how passionately I make advances of love, and how disdainfully you receive 'em.

Har. When your love's grown strong enough to make you bear being laughed at, I'll give you leave to trouble me with it: till when, pray forbear, sir.

Y

Enter SIR FOPLING *and others in masks.*

Dor. What's here, masquerades?

Har. I thought that foppery had been left off and people might have been in private with a fiddle.

Dor. 'Tis endeavoured to be kept on foot still by some who find themselves the more acceptable the less they are known.

Y. Bell. This must be Sir Fopling.

Med. That extraordinary habit shows it.

Y. Bell. What are the rest?

Med. A company of French rascals whom he picked up in Paris and has brought over to be his dancing equipage on these occasions. Make him own himself; a fool is very troublesome when he presumes he is incognito.

Sir Fop. (*to* HARRIET). Do you know me?

Har. Ten to one but I guess at you.

Sir Fop. Are you women as fond of a vizard as we men are?

Har. I am very fond of a vizard that covers a face I do not like, sir.

Y. Bell. Here are no masks, you see, sir, but those which came with you; this was intended a private meeting, but because you look like a gentleman, if you discover yourself, and we know you to be such, you shall be welcome.

Sir Fop. (*pulling off his mask*). Dear Bellair.

Med. Sir Fopling! how came you hither?

Sir Fop. Faith, I was coming late from Whitehall, after the King's *couchée,* one of my people told me he had heard fiddles at my Lady Townley's, and——

Dor. You need not say any more, sir.

Sir Fop. Dorimant, let me kiss thee.

Dor. (*whispers*). Hark you, Sir Fopling.

Sir Fop. Enough, enough—Courtage. A pretty kind of young woman that, Medley; I observed her in the Mall; more *éveillée* [1] than our English women commonly are; prithee, what is she?

Med. The most noted *coquette* in town; beware of her.

Sir Fop. Let her be what she will, I know how to take my measures; in Paris the *mode* is to flatter the *prude*, laugh at the *faux-prude*, make serious love to the *demi-prude*, and only rally with the *coquette*. Medley, what think you?

Med. That for all this smattering of the mathematics, you may be out in your judgment at tennis.

Sir Fop. What a *coq-à-l'âne* is this! I talk of women, and thou answer'st tennis.

Med. Mistakes will be for want of apprehension.

Sir Fop. I am very glad of the acquaintance I have with this family.

Med. My lady truly is a good woman.

Sir Fop. Ah! Dorimant—Courtage I would say— would thou hadst spent the last winter in Paris with me. When thou wert there La Corneus and Sallyes [2] were

---

[1] Cf. the *Spectator*, No. 45, on the "Invasion of French Manners": "The whole behaviour of the French is to make the sex (women) more fantastical, or (as they are pleased to call it) more *awakened*."

[2] So the old editions. Possibly Etheredge wrote *Cornuel* and *Selles*. Readers of Madame de Sévigné will remember allusions to

the only habitudes we had; a comedian would have been a *bonne fortune.* No stranger ever passed his time so well as I did some months before I came over. I was well received in a dozen families where all the women of quality used to visit; I have intrigues to tell thee more pleasant than ever thou read'st in a novel.

Har. Write 'em, sir, and oblige us women; our language wants such little stories.

Sir Fop. Writing, madam, is a mechanic part of wit; a gentleman should never go beyond a song or a billet.

Har. Bussy was a gentleman.

Sir Fop. Who, d'Ambois?[1]

Med. Was there ever such a brisk blockhead?

Har. Not d'Ambois, sir, but Rabutin[2]—he who writ *The Loves of France.*

Sir Fop. That may be, madam: many gentlemen

---

a Madame Cornuel whose epigrams were deservedly admired. She is mentioned in Bussy's letters, plays some part in the *Histoire Amoureuse* (*Mémoires,* vol. ii. pp. 350-358), and altogether seems to have been a distinguished figure in French society. Very probably Etheredge knew her, at least by fame, and may be referring to her here. Madame Selles is less tangible. Bussy, however, mentions a lady of that name who had attracted some attention by " une petite histoire de ses amours." This *histoire* is spoken of several times in the *Correspondance* (vol. ii. pp. 134-7), and its author may have presided over one of the fashionable *salons* of the time. At any rate, it should be noticed that all the names which occur in the play—Candale, Merille, Lambert, &c.—are those of contemporaries, and all through Etheredge is bent on showing his close familiarity with the great world of Paris.

[1] To whom is Etheredge referring?—the great French cardinal and minister, or the nobleman whose adventures are chronicled in Dumas' *La Dame de Monsoreau?*

[2] Bussy-Rabutin, Roger, Comte de; born 1618, died 1693;

do things that are below 'em. Damn your authors, Courtage; women are the prettiest things we can fool away our time with.

Har. I hope ye have wearied yourself to-night at Court, sir, and will not think of fooling with anybody here.

Sir Fop. I cannot complain of my fortune there, madam——Dorimant——

Dor. Again!

Sir Fop. Courtage, a pox on't! I have something to tell thee. When I had made my court within, I came out and flung myself upon the mat, under the State i' th' outward room, i' th' midst of half-a-dozen beauties who were withdrawn to jeer among themselves, as they called it.

Dor. Did you know 'em?

Sir Fop. Not one of 'em, by heavens! not I. But they were all your friends.

Dor. How are you sure of that?

Sir Fop. Why, we laughed at all the town; spared nobody but yourself; they found me a man for their purpose.

a cousin of Madame de Sévigné, with whom he corresponded. A complete edition of his *Mémoires* and *Correspondance* was published at Paris, 1857-59. Etheredge speaks so familiarly of him that one is tempted to think he knew the author of the *Histoire Amoureuse*, and I hoped—vainly, however—to find some reference in the letters to the English dramatist. Of Bussy's numerous works the fame of the *Histoire Amoureuse des Gaules* alone has survived. It appears to have been extremely popular, possessing "a thousand irresistible graces," according to the dictum of that politest of eighteenth century critics, the ingenious and courtly Major Pack (*Works,* ed. 1729).

Dor. I know you are malicious to your power.

Sir Fop. And, faith, I had occasion to show it, for I never saw more gaping fools at a ball or on a Birthday.

Dor. You learned who the women were?

Sir Fop. No matter; they frequent the Drawing-room.

Dor. And entertain themselves pleasantly at the expense of all the fops who come there.

Sir Fop. That's their business; faith, I sifted 'em, and find they have a sort of wit among them——Ah! filthy.   [*Pinches a tallow candle.*

Dor. Look, he has been pinching the tallow candle.

Sir Fop. How can you breathe in a room where there's grease frying? Dorimant, thou art intimate with my lady, advise her for her own sake, and the good company that comes hither, to burn wax lights.

Har. What are these masquerades who stand so obsequiously at a distance?

Sir Fop. A set of *balladins* whom I picked out of the best in France, and brought over with a *flûtes douces* or two, my servants; they shall entertain you.

Har. I had rather see you dance yourself, Sir Fopling.

Sir Fop. And I had rather do it——all the company knows it——but, madam——

Med. Come, come, no excuses, Sir Fopling.

Sir Fop. By heavens, Medley!

Med. Like a woman, I find you must be struggled with before one brings you to what you desire.

Har. (*aside*). Can he dance?

Emil. And fence and sing too, if you'll believe im.

Dor. He has no more excellence in his heels than his head. He went to Paris a plain bashful English ockhead, and is returned a fine undertaking French p.

Med. I cannot prevail.

Sir Fop. Do not think it want of complaisance, adam.

Har. You are too well bred to want that, Sir opling. I believe it want of power.

Sir Fop. By heavens! and so it is. I have sat up) damned late and drunk so cursed hard since I me to this lewd town, that I am fit for nothing but w dancing now, a *corant*, a *bourée*,[1] or a *menuet;* but t. André tells me, if I will but be regular, in one onth I shall rise again. Pox on this debauchery!
      [*Endeavours at a caper.*

Emil. I have heard your dancing much commended.

Sir Fop. It had the good fortune to please in Paris: was judged to rise within an inch as high as the isque, in an entry I danced there.

Har. I am mightily taken with this fool, let us sit. Iere's a seat, Sir Fopling.

Sir Fop. At your feet, madam; I can be nowhere) much at ease: by your leave, gown.

Har. and Emil. Ah! you'll spoil it.

---

[1] For the former, cf. *Henry V.*, iii. 5, 33:
    And teach lavoltas high and swift corantos.

or a note on the *bourée* Mr. Ashton's *Social Life in the Reign* *Queen Anne* (i. 100) may be consulted.

Sir Fop. No matter, my clothes are my creatures; I make 'em to make my court to you ladies, hey——
[*Dance.*
Qu'on commence—to an English dancer English motions. I was forced to entertain this fellow, one of my set miscarrying——Oh, horrid! leave your damned manner of dancing, and put on the French air; have you not a pattern before you——pretty well! Imitation in time may bring him to something.

After the dance enter OLD BELLAIR, LADY WOODVIL, *and* LADY TOWNLEY.

O. Bell. Hey, adod! what have we here, a mumming?

Lady Wood. Where's my daughter——Harriet?

Dor. Here, here, madam. I know not but under these disguises there may be dangerous sparks; I gave the young lady warning.

Lady Wood. Lord! I am so obliged to you, Mr. Courtage.

Har. Lord! how you admire this man.

Lady Wood. What have you to except against him?

Har. He's a fop.

Lady Wood. He's not a Dorimant, a wild extravagant fellow of the times.

Har. He's a man made up of forms and commonplaces sucked out of the remaining lees of the last age.

Lady Wood. He's so good a man, that were you not engaged——

Lady Town. You'll have but little night to sleep in.

Lady Wood. Lord! 'tis perfect day——

Dor. (*aside*). The hour is almost come I appointed Belinda, and I am not so foppishly in love here to forget: I am flesh and blood yet.

Lady Town. I am very sensible, madam.

Lady Wood. Lord, madam!

Har. Look, in what struggle is my poor mother yonder?

Y. Bell. She has much ado to bring out the compliment.

Dor. She strains hard for it.

Har. See, see! her head tottering, her eyes staring, and her under lip trembling——

Dor. (*aside*). Now, now she's in the very convulsions of her civility. 'Sdeath, I shall lose Belinda. I must fright her hence; she'll be an hour in this fit of good manners else. [*To* LADY WOODVIL.] Do you not know Sir Fopling, madam?

Lady Wood. I have seen that face——Oh, heaven! 'tis the same we met in the Mall; how came he here?

Dor. A fiddle in this town is a kind of fop-call; no sooner it strikes up but the house is besieged with an army of masquerades straight.

Lady Wood. Lord! I tremble, Mr. Courtage; for certain Dorimant is in the company.

Dor. I cannot confidently say he is not; you had best begone. I will wait upon you; your daughter is in the hands of Mr. Bellair.

Lady Wood. I'll see her before me. Harriet, come away.

Y. Bell. Lights! lights!

Lady Town. Light down there.

O. Bell. Adod, it needs not——

Dor. Call my Lady Woodvil's coach to the door quickly.

[*Exeunt* DORIMANT *and* YOUNG BELLAIR, *with the Ladies.*

O. Bell. Stay, Mr. Medley, let the young fellows do that duty; we will drink a glass of wine together. 'Tis good after dancing; what mumming spark is that?

Med. He is not to be comprehended in few words.

Sir Fop. Hey! La Tour.

Med. Whither away, Sir Fopling?

Sir Fop. I have business with Courtage——

Med. He'll but put the ladies into their coach, and come up again.

O. Bell. In the meantime I'll call for a bottle.

[*Exit* OLD BELLAIR.

Enter YOUNG BELLAIR.

Med. Where's Dorimant?

Y. Bell. Stolen home; he has had business waiting for him there all this night, I believe, by an impatience I observed in him.

Med. Very likely; 'tis but dissembling drunkenness, railing at his friends, and the kind soul will embrace the blessing and forget the tedious expectation.

Sir Fop. I must speak with him before I sleep.

Y. Bell. Emilia and I are resolved on that business.

Med. Peace, here's your father.

Enter OLD BELLAIR *and Butler, with a bottle of wine.*

O. Bell. The women are all gone to bed. Fill, boy; Mr. Medley, begin a health.

Med. (*whispers*). To Emilia.

O. Bell. Out, a pise! she's a rogue, and I'll not pledge you.

Med. I know you will.

O. Bell. Adod, drink it then.

Sir Fop. Let us have the new *bachique*.

O. Bell. Adod, that is a hard word; what does it mean, sir?

Med. A catch or drinking song.

O. Bell. Let us have it then.

Sir Fop. Fill the glasses round, and draw up in a body. Hey! music!

They sing.

The pleasures of love and the joys of good wine
To perfect our happiness wisely we join.
We to beauty all day
Give the sovereign sway,
And her favourite nymphs devoutly obey.
At the plays we are constantly making our court,
And when they are ended we follow the sport,
To the Mall and the Park,
Where we love till 'tis dark;
Then sparkling champagne
Puts an end to their reign;
It quickly recovers
Poor languishing lovers,

Makes us frolic and gay, and drowns all our sorrow;
But, alas! we relapse again on the morrow.
Let ev'ry man stand
With his glass in his hand,
And briskly discharge at the word of command.
Here's a health to all those
Whom to-night we depose:
Wine and beauty by turns great souls should inspire.
Present altogether, and now, boys, give fire!

O. Bell. Adod, a pretty business, and very merry.

Sir Fop. Hark you, Medley, let you and I take the fiddles, and go waken Dorimant.

Med. We shall do him a courtesy, if it be as I guess. For after the fatigue of this night, he'll quickly have his bellyful, and be glad of an occasion to cry, *Take away, Handy.*

Y. Bell. I'll go with you, and there we'll consult about affairs, Medley.

O. Bell. (*looks at his watch*). Adod, 'tis six o'clock.

Sir Fop. Let's away then.

O. Bell. Mr. Medley, my sister tells me you are an honest man, and, adod, I love you. Few words and hearty—that's the way with old Harry, old Harry.

Sir Fop. Light your *flambeaux*. Hey!

O. Bell. What does the man mean?

Med. 'Tis day, Sir Fopling.

Sir Fop. No matter. Our serenade will look the greater. [*Exeunt omnes.*

SCENE II.—DORIMANT'S LODGING. *A table, a candle, a toilet, &c.* HANDY *tying up linen.*

Enter DORIMANT *in his gown, and* BELINDA.

Dor. Why will you be gone so soon?

Bel. Why did you stay out so late?

Dor. Call a chair, Handy. [*Exit* HANDY. What makes you tremble so?

Bel. I have a thousand fears about me. Have I not been seen, think you?

Dor. By nobody but myself and trusty Handy.

Bel. Where are all your people?

Dor. I have dispersed 'em on sleeveless [1] errands. What does that sigh mean?

Bel. Can you be so unkind to ask me?—Well— [*Sighs.*] were it to do again——

Dor. We should do it, should we not?

Bel. I think we should; the wickeder man you to make me love so well. Will you be discreet now?

Dor. I will.

Bel. You cannot.

Dor. Never doubt it.

Bel. I will not expect it.

Dor. You do me wrong.

Bel. You have no more power to keep the secret than I had not to trust you with it.

---

[1] *i.e.* fruitless: "on a sleeveless errand."—*Troilus and Cressida*, v. 4.

Dor. By all the joys I have had, and those you keep in store——

Bel. You'll do for my sake what you never did before——

Dor. By that truth thou hast spoken, a wife shall sooner betray herself to her husband——

Bel. Yet I had rather you should be false in this, than in any other thing you promised me.

Dor. What's that?

Bel. That you would never see Loveit more but in public places, in the Park, at Court, and plays.

Dor. 'Tis not likely a man should be fond of seeing a damned old play when there is a new one acted.

Bel. I dare not trust your promise.

Dor. You may.

Bel. This does not satisfy me. You shall swear you never will see her more.

Dor. I will! a thousand oaths——By all——

Bel. Hold——You shall not, now I think on't better.

Dor. I will swear.

Bel. I shall grow jealous of the oath, and think I owe your truth to that, not to your love.

Dor. Then, by my love, no other oath I'll swear.

Enter HANDY.

Handy. Here's a chair.

Bel. Let me go.

Dor. I cannot.

Bel. Too willingly, I fear.

Dor. Too unkindly feared. When will you promise me again?

Bel. Not this fortnight.

Dor. You will be better than your word.

Bel. I think I shall. Will it not make you love me less? [*Starting.*] Hark! what fiddles are these?

[*Fiddles without.*

Dor. Look out, Handy.

[*Exit* HANDY, *and returns.*

Handy. Mr. Medley, Mr. Bellair, and Sir Fopling; they are coming up.

Dor. How got they in?

Handy. The door was open for the chair.

Bel. Lord! let me fly——

Dor. Here, here, down the back stairs. I'll see you into your chair.

Bel. No, no, stay and receive 'em, and be sure you keep your word and never see Loveit more: let it be a proof of your kindness.

Dor. It shall——Handy, direct her. Everlasting love go along with thee. [*Kissing her hand.*

[*Exeunt* BELINDA *and* HANDY.

Enter YOUNG BELLAIR, MEDLEY, *and* SIR FOPLING.

Y. Bell. Not a-bed yet!

Med. You have had an irregular fit, Dorimant?

Dor. I have.

Y. Bell. And is it off already?

Dor. Nature has done her part, gentlemen; when she falls kindly to work, great cures are effected in little time, you know.

Sir Fop. We thought there was a wench in the case by the chair that waited. Prithee make us a *confidence.*

Dor. Excuse me.

Sir Fop. Le sage Dorimant! was she pretty?

Dor. So pretty she may come to keep her coach and pay parish duties if the good humour of the age continue.

Med. And be of the number of the ladies kept by public-spirited men for the good of the whole town.

Sir Fop. Well said, Medley.

[SIR FOPLING *dancing by himself.*

Y. Bell. See, Sir Fopling dancing.

Dor. You are practising and have a mind to recover, I see.

Sir Fop. Prithee, Dorimant, why hast not thou a glass hung up here? A room is the dullest thing without one.

Y. Bell. Here is company to entertain you.

Sir Fop. But I mean in case of being alone. In a glass a man may entertain himself——

Dor. The shadow of himself indeed.

Sir Fop. Correct the errors of his motions and his dress.

Med. I find, Sir Fopling, in your solitude you remember the saying of the wise man, and study yourself.

Sir Fop. 'Tis the best diversion in our retirements. Dorimant, thou art a pretty fellow, and wear'st thy clothes well, but I never saw thee have a handsome cravat. Were they made up like mine, they'd give another air to thy face. Prithee let me send my man to dress thee but one day. By heavens! an Englishman cannot tie a ribbon.

Dor. They are something clumsy-fisted——

Sir Fop. I have brought over the prettiest fellow that ever spread a toilet; he served some time under Merille,[1] the greatest *génie* in the world for a *valet-de-chambre*.

Dor. What, he who formerly belonged to the Duke of Candale?[2]

Sir Fop. The same, and got him his immortal reputation.

Dor. You've a very fine *brandenburgh* on, Sir Fopling.

Sir Fop. It serves to wrap me up after the fatigue of a ball.

Med. I see you often in it, with your periwig tied up.

---

[1] Mentioned in the *Histoire Amoureuse* as "le principal confident du duc" (*i.e.* Candale).—Bussy's *Mémoires*, vol. ii. p. 322. Subsequently he passed into the service of the Duke of Orleans; cf. the *Correspondance*, vol. ii. p. 313 ("valet de chambre de M. le duc d'Orléans"), and vol. iii. p. 240, where he has risen to the dignity of "premier valet de chambre de Monsieur."

[2] Often referred to in Bussy's *Mémoires*. The allusion to his "immortal reputation" is explained by a passage in the *Histoire Amoureuse*: "Le duc de Candale avait les yeux bleus, le nez bien fait, les traits irréguliers, la bouche grande et désagréable mais de fort belles dents, les cheveux blonds-dorés, en la plus grande quantité du monde. Sa taille était admirable et s'habillait bien, et les plus propres tâchaient de l'imiter. Il avait l'air d'un homme de grande qualité, il tenait un des premiers rangs en France." Doubtless the duke's-love-affair with Madame Olonne served as a title to distinction.

z

Sir Fop. We should not always be in a set dress; 'tis more *en cavalier* to appear now and then in a *déshabillé*.

Med. Pray how goes your business with Loveit?

Sir Fop. You might have answered yourself in the Mall last night. Dorimant! did you not see the advances she made me? I have been endeavouring at a song.

Dor. Already!

Sir Fop. 'Tis my *coup d'essai* in English; I would fain have thy opinion of it.

Dor. Let's see it.

Sir Fop. Hey, Page! give me my song——Bellair, here, thou hast a pretty voice, sing it.

Y. Bell. Sing it yourself, Sir Fopling.

Sir Fop. Excuse me.

Y. Bell. You learnt to sing in Paris.

Sir Fop. I did, of Lambert,[1] the greatest master in the world; but I have his own fault, a weak voice, and care not to sing out of a *ruelle*.[2]

Dor. A *ruelle* is a pretty cage for a singing fop, indeed.

---

[1] Michel Lambert, "maître de la musique de la chambre du roi;" born 1610, died July, 1696.

[2] Properly the *ruelle* was the space in a bedroom between the bed and the wall: "Se disait particulièrement des chambres à coucher sous Louis XIV., des alcôves de certaines dames de qualité, servant de salon de conversation et où régnait souvent le ton précieux."—Littré. Turning to *Les Précieuses* (scene ix.), we find Mascarille saying, "Et vous verrez courir de ma façon, dans les belles ruelles de Paris, deux cents chansons, autant de sonnets." The use of the word here is one of those intimate touches in which Etheredge delights.

YOUNG BELLAIR *reads the song.*

How charming Phyllis is! how fair!
  Ah, that she were as willing
To ease my wounded heart of care,
  And make her eyes less killing!
I sigh! I sigh! I languish now,
  And love will not let me rest;
I drive about the Park, and bow
  Still as I meet my dearest.

Sir Fop. Sing it, sing it, man; it goes to a pretty new tune, which I am confident was made by Baptiste.[1]

Med. Sing it yourself, Sir Fopling; he does not know the tune.

Sir Fop. I'll venture. [SIR FOPLING *sings.*

Dor. Ay, marry, now 'tis something. I shall not flatter you, Sir Fopling; there is not much thought in't, but 'tis passionate, and well turned.

Med. After the French way.

Sir Fop. That I aimed at. Does it not give you a lively image of the thing? Slap down goes the glass, and thus we are at it.

Dor. It does indeed. I perceive, Sir Fopling, you'll be the very head of the sparks who are lucky in compositions of this nature.

---

[1] "The present great composer," says Pepys, June 18th, 1666. Baptiste—his real name was Baptiste Anet—was a pupil of Corelli; as a violinist he had a great reputation. He settled in Paris, but being badly received by Louis XIV. eventually retired into Poland, where he died.

Enter SIR FOPLING'S *Footman*.

Sir Fop. La Tour, is the bath ready?

Footman. Yes, sir.

Sir Fop. Adieu donc, mes chers. [*Exit* SIR FOPLING.

Med. When have you your revenge on Loveit, Dorimant?

Dor. I will but change my linen, and about it.

Med. The powerful considerations which hindered have been removed then?

Dor. Most luckily this morning; you must along with me, my reputation lies at stake there.

Med. I am engaged to Bellair.

Dor. What's your business?

Med. Ma-tri-mony, an't like you.

Dor. It does not, sir.

Y. Bell. It may in time, Dorimant; what think you of Mrs. Harriet?

Dor. What does she think of me?

Y. Bell. I am confident she loves you.

Dor. How does it appear?

Y. Bell. Why, she's never well but when she's talking of you; but then she finds all the faults in you she can. She laughs at all who commend you; but then she speaks ill of all who do not.

Dor. Women of her temper betray themselves by their over-cunning. I had once a growing love with a lady who would always quarrel with me when I came to see her, and yet was never quiet if I stayed a day from her.

Y. Bell. My father is in love with Emilia.

Dor. That is a good warrant for your proceedings: go on and prosper; I must to Loveit. Medley, I am sorry you cannot be a witness.

Med. Make her meet Sir Fopling again in the same place, and use him ill before me.

Dor. That may be brought about, I think. I'll be at your aunt's anon, and give you joy, Mr. Bellair.

Y. Bell. You had not best think of Mrs. Harriet too much; without church security there's no taking up there.

Dor. I may fall into the snare too. But——
The wise will find a difference in our fate;
You wed a woman, I a good estate. [*Exeunt.*

Scene III.

Enter the Chair with Belinda; *the Men set it down and open it.* Belinda *starting.*

Bel. (*surprised*). Lord! where am I? in the Mall? Whither have you brought me?

1 *Chairman.* You gave us no directions, madam.

Bel. (*aside*). The fright I was in made me forget it.

1 *Chairman.* We use to carry a lady from the squire's hither.

Bel. (*aside*). This is Loveit; I am undone if she sees me. Quickly carry me away.

1 *Chairman.* Whither, an't like your honour?

Bel. Ask no questions.

Enter LOVEIT'S *Footman.*

Footman. Have you seen my lady, madam?

Bel. I am just come to wait upon her.

Footman. She will be glad to see you, madam. She sent me to you this morning to desire your company, and I was told you went out by five o'clock.

Bel. (*aside*). More and more unlucky!

Footman. Will you walk in, madam?

Bel. I'll discharge my chair and follow. Tell your mistress I am here. [*Exit Footman.*
[*Gives the Chairmen money.*
Take this, and if ever you should be examined, be sure you say you took me up in the Strand, over against the Exchange, as you will answer it to Mr. Dorimant.

Chairmen. We will, an't like your honour.
[*Exeunt Chairmen.*

Bel. Now to come off, I must on——
In confidence and lies some hope is left;
'Twere hard to be found out in the first theft. [*Exit.*

ACT V.

Scene I.

Enter MISTRESS LOVEIT *and* PERT, *her woman.*

Pert.

WELL, in my eyes Sir Fopling is no such despicable person.

Lov. You are an excellent judge!

Pert. He's as handsome a man as Mr. Dorimant, and as great a gallant.

Lov. Intolerable! is't not enough I submit to his impertinences, but I must be plagued with yours too?

Pert. Indeed, madam——

Lov. 'Tis false, mercenary malice——

Enter her Footman.

Footman. Mrs. Belinda, madam——

Lov. What of her?

Footman. She's below.

Lov. How came she?

Footman. In a chair; ambling Harry brought her.

Lov. He bring her! His chair stands near Dorimant's door, and always brings me from thence—— Run and ask him where he took her up; go, there is no truth in friendship neither. Women as well as men—all are false, or all are so to me at least.

Pert. You are jealous of her too.

Lov. You had best tell her I am. 'Twill become the liberty you take of late. This fellow's bringing of her, her going out by five o'clock——I know not what to think.

Enter BELINDA.

Belinda, you are grown an early riser, I hear.

Bel. Do you not wonder, my dear, what made me abroad so soon?

Lov. You do not use to be so.

Bel. The country gentlewomen I told you of (Lord! they have the oddest diversions!) would never let me rest till I promised to go with them to the markets this morning to eat fruit and buy nosegays.

Lov. Are they so fond of a filthy nosegay?

Bel. They complain of the stinks of the town, and are never well but when they have their noses in one.

Lov. There are essences and sweet waters.

Bel. Oh! they cry out upon perfumes they are unwholesome; one of 'em was falling into a fit with the smell of these *narolii*.

Lov. Methinks, in complaisance you should have had a nosegay too.

Bel. Do you think, my dear, I could be so loathsome to trick myself up with carnations and stock gillyflowers? I begged their pardon, and told them I never wore anything but orange flowers and tuberose.

That which made me willing to go was a strange desire I had to eat some fresh nectarines.

Lov. And had you any?

Bel. The best I ever tasted.

Lov. Whence came you now?

Bel. From their lodgings, where I crowded out of a coach, and took a chair to come and see you, my dear.

Lov. Whither did you send for that chair?

Bel. 'Twas going by empty.

Lov. Where do these country gentlewomen lodge, I pray?

Bel. In the Strand, over against the Exchange.

Pert. That place is never without a nest of 'em; they are always as one goes by fleering in balconies or staring out of windows.

Enter Footman.

Lov. (*whispers to the Footman*). Come hither.

Bel. (*aside*). This fellow by her order has been questioning the chairmen—I threatened 'em with the name of Dorimant; if they should have told truth I am lost for ever.

Lov. In the Strand, said you?

Footman. Yes, madam, over against the Exchange.
[*Exit Footman.*

Lov. She's innocent, and I am much to blame.

Bel. (*aside*). I am so frighted my countenance will betray me.

Lov. Belinda! what makes you look so pale?

Bel. Want of my usual rest, and jolting up and down so long in an odious hackney.

Enter Footman.

Footman. Madam, Mr. Dorimant!

Lov. What makes him here?

Bel. (*aside*). Then I am betrayed indeed; he's broke his word, and I love a man that does not care for me.

Lov. Lord! you faint, Belinda.

Bel. I think I shall; such an oppression here on the sudden.

Pert. She has eaten too much fruit, I warrant you.

Lov. Not unlikely!

Pert. 'Tis that lies heavy on her stomach.

Lov. Have her into my chamber, give her some surfeit water, and let her lie down a little.

Pert. Come, madam, I was a strange devourer of fruit when I was young, so ravenous——

[*Exit* BELINDA, PERT *leading her off.*

Lov. Oh, that my love would be but calm awhile! that I might receive this man with all the scorn and indignation he deserves.

Enter DORIMANT.

Dor. Now for a touch of Sir Fopling to begin with. Hey——page——give positive order that none of my people stir——let the *canaille* wait as they should do: since noise and nonsense have such powerful charms,

*I, that I may successful prove,
Transform myself to what you love.*

Lov. If that would do, you need not change from at you are; you can be vain and loud enough.

Dor. But not with so good a grace as Sir Fopling. ey, Hampshire!——Oh! that sound! that sound comes the mouth of a man of quality.

Lov. Is there a thing so hateful as a senseless imic?

Dor. He's a great grievance indeed to all who like urself, madam, love to play the fool in quiet.

Lov. A ridiculous animal who has more of the ape an the ape has of the man in him.

Dor. I have as mean an opinion of a sheer mimic yourself; yet were he all ape I should prefer him the gay, the giddy, brisk, insipid, noisy fool you te on.

Lov. Those noisy fools, however you despise 'em, ve good qualities, which weigh more (or ought at ast) with us women than all the pernicious wit you ve to boast of.

Dor. That I may hereafter have a just value for eir merit, pray do me the favour to name 'em.

Lov. You'll despise 'em as the dull effects of ignonce and vanity, yet I care not if I mention some. rst, they really admire us, while you at best but tter us well.

Dor. Take heed! fools can dissemble too——

Lov. They may, but not so artificially as you: ere is no fear they should deceive us. Then they are assiduous, sir; they are ever offering us their service, and always waiting on our will.

Dor. You owe that to their excessive idleness; they know not how to entertain themselves at home, and find so little welcome abroad, they are fain to fly to you who countenance 'em as a refuge against the solitude they would be otherwise condemned to.

Lov. Their conversation too diverts us better.

Dor. Playing with your fan, smelling to your gloves, commending your hair, and taking notice how 'tis cut and shaded after the new way.

Lov. Were it sillier than you can make it, you must allow 'tis pleasanter to laugh at others than to be laughed at ourselves, though never so wittily. Then though they want skill to flatter us, they flatter themselves so well they save us the labour; we need not take that care and pains to satisfy 'em of our love, which we so often lose on you.

Dor. They commonly indeed believe too well of themselves, and always better of you than you deserve.

Lov. You are in the right; they have an implicit faith in us which keeps 'em from prying narrowly into our secrets, and saves us the vexatious trouble of clearing doubts which your subtle and causeless jealousies every moment raise.

Dor. There is an inbred falsehood in women which inclines 'em still to them whom they may most easily deceive.

Lov. The man who loves above his quality does not suffer more from the insolent impertinence of his mistress than the woman who loves above her understanding does from the arrogant presumptions of her friend.

Dor. You mistake the use of fools: they are designed for properties, and not for friends. You have an indifferent stock of reputation left yet. Lose it all like a frank gamester on the square; 'twill then be time enough to turn rook and cheat it up again on a good substantial bubble.

Lov. The old and the ill-favoured are only fit for properties indeed, but young and handsome fools have met with kinder fortunes.

Dor. They have, to the shame of your sex be it spoken; 'twas this, the thought of this, made me, by a timely jealousy, endeavour to prevent the good fortune you are providing for Sir Fopling——but against a woman's frailty all our care is vain.

Lov. Had I not with a dear experience bought the knowledge of your falsehood, you might have fooled me yet. This is not the first jealousy you have feigned to make a quarrel with me and get a week to throw away on some such unknown inconsiderable slut as you have been lately lurking with at plays.

Dor. Women, when they would break off with a man, never want th' address to turn the fault on him.

Lov. You take a pride of late in using of me ill, that the town may know the power you have over me, which now (as unreasonably as yourself) expects that I (do me all the injuries you can) must love you still.

Dor. I am so far from expecting that you should, I begin to think you never did love me.

Lov. Would the memory of it were so wholly worn

out in me that I did doubt it too! What made you come to disturb my growing quiet?

Dor. To give you joy of your growing infamy.

Lov. Insupportable! insulting devil! this from you, the only author of my shame! This from another had been but justice, but from you 'tis a hellish and inhuman outrage. What have I done?

Dor. A thing that puts you below my scorn and makes my anger as ridiculous as you have made my love.

Lov. I walked last night with Sir Fopling.

Dor. You did, madam, and you talked and laughed aloud, ha, ha, ha!——Oh! that laugh! that laugh becomes the confidence of a woman of quality.

Lov. You, who have more pleasure in the ruin of a woman's reputation than in the endearments of her love, reproach me not with yourself, and I defy you to name the man can lay a blemish on my fame.

Dor. To be seen publicly so transported with the vain follies of that notorious fop, to me is an infamy below the sin of prostitution with another man.

Lov. Rail on, I am satisfied in the justice of what I did; you had provoked me to't.

Dor. What I did was the effect of a passion whose extravagances you have been willing to forgive.

Lov. And what I did was the effect of a passion you may forgive if you think fit.

Dor. Are you so indifferent grown?

Lov. I am.

Dor. Nay! then 'tis time to part. I'll send you

back your letters you have so often asked for. I have two or three of 'em about me.

Lov. Give 'em me.

Dor. You snatch as if you thought I would not—— there——and may the perjuries in 'em be mine if e'er I see you more. [*Offers to go, she catches him.*

Lov. Stay!

Dor. I will not.

Lov. You shall.

Dor. What have you to say?

Lov. I cannot speak it yet.

Dor. Something more in commendation of the fool. Death! I want patience, let me go.

Lov. (*aside*). I cannot. I can sooner part with the limbs that hold him.——I hate that nauseous fool, you know I do.

Dor. Was it the scandal you were fond of then?

Lov. You'd raised my anger equal to my love, a thing you ne'er could do before, and in revenge I did ——I know not what I did.——Would you would not think on't any more!

Dor. Should I be willing to forget it, I shall be daily minded of it, 'twill be a commonplace for all the town to laugh at me; and Medley, when he is rhetorically drunk, will ever be declaiming on it in my ears.

Lov. 'Twill be believed a jealous spite! Come, forget it.

Dor. Let me consult my reputation; you are too careless of it. [*Pauses.*] You shall meet Sir Fopling in the Mall again to-night.

Lov. What mean you?

Dor. I have thought on't, and you must: 'tis necessary to justify my love to the world; you can handle a coxcomb as he deserves when you are not out of humour, madam.

Lov. Public satisfaction for the wrong I have done you! This is some new device to make me more ridiculous.

Dor. Hear me.

Lov. I will not.

Dor. You will be persuaded.

Lov. Never.

Dor. Are you so obstinate?

Lov. Are you so base?

Dor. You will not satisfy my love?

Lov. I would die to satisfy that, but I will not to save you from a thousand racks do a shameless thing to please your vanity.

Dor. Farewell, false woman!

Lov. Do! go!

Dor. You will call me back again.

Lov. Exquisite fiend! I knew you came but to torment me.

Enter BELINDA *and* PERT.

Dor. (*surprised*). Belinda here!

Bel. (*aside*). He starts and looks pale; the sight of me has touched his guilty soul.

Pert. 'Twas but a qualm, as I said, a little indigestion; the surfeit water did it, madam, mixed with a little *mirabilis*.

Dor. I am confounded, and cannot guess how she came hither!

Lov. 'Tis your fortune, Belinda, ever to be here when I am abused by this prodigy of ill-nature.

Bel. I am amazed to find him here! How has he the face to come near you?

Dor. (*aside*). Here is fine work towards! I never was at such a loss before.

Bel. One who makes a public profession of breach of faith and ingratitude; I loathe the sight of him.

Dor. (*aside*). There is no remedy; I must submit to their tongues now, and some other time bring myself off as well as I can.

Bel. Other men are wicked, but then they have some sense of shame: he is never well but when he triumphs, nay, glories to a woman's face in his villainies.

Lov. You are in the right, Belinda; but methinks your kindness for me makes you concern yourself too much with him.

Bel. It does indeed, my dear; his barbarous carriage to you yesterday made me hope you ne'er would see him more, and the very next day to find him here again provokes me strangely; but, because I know you love him, I have done.

Dor. You have reproached me handsomely, and I deserve it for coming hither, but——

Pert. You must expect it, sir; all women will hate you for my lady's sake.

Dor. (*aside to* BELINDA). Nay, if she begins too, 'tis time to fly; I shall be scolded to death else.—I am to blame in some circumstances, I confess; but as to the main, I am not so guilty as you imagine. I shall seek a more convenient time to clear myself.

Lov. Do it now ! what impediments are here ?

Dor. I want time, and you want temper.

Lov. These are weak pretences !

Dor. You were never more mistaken in your life, and so farewell. [DORIMANT *flings off.*

Lov. Call a footman, Pert, quickly ; I will have him dogged.

Pert. I wish you would not for my quiet and your own.

Lov. I'll find out the infamous cause of all our quarrels, pluck her mask off, and expose her barefaced to the world.

Bel. (aside). Let me but escape this time I'll never venture more.

Lov. Belinda ! you shall go with me.

Bel. I have such a heaviness hangs on me with what I did this morning, I would fain go home and sleep, my dear.

Lov. Death and eternal darkness ! I shall never sleep again. Raging fevers seize the world, and make mankind as restless all as I am ! [*Exit* LOVEIT.

Bel. I knew him false, and helped to make him so. Was not her ruin enough to fright me from the danger ? It should have been, but love can take no warning.
[*Exit* BELINDA.

SCENE II.—LADY TOWNLEY'S HOUSE.

Enter MEDLEY, YOUNG BELLAIR, LADY TOWNLEY, EMILIA, *and Chaplain.*

Med. Bear up, Bellair, and do not let us see that repentance in thine we daily do in married faces.

Lady Town. This wedding will strangely surprise my brother when he knows it.

Med. Your nephew ought to conceal it for a time, madam, since marriage has lost its good name; prudent men seldom expose their own reputations till 'tis convenient to justify their wives.

O. Bell. (*without*). Where are you all there? Out, adod, will nobody hear?

Lady Town. My brother! quickly, Mr. Smirk, into this closet; you must not be seen yet.

[*He goes into the closet.*

Enter OLD BELLAIR *and* LADY TOWNLEY'S *Page.*

O. Bell. Desire Mr. Fourbes to walk into the lower parlour, I will be with him presently. [*To* YOUNG BELLAIR.] Where have you been, sir, you could not wait on me to-day?

Y. Bell. About a business.

O. Bell. Are you so good at business? Adod, I have a business too you shall despatch out of hand, sir. Send for a parson, sister; my Lady Woodvil and her daughter are coming.

Lady Town. What need you huddle up things thus?

O. Bell. Out a pise! youth is apt to play the fool, and 'tis not good it should be in their power.

Lady Town. You need not fear your son.

O. Bell. He's been idling this morning, and, adod, I do not like him. [*To* EMILIA.] How dost thou do, sweetheart?

Emil. You are very severe, sir; married in such haste.

O. Bell. Go to, thou'rt a rogue, and I will talk with thee anon. Here's my Lady Woodvil come.

Enter LADY WOODVIL, HARRIET, *and* BUSY.

Welcome, madam; Mr. Fourbes is below with the writings.

Lady Wood. Let us down, and make an end then.

O. Bell. Sister, show the way. [*To* YOUNG BELLAIR, *who is talking to* HARRIET.] Harry, your business lies not there yet; excuse him till we have done, lady, and then, adod, he shall be for thee. Mr. Medley, we must trouble you to be a witness.

Med. I luckily came for that purpose, sir.

[*Exeunt* OLD BELLAIR, MEDLEY, YOUNG BELLAIR, LADY TOWNLEY, *and* LADY WOODVIL.

Busy. What will you do, madam?

Har. Be carried back and mewed up in the country again, run away here, anything rather than be married to a man I do not care for——Dear Emilia, do thou advise me.

Emil. Mr. Bellair is engaged, you know.

Har. I do; but know not what the fear of losing an estate may fright him to.

Emil. In the desperate condition you are in you should consult with some judicious man; what think you of Mr. Dorimant?

Har. I do not think of him at all.

Busy. She thinks of nothing else, I am sure.

Emil. How fond your mother was of Mr. Courtage!

Har. Because I contrived the mistake to make a little mirth you believe I like the man.

Emil. Mr. Bellair believes you love him.

Har. Men are seldom in the right when they guess at a woman's mind; would she whom he loves loved him no better!

Busy (aside). That's e'en well enough, on all conscience.

Emil. Mr. Dorimant has a great deal of wit.

Har. And takes a great deal of pains to show it.

Emil. He's extremely well-fashioned.

Har. Affectedly grave or ridiculously wild and apish.

Busy. You defend him still against your mother.

Har. I would not were he justly rallied, but I cannot hear anyone undeservedly railed at.

Emil. Has your woman learnt the song you were so taken with?

Har. I was fond of a new thing; 'tis dull at second hearing.

Emil. Mr. Dorimant made it.

Busy. She knows it, madam, and has made me sing it at least a dozen times this morning.

Har. Thy tongue is as impertinent as thy fingers.

Emil. You have provoked her.

Busy. 'Tis but singing the song,[1] and I shall appease her.

Emil. Prithee do.

Har. She has a voice will grate your ears worse than a cat-call, and dresses so ill she's scarce fit to trick up a yeoman's daughter on a holiday.

Busy *sings.*

As Amoret with Phyllis sat
  One evening on the plain,
And saw the charming Strephon wait
  To tell the nymph his pain,

The threatening danger to remove
  She whisper'd in her ear,
Ah, Phyllis! if you would not love,
  This shepherd do not hear.

None ever had so strange an art
  His passion to convey
Into a listening virgin's heart,
  And steal her soul away.

---

[1] "A translation," says Coxeter (MS. note in his copy of Gildon's *Lives*), "from the French of Madame la Comtesse de la Suze in Le Recüeil des Pièces Gallantes." The version was by Sir Car Scroope; indeed all the old editions prefix to the verses a note—"Song by Sir C. S."

Fly, fly betimes, for fear you give
Occasion for your fate.
In vain, said she, in vain I strive,
Alas! 'tis now too late.

Enter DORIMANT.

Dor. Music so softens and disarms the mind——

Har. That not one arrow does resistance find.

Dor. Let us make use of the lucky minute then.

Har. (*aside, turning from* DORIMANT). My love springs with my blood into my face, I dare not look upon him yet.

Dor. What have we here, the picture of celebrated beauty giving audience in public to a declared lover?

Har. Play the dying fop and make the piece complete, sir.

Dor. What think you if the hint were well improved—the whole mystery of making love pleasantly designed and wrought in a suit of hangings?

Har. 'Twere needless to execute fools in effigy who suffer daily in their own persons.

Dor. (*aside to* EMILIA). Mrs. Bride, for such I know this happy day has made you.

Emil. Defer the formal joy you are to give me and mind your business with her. [*Aloud.*] Here are dreadful preparations, Mr. Dorimant, writings sealing, and a parson sent for.

Dor. To marry this lady?

Busy. Condemned she is, and what will become of her I know not, without you generously engage in a rescue.

Dor. In this sad condition, madam, I can do no less than offer you my service.

Har. The obligation is not great; you are the common sanctuary for all young women who run from their relations.

Dor. I have always my arms open to receive the distressed. But I will open my heart, and receive you where none yet did ever enter: you have filled it with a secret, might I but let you know it——

Har. Do not speak it if you would have me believe it; your tongue is so famed for falsehood 'twill do the truth an injury. [*Turns away her head.*

Dor. Turn not away then; but look on me and guess it.

Har. Did you not tell me there was no credit to be given to faces? that women now-a-days have their passions as much at will as they have their complexions, and put on joy and sadness, scorn and kindness, with the same ease they do their paint and patches[1]——Are they the only counterfeits?

Dor. You wrong your own while you suspect my eyes; by all the hope I have in you, the inimitable colour in your cheeks is not more free from art than are the sighs I offer.

Har. In men who have been long hardened in sin we have reason to mistrust the first signs of repentance.

---

[1] When the custom of patching (to which the *Spectator* objected so wrongly, No. 81) first became fashionable is not quite clear. Shadwell, however, in *The Virtuoso*, writes: "They have so many tricks to disguise themselves, washing, painting, patching."

Dor. The prospect of such a heaven will make me persevere and give you marks that are infallible.

Har. What are those?

Dor. I will renounce all the joys I have in friendship and in wine, sacrifice to you all the interest I have in other women——

Har. Hold!—though I wish you devout I would not have you turn fanatic——Could you neglect these awhile and make a journey into the country?

Dor. To be with you I could live there and never send one thought to London.

Har. Whate'er you say, I know all beyond High Park's a desert to you, and that no gallantry can draw you farther.

Dor. That has been the utmost limit of my love, but now my passion knows no bounds, and there's no measure to be taken of what I'll do for you from anything I ever did before.

Har. When I hear you talk thus in Hampshire I shall begin to think there may be some truth enlarged upon.

Dor. Is this all?——will you not promise me?——

Har. I hate to promise! what we do then is expected from us, and wants much of the welcome it finds when it surprises.

Dor. May I not hope?

Har. That depends on you and not on me, and 'tis to no purpose to forbid it.   [*Turns to* BUSY.

Busy. Faith, madam, now I perceive the gentleman loves you too; e'en let him know your mind, and torment yourselves no longer.

Har. Dost think I have no sense of modesty?

Busy. Think, if you lose this you may never have another opportunity.

Har. May he hate me—a curse that frights me when I speak it—if ever I do a thing against the rules of decency and honour!

Dor. (*to* EMILIA). I am beholding to you for your good intentions, madam.

Emil. I thought the concealing of our marriage from her might have done you better service.

Dor. Try her again.

Emil. What have you resolved, madam? The time draws near.

Har. To be obstinate, and protest against this marriage.

Enter LADY TOWNLEY *in haste.*

Lady Town. (*to* EMILIA). Quickly, quickly, let Mr. Smirk out of the closet. [SMIRK *comes out of the closet.*

Har. A parson! had you laid him in here?

Dor. I knew nothing of him.

Har. Should it appear you did, your opinion of my easiness may cost you dear.

Enter OLD BELLAIR, YOUNG BELLAIR, MEDLEY, *and* LADY WOODVIL.

O. Bell. Out a pise! the canonical hour is almost past. Sister, is the man of God come?

Lady Town. He waits your leisure.

O. Bell. By your favour, sir. Adod, a pretty spruce fellow! what may we call him?

Lady Town. Mr. Smirk, my Lady Biggot's chaplain.

O. Bell. A wise woman ! adod, she is. The man will serve for the flesh as well as the spirit. Please you, sir, to commission a young couple to go to bed together i' God's name ?—Harry.

Y. Bell. Here, sir.

O. Bell. Out a pise ! without your mistress in your hand !

Smirk. Is this the gentleman ?

O. Bell. Yes, sir.

Smirk. Are you not mistaken, sir ?

O. Bell. Adod, I think not, sir.

Smirk. Sure you are, sir.

O. Bell. You look as if you would forbid the banes ; Mr. Smirk, I hope you have no pretension to the lady ?

Smirk. Wish him joy, sir ! I have done him the good office to-day already.

O. Bell. Out a pise ! what do I hear ?

Lady Town. Never storm, brother, the truth is out.

O. Bell. How say you, sir ? is this your wedding-day ?

Y. Bell. It is, sir.

O. Bell. And, adod, it shall be mine too ; give me thy hand, sweetheart. [*To* EMILIA.] What dost thou mean ? give me thy hand, I say.

[EMILIA *kneels, and* YOUNG BELLAIR.

Lady Town. Come, come, give her your blessing; this is the woman your son loved and is married to.

O. Bell. Ha ! cheated ! cozened ! and by your contrivance, sister !

Lady Town. What would you do with her? She's a rogue, and you can't abide her.

Med. Shall I hit her a pat for you, sir?

O. Bell. Adod, you are all rogues, and I never will forgive you.

Lady Town. Whither! whither away?

Med. Let him go and cool awhile.

Lady Wood. (*to* DORIMANT). Here's a business broke out now; Mr. Courtage, I am made a fine fool of.

Dor. You see the old gentleman knows nothing of it.

Lady Wood. I find he did not. I shall have some trick put upon me if I stay in this wicked town any longer. Harriet! dear child! where art thou? I'll into the country straight.

O. Bell. Adod, madam, you shall hear me first.

Enter LOVEIT *and* BELINDA.

Lov. Hither my man dogged him.

Bel. Yonder he stands, my dear.

Lov. I see him. [*Aside.*] And with the face that has undone me! Oh, that I were but where I might throw out the anguish of my heart! here it must rage within and break it.

Lady Town. Mrs. Loveit, are you afraid to come forward?

Lov. I was amazed to see so much company here in a morning, the occasion sure is extraordinary.

Dor. (*aside*). Loveit and Belinda! the devil owes

me a shame to-day, and I think never will have done paying it.

Lov. Married! dear Emilia! how am I transported with the news?

Har. (*to* DORIMANT). I little thought Emilia was the woman Mr. Bellair was in love with; I'll chide her for not trusting me with the secret.

Dor. How do you like Mrs. Loveit?

Har. She's a famed mistress of yours, I hear.

Dor. She has been on occasion.

O. Bell. (*to* LADY WOODVIL). Adod, madam, I cannot help it.

Lady Wood. You need make no more apologies, sir.

Emil. (*to* LOVEIT). The old gentleman's excusing himself to my Lady Woodvil.

Lov. Ha, ha, ha! I never heard of anything so pleasant.

Har. (*to* DORIMANT). She's extremely overjoyed at something.

Dor. At nothing; she is one of those hoiting ladies who gaily fling themselves about and force a laugh when their aching hearts are full of discontent and malice.

Lov. Oh, heaven! I was never so near killing myself with laughing.—Mr. Dorimant, are you a brideman?

Lady Wood. Mr. Dorimant! is this Mr. Dorimant, madam?

Lov. If you doubt it, your daughter can resolve you, I suppose.

Lady Wood. I am cheated too, basely cheated.

O. Bell. Out a pise! what's here? more knavery yet?

Lady Wood. Harriet! on my blessing, come away, I charge you.

Har. Dear mother, do but stay and hear me.

Lady Wood. I am betrayed, and thou art undone, I fear.

Har. Do not fear it. I have not, nor never will do anything against my duty; believe me, dear mother, do.

Dor. (*to* LOVEIT). I had trusted you with this secret, but that I knew the violence of your nature would ruin my fortune, as now unluckily it has. I thank you, madam.

Lov. She's an heiress, I know, and very rich.

Dor. To satisfy you I must give up my interest wholly to my love; had you been a reasonable woman, I might have secured 'em both and been happy.

Lov. You might have trusted me with anything of this kind, you know you might. Why did you go under a wrong name?

Dor. The story is too long to tell you now—be satisfied, this is the business, this is the mask has kept me from you.

Bel. (*aside*). He's tender of my honour, though he's cruel to my love.

Lov. Was it no idle mistress then?

Dor. Believe me, a wife, to repair the ruins of my estate that needs it.

Lov. The knowledge of this makes my grief hang lighter on my soul; but I shall never more be happy.

Dor. Belinda!

Bel. Do not think of clearing yourself with me, it is impossible. Do all men break their words thus?

Dor. Th' extravagant words they speak in love; 'tis as unreasonable to expect we should perform all we promise then, as do all we threaten when we are angry. When I see you next——

Bel. Take no notice of me, and I shall not hate you.

Dor. How came you to Mrs. Loveit?

Bel. By a mistake the chairmen made for want of my giving them directions.

Dor. 'Twas a pleasant one. We must meet again.

Bel. Never.

Dor. Never?

Bel. When we do, may I be as infamous as you are false.

Lady Town. Men of Mr. Dorimant's character always suffer in the general opinion of the world.

Med. You can make no judgment of a witty man from common fame, considering the prevailing faction, madam.

O. Bell. Adod, he's in the right.

Med. Besides, 'tis a common error among women to believe too well of them they know and too ill of them they don't.

O. Bell. Adod, he observes well.

Lady Town. Believe me, madam, you will find Mr. Dorimant as civil a gentleman as you thought Mr. Courtage.

Har. If you would but know him better——

Lady Wood. You have a mind to know him better; come away! You shall never see him more.

Har. Dear mother, stay!

Lady Wood. I won't be consenting to your ruin.

Har. Were my fortune in your power——

Lady Wood. Your person is.

Har. Could I be disobedient I might take it out of yours, and put it into his.

Lady Wood. 'Tis that you would be at; you would marry this Dorimant?

Har. I cannot deny it; I would, and never will marry any other man.

Lady Wood. Is this the duty that you promised?

Har. But I will never marry him against your will——

Lady Wood. (*aside*). She knows the way to melt my heart. [*To* HARRIET.] Upon yourself light your undoing.

Med. (*to* OLD BELLAIR). Come, sir, you have not the heart any longer to refuse your blessing.

O. Bell. Adod, I ha' not——Rise, and God bless you both! Make much of her, Harry, she deserves thy kindness. [*To* EMILIA.] Adod, sirrah, I did not think it had been in thee.

Enter SIR FOPLING *and his Page.*

Sir Fop. 'Tis a damned windy day; hey, page? Is my periwig right?

Page. A little out of order, sir.

Sir Fop. Pox o' this apartment! it wants an antechamber to adjust oneself in. [*To* LOVEIT.] Madam, I came from your house, and your servants directed me hither.

Lov. I will give order hereafter they shall direct you better.

Sir Fop. The great satisfaction I had in the Mall last night has given me much disquiet since.

Lov. 'Tis likely to give me more than I desire.

Sir Fop. What the devil makes her so reserved? Am I guilty of an indiscretion, madam?

Lov. You will be of a great one if you continue your mistake, sir.

Sir Fop. Something puts you out of humour.

Lov. The most foolish inconsiderable thing that ever did.

Sir Fop. Is it in my power?

Lov. To hang or drown it; do one of 'em, and trouble me no more.

Sir Fop. So *fière*? *Serviteur, madame.* Medley, where's Dorimant?

Med. Methinks the lady has not made you those advances to-day she did last night, Sir Fopling.

Sir Fop. Prithee do not talk of her.

Med. She would be a *bonne fortune*.

Sir Fop. Not to me, at present.

Med. How so?

Sir Fop. An intrigue now would be but a temptation to me to throw away that vigour on one which I mean shall shortly make my court to the whole sex in a *ballet*.

Med. Wisely considered, Sir Fopling.

Sir Fop. No one woman is worth the loss of a cut in a caper.

Med. Not when 'tis so universally designed.

Lady Wood. Mr. Dorimant, everyone has spoke so much in your behalf that I can no longer doubt but I was in the wrong.

Lov. There's nothing but falsehood and impertinence in this world, all men are villains or fools; take example from my misfortunes, Belinda; if thou wouldst be happy, give thyself wholly up to goodness.

Har. (*to* LOVEIT). Mr. Dorimant has been your God Almighty long enough; 'tis time to think of another.

Lov. Jeered by her! I will lock myself up in my house, and never see the world again.

Har. A nunnery is the more fashionable place for such a retreat, and has been the fatal consequence of many a *belle passion.*

Lov. Hold, heart! till I get home; should I answer 'twould make her triumph greater. [*Is going out.*

Dor. Your hand, Sir Fopling——

Sir Fop. Shall I wait upon you, madam?

Lov. Legion of fools, as many devils take thee!

[*Exit* LOVEIT.

Med. Dorimant! I pronounce thy reputation clear, and henceforward when I would know anything of woman, I will consult no other oracle.

Sir Fop. Stark mad, by all that handsome! Dorimant, thou hast engaged me in a pretty business.

Dor. I have not leisure now to talk about it.

O. Bell. Out a pise! what does this Man of Mode do here again?

Lady Town. He'll be an excellent entertainment within, brother, and is luckily come to raise the mirth of the company.

Lady Wood. Madam, I take my leave of you.

Lady Town. What do you mean, madam?

Lady Wood. To go this afternoon part of my way to Hartley.

O. Bell. Adod, you shall stay and dine first; come, we will all be good friends, and you shall give Mr. Dorimant leave to wait upon you and your daughter in the country.

Lady Wood. If his occasions bring him that way, I have now so good an opinion of him he shall be welcome.

Har. To a great rambling lone house that looks as it were not inhabited, the family's so small; there you'll find my mother, an old lame aunt, and myself, sir, perched up on chairs at a distance in a large parlour, sitting moping like three or four melancholy birds in a spacious volery. Does not this stagger your resolution?

Dor. Not at all, madam. The first time I saw you you left me with the pangs of love upon me, and this day my soul has quite given up her liberty.

Har. This is more dismal than the country, Emilia; pity me who am going to that sad place. Methinks I hear the hateful noise of rooks already—knaw, knaw, knaw. There's music in the worst cry in London, *My dill and cucumbers to pickle.*[1]

---

[1] Addison thought differently: "I am always pleased with that particular time of the year which is proper for the pickling of dill and cucumbers; but, alas! this cry, like the song of the nightingale, is not heard above two months. It would therefore be worth while to consider whether the same air might not in some cases be adapted to other words."—In the classic dissertation on London "Cries," *Spectator*, No. 251.

O. Bell. Sister, knowing of this matter, I hope you have provided us some good cheer.

Lady Town. I have, brother, and the fiddles too.

O. Bell. Let 'em strike up then; the young lady shall have a dance before she departs. [*Dance.*
[*After the dance.*] So, now we'll in and make this an arrant wedding-day——

[*To the pit.*] And if these honest gentlemen rejoice,
Adod, the boy has made a happy choice.
[*Exeunt omnes.*

THE EPILOGUE.

By Mr. Dryden.

*MOST modern wits such monstrous fools have
    shown,
They seem'd not of heaven's making, but their own.
Those nauseous harlequins in farce may pass,
But there goes more to a substantial ass;
Something of man must be exposed to view,
That, gallants, they may more resemble you:
Sir Fopling is a fool so nicely writ,
The ladies would mistake him for a wit,
And when he sings, talks loud, and cocks, would cry,
I vow, methinks he's pretty company!
So brisk, so gay, so travell'd, so refined,
As he took pains to graft upon his kind.
True fops help nature's work, and go to school
To file and finish God Almighty's fool.
Yet none Sir Fopling him, or him, can call;*[1]

---

[1] This, with what follows, is not unsuggestive of Shadwell's prologue to *The Virtuoso*:—

>   Yet no one coxcomb in this play is shown,
>   No one man's humour makes a part alone,
>   But scatter'd follies gather'd into one.

He's knight o' th' shire, and represents ye all.
From each he meets he culls whate'er he can,
Legion's his name, a people in a man :
His bulky folly gathers as it goes,
And, rolling o'er you, like a snowball grows.
His various modes from various fathers follow ;
One taught the toss, and one the new French wallow.
His sword-knot this, his cravat this design'd,
And this the yard-long snake he twirls behind.
From one the sacred periwig he gain'd,
Which wind ne'er blew, nor touch of hat profaned.
Another's diving bow he did adore,
Which with a shog casts all the hair before ;
Till he, with full decorum, brings it back,
And rises with a water-spaniel shake.
As for his songs (the ladies' dear delight)
Those sure he took from most of you who write.
Yet every man is safe from what he fear'd,
For no one fool is hunted from the herd.

POEMS.

POEMS.

A LETTER TO THE EARL OF MIDDLETON.[1]

SINCE love and verse, as well as wine,
  Are brisker where the sun does shine,
'Tis something to lose two degrees,
Now age itself begins to freeze:
Yet this I patiently could bear,
If the rough Danube's beauties were
But only two degrees less fair
Than the bright nymphs of gentle Thames,
Who warm me hither with their beams:
Such power they have, they can dispense
Five hundred miles their influence.
But hunger forces men to eat,
Though no temptation's in the meat.
How would the ogling sparks despise
The darling damsel of my eyes,
Should they behold her at a play
As she's trick'd up on holiday,

---

[1] A man of letters of some little note. Like Etheredge, he had served as representative of the English Court in Germany.

When the whole family combine
For public pride to make her shine!
Her locks, which long before lay matted,
Are on this day comb'd out and plaited;
A diamond bodkin in each tress,
The badges of her nobleness;
For every stone, as well as she,
Can boast an ancient pedigree.
These form'd the jewel erst did grace
The cap of the first *Graf* o' th' race,
Preferr'd by *Gräfin Marian*
T'adorn the handle of her fan,
And, as by old record appears,
Worn since in Renigunda's years,
Now sparkling in the *Fräulein's* hair;
No rocket breaking in the air
Can with her starry head compare.
Such ropes of pearl her arms encumber
She scarce can deal the cards at ombre;
So many rings each finger freight
They tremble with the mighty weight;
The like in England ne'er was seen
Since Holbein drew Hal and his Queen.
But after these fantastic flights
The lustre's meaner than the lights;
The thing that bears this glittering pomp
Is but a tawdry ill-bred ramp,
Whose brawny limbs and martial face
Proclaim her of the Gothic race,
More than the mangled pageantry
Of all the father's heraldry.

But there's another sort of creatures,
Whose ruddy look and grotesque features
Are so much out of nature's way,
You'd think 'em stamp'd on other clay:
No lawful daughters of old Adam.
'Mongst these behold a city madam,
With arms in mittens, head in muff,
A dapper cloak and reverend ruff:
No farce so pleasant as this malkin,
And the soft sound of High-Dutch talking.
Here unattended by the Graces,
The Queen of Love in a sad case is.
Nature, her active minister,
Neglects affairs, and will not stir;
Thinks it not worth the while to please,
But when she does it for her ease.
Even I, her most devout adorer,
With wandering thoughts appear before her;
And when I'm making an oblation,
Am fain to spur imagination
With some sham London inclination.
The bow is bent at German dame,
The arrow flies at English game.
Kindness, that can indifference warm,
And blow that calm into a storm,
Has in the very tenderest hour
Over my gentleness a power:
True to my countrywomen's charms
When kiss'd and press'd in foreign arms.

A SECOND LETTER TO THE LORD MIDDLETON.

FROM hunting whores, and haunting play,
 And minding nothing else all day,
And all the night too, you will say;
To make grave legs in formal fetters,
Converse with fools, and write dull letters;
To go to bed 'twixt eight and nine,
And sleep away my precious time
In such a sneaking idle place,
Where vice and folly hide their face,
And in a troublesome disguise
The wife seems honest, husband wise.
For pleasure here has the same fate
Which does attend affairs of state,
The plague of ceremony infects,
Even in love, the softer sex;
Who an essential will neglect
Rather than lose the least respect.
In regular approach we storm,
And never visit but in form,
That is, sending to know before
At what o'clock she'll play the whore.
The nymphs are constant, gallants private,
One scarce can guess what 'tis they drive at.
This seems to me a scurvy fashion,
Which have been bred in a free nation

With liberty of speech and passion.
Yet I cannot forbear to spark it,
And make the best of a bad market.
Meeting with one, by chance, kind-hearted,
Who no preliminaries started,
I enter'd, beyond expectation,
Into a close negotiation:
Of which hereafter a relation.
Humble to fortune, not her slave,
I still was pleased with what she gave;
And, with a firm and cheerful mind,
I steer my course with every wind,
To all the ports she has design'd.

A SONG.

YE happy swains, whose hearts are free
    From love's imperial chain,
Take warning and be taught by me,
    T'avoid th' enchanting pain.
Fatal the wolves to trembling flocks,
    Fierce winds to blossoms prove,
To careless seamen hidden rocks,
    To human quiet love.

Fly the fair sex, if bliss you prize;
    The snake's beneath the flower:
Who ever gazed on beauteous eyes
    That tasted quiet more?

How faithless is the lover's joy !
How constant is their care,
The kind with falsehood to destroy,
The cruel with despair !

THE FORSAKEN MISTRESS.

A DIALOGUE BETWEEN PHYLLIS AND STREPHON.

Phyllis.

TELL me, gentle Strephon, why
You from my embraces fly ?
Does my love thy love destroy ?
Tell me, I will yet be coy.
Stay, oh, stay ! and I will feign
(Though I break my heart) disdain ;
But, lest I too unkind appear,
For every frown I'll shed a tear.
And if in vain I court thy love,
Let mine at least thy pity move :
Ah ! while I scorn vouchsafe to woo ;
Methinks you may dissemble too.

Strephon.

Ah, Phyllis ! that you would contrive
A way to keep my love alive !
But all your other charms must fail,
When kindness ceases to prevail.
Alas ! no less than you I grieve,
My dying flame has no reprieve ;

For I can never hope to find,
Should all the nymphs I court be kind,
One beauty able to renew
Those pleasures I enjoy'd in you,
When love and youth did both conspire
To fill our breasts and veins with fire.
'Tis true some other nymph may gain
That heart which merits your disdain;
But second love has still allay,
The joys grow aged and decay.
Then blame me not for losing more
Than love and beauty can restore;
And let this truth thy comfort prove,
I would, but can no longer love.

SONG OF BASSET.[1]

LET equipage and dress despair,
    Since Basset is come in;
For nothing can oblige the fair
    Like money and moreen.

Is any countess in distress,
    She flies not to the *beau;*

---

[1] A popular game. In the "Diary of a Lady of Quality" (*Spectator*, No. 383), we find: "*From six to eleven,* at basset. *Mem.* Never set again upon the ace of diamonds." Apparently the amusement was equally affected in France; a friend writes to Bussy-Rabutin, in December, 1678: "On ne parle à Versailles que de bassette, et le roi qui taille ruine tout le monde."—Bussy's *Correspondance,* iv. 255. *The Basset Table* provided the prolific Mrs. Centlivre with the title of a comedy.

'Tis only coney can redress
    Her grief with a *rouleau*.

By this bewitching game betray'd,
    Poor love is bought and sold;
And that which should be a free trade,
    Is now engross'd by gold.

Even sense is brought into disgrace
    Where company is met,
Or silent stands, or leaves the place,
    While all the talk's Basset.

Why, ladies, will you stake your hearts,
    Where a plain cheat is found?
You first are rook'd out of those darts
    That gave yourselves the wound.

The time, which should be kindly lent
    To plays and witty men,
In waiting for a knave is spent,
    Or wishing for a ten.

Stand in defence of your own charms,
    Throw down this favourite,
That threatens, with his dazzling arms,
    Your beauty and your wit.

What pity 'tis, those conquering eyes,
    Which all the world subdue,
Should, while the lover gazing dies,
    Be only on Alpue!

CEASE, anxious world, your fruitless pain
    To grasp forbidden store;
Your studied labours shall prove vain,
    Your alchemy unblest;
Whilst seeds of far more precious ore
    Are ripen'd in my breast.

My breast the forge of happier love,
    Where my Lucinda lives,
And the rich stock does so improve,
    As she her art employs,
That every smile and touch she gives
    Turns all to golden joys.

Since then we can such treasures raise,
    Let's no expense refuse;
In love let's lay out all our days;
    How can we e'er be poor,
When every blessing that we use
    Begets a thousand more?

A SONG.

IN some kind dream upon her, slumber, steal,
  And to Lucinda all, I beg, reveal;
Breathe gentlest words into her ears,
Words full of love, but full of fears,

Such words as may prevail, like prayers
From a poor dying martyr's tongue,
By the sweet voice of pity sung.
Touch with the voice the more enchanting lute
To make the charms strike all repulses mute.
These may insensibly impart
My tender wishes to her heart,
And by a sympathetic force
So tune its strings to love's discourse,
That when my griefs compel a groan,
Her sighs may echo to my moan.

GARDE le secret de ton ame,
    Et ne te laisse pas flatter,
Qu'Iris espargnera ta flamme,
    Si tu luy permets d'éclater ;
Son humeur, à l'amour rebelle,
    Exile tous ses doux desirs,
Et la tendresse est criminelle
    Qui veut luy parler en soupirs.

Puis que tu vis sous son empire,
    Il faut luy cacher ton destin,
Si tu ne veux le rendre pire
    Percé du trait de son dédain ;
D'une rigeur si delicate
    Ton cœur ne peut rien esperer,
Derobe donc à cette ingrate
    La vanité d'en trionfer.

UPON the downs when shall I breathe at ease,
    Have nothing else to do but what I please?
In a fresh cooling shade upon the brink
Of Arden's spring have time to read and think,
And stretch, and sleep, when all my care shall be
For health, and pleasure my philosophy?
When shall I rest from business, noise, and strife,
Lay down the soldier's and the courtier's life,
And in a little melancholy seat
Begin at last to live and to forget
The nonsense and the farce of what the fools call
    great?

TO MR. J. N., ON HIS TRANSLATIONS OUT OF FRENCH AND ITALIAN.

WHILE others toil our country to supply
    With what we need only for luxury,
Spices and silk in the rich East provide,
To glut our avarice and feed our pride;
You foreign learning prosperously transmit,
To raise our virtue and provoke our wit:
Such brave designs your generous soul inflame
To be a bold adventurer for fame.
How much obliged are Italy and France
While with your voice their music you advance!

Your growing fame with envy can oppose,
Who sing with no less art than they compose.
In these attempts so few have had success,
Their beauties suffer in our English dress;
By artless hands spoil'd of their native air,
They seldom pass from moderately fair.
As if you meant these injuries to atone,
You give them charms more conquering than their
    own;
Not like the dull laborious flatterer,
With secret art those graces you confer;
The skilful painters with slight strokes impart
That subtle beauty which affects the heart.
There are who publicly profess they hate
Translations, and yet all they write translate:
So proud, they scorn to drive a lawful trade,
Yet by their wants are shameless pirates made.
These you incense, while you their thefts reveal,
Or else prevent in what they meant to steal.
From all besides you are secure of praise;
But you so high our expectation raise,
A general discontent we shall declare
If such a workman only should repair;
You to the dead your piety have shown,
Adorn'd their monuments; now build your own.
Drawn in the East, we in your lines may trace
That genius which of old inspired the place;
The banished Muses back to Greece you bring,
Where their best airs you so divinely sing.
The world must own they are by you restored
To sacred shades where they were first adored.

VOITURE'S URANIA.

HOPELESS I languish out my days
Struck with Urania's conquering eyes;
The wretch at whom she darts these rays
Must feel the wound until he dies.

Though endless be her cruelty,
Calling her beauties to my mind,
I bow beneath her tyranny,
And dare not murmur she's unkind.

Reason this tameness does upbraid,
Proffering to arm in my defence;
But when I call her to my aid
She's more a traitor than my sense.

No sooner I the war declare,
But straight her functions she denies,
And joining forces with the fair
Confirms the conquest of her eyes.

SILVIA.

THE nymph that undoes me is fair and unkind,
No less than a wonder by nature design'd;
She's the grief of my heart, the joy of my eye,
And the cause of a flame that never can die.

Her mouth from whence wit still obligingly flows,
Has the beautiful blush and the smell of the rose;
Love and destiny both attend on her will,
She wounds with a look, with a frown she can kill.

The desperate lover can hope no redress,
When beauty and rigour are both in excess;
In Silvia they meet, so unhappy am I,
Who sees her must love, and who loves her must die.

TO A LADY WHO FLED THE SIGHT OF HIM.

IF I my Celia could persuade
To see those wounds her eyes have made,
And hear whilst I that passion tell
Which, like herself, does so excel,
How soon we might be freed from care!
She need not fear, nor I despair.
Such beauty does the nymph protect
That all approach her with respect;
And can I offer violence
Where love does join in her defence?
This guard might all her fears disperse,
Did she with savages converse.
Then my Celia would surprise
With what's produced by her own eyes;

Those matchless flames which they inspire
In her own breast should raise a fire.
For love, but with more subtle art,
As well as beauty charms the heart.

TO A LADY, ASKING HIM HOW LONG HE WOULD LOVE HER.

IT is not, Celia, in our power
  To say how long our love will last;
It may be we within this hour
May lose those joys we now do taste;
The blessed, that immortal be,
From change in love are only free.
Then, since we mortal lovers are,
Ask not how long our love will last;
But while it does, let us take care
Each minute be with pleasure pass'd:
Were it not madness to deny
To live because we're sure to die?

SONG.

TELL me no more you love; in vain,
  Fair Celia, you this passion feign.
Can they pretend to love who do
Refuse what love persuades them to?

Who once hath felt his active flame,
Dull laws of honour will disclaim;
You would be thought his slave, and yet
You will not to his power submit,
More cruel than those beauties are
Whose coyness wounds us to despair;
For all the kindness which you show,
Each smile and kiss which you bestow,
Are like those cordials which we give
To dying men to make them live,
And languish out an hour in pain.
Be kinder, Celia, or disdain.

TO A VERY YOUNG LADY.

SWEETEST bud of beauty, may
No untimely frost decay
Th' early glories which we trace
Blooming in thy matchless face!
But kindly opening like the rose
Fresh beauties every day disclose,
Such as by nature are not shown
In all the blossoms she has blown.
And then what conquests shall you make
Who hearts already daily take!
Scorch'd in the morning with thy beams,
How shall we bear those sad extremes,
Which must attend thy threatening eyes
When thou shalt to thy noon arise!

THE DIVIDED HEART.

AH, Celia! that I were but sure
Thy love, like mine, could still endure;
That time and absence, which destroy
The cares of lovers and their joy,
Could never rob me of that part
Which you have given me of your heart:
Others unenvied might possess
Whole hearts, and boast that happiness.
'Twas nobler fortune to divide
The Roman empire in her pride,
Than on some low and barbarous throne
Obscurely placed to rule alone.
Love only from thy heart exacts
The several debts thy face contracts,
And by that new and juster way
Secures thy empire and his sway:
Favouring but one he might compel
The hopeless lover to rebel.
But should he other hearts thus share
That in the whole so worthless are,
Should into several squadrons draw
That strength which, kept entire, could awe,
Men would his scatter'd powers deride,
And conquering him those spoils divide.

To Her Excellency
THE MARCHIONESS OF NEWCASTLE,[1]
After the Reading of her Incomparable Poems.

MADAM, with so much wonder we are struck
When we begin to read your matchless book;
Awhile your own excess of merit stays
Our forward pens, and does suspend your praise,
Till time our minds does gently recompose,
Allays this wonder, and our duty shows,
Instructs us how your virtues to proclaim,
And what we ought to pay to your great fame;
Your fame which in your country has no bounds,
But wheresoever learning's known resounds.
Those graces nature did till now divide,
Your sex's glory and our sex's pride,
Are join'd in you, and all to you submit,
The brightest beauty and the sharpest wit.
No faction here or fiery envy sways,
They give you myrtle while we offer bays.

---

[1] The very famous authoress. Her *Life* of the duke (which Pepys disliked so much, March 18th, 1668) was published in 1667. She died in December, 1673; he, in December, 1676. She wrote in every possible style, plays, poems, essays on natural philosophy, and what not; he was responsible for four plays and an adaptation of *L'Etourdi*.

What mortal dares dispute those wreaths with you,
Arm'd thus with lightning, and with thunder too?
This made the great Newcastle's heart your prize;
Your charming soul and your victorious eyes
Had only power his martial mind to tame
And raise in his heroic breast a flame:
A flame which with his courage still aspires,
As if immortal fuel fed those fires.
This mighty chief and your great self made one
Together the same race of glory run;
Together in the wings of fame you move,
Like yours his virtue, and like yours his love.
While we your praise endeavouring to rehearse
Pay that great duty in our humble verse,
Such as may justly move your anger, you,
Like heaven, forgive them and accept them too.
But what we cannot, your brave hero pays,
He builds those monuments we strive to raise;
Such as to after-ages shall make known,
While he records your deathless fame, his own.
So when an artist some rare beauty draws,
Both in our wonder share and our applause:
His skill from time secures the glorious dame,
And makes himself immortal in her fame.

A PROLOGUE,[1]

Spoken at the Opening of the Duke's New Playhouse.

'TIS not in this as in the former age,
  When wit alone sufficed t'adorn the stage;
When things well said an audience could invite,
Without the hope of such a gaudy sight.
What with your fathers took would take with you,
If wit had still the charm of being new;
Had not enjoyment dull'd your appetite,
She in her homely dress would yet delight;
Such stately theatres we need not raise,
Our old house would put off our dullest plays.
You gallants know a fresh wench of sixteen
May drive the trade in honest bombasine,
And never want good custom should she lie
In a back room, two or three storeys high.
But such a beauty as has long been known,
Though not decay'd, but to perfection grown,
Must, if she mean to thrive in this lewd town,
Wear points, laced petticoats, and a rich gown;
Her lodgings, too, must with her dress agree,
Be hung with damask or with tapestry,

---

[1] For this prologue, and the probable occasion of its being spoken, see note on the "Duke's House," *She Would if She Could*, iv. 1.

Have china, cabinets, and a great glass,
To strike respect into an amorous ass.
Without the help of stratagems and arts
An old acquaintance cannot touch your hearts.
Methinks 'tis hard our authors should submit
So tamely to their predecessors' wit,
Since, I am sure, among you there are few
Would grant your grandfathers had more than you.
But hold! I in this business may proceed too far,
And raise a storm against our theatre,
And then what would the wise adventurers say
Who are in a much greater fright to-day
Than ever poet was about his play?
Our apprehensions none can justly blame,
Money is dearer much to us than fame.
This thought on, let our poets justify
The reputation of their poetry;
We are resolved we will not have to do
With what's between those gentlemen and you.
Be kind, and let our house have but your praise,
You're welcome every day to damn their plays.

THE IMPERFECT ENJOYMENT.

AFTER a pretty amorous discourse,
She does resist my love with pleasing force;
Moved not with anger, but with modesty,
Against her will she is my enemy.

Her eyes the rudeness of her arms excuse,
Whilst those accept what these seem to refuse;
To ease my passion and to make me blest
The obliging smock falls from her whiter breast.
Then with her lovely hands she does conceal
Those wonders chance so kindly did reveal.
In vain, alas! her nimble fingers strove
To shield her beauties from my greedy love:
Guarding her breasts, her lips she did expose,
To save a lily she must lose a rose.
So many charms she has in every place,
A hundred hands cannot defend each grace.
Sighing at length her force she does recall,
For since I must have part she'll give me all.
Her arms the joyful conqueror embrace,
And seem to guide me to the sought-for place:
Her love is in her sparkling eyes express'd,
She falls o' the bed for pleasure more than rest.
But oh, strange passion! oh, abortive joy!
My zeal does my devotion quite destroy:
Come to the temple where I should adore
My saint, I worship at the sacred door;
Oh, cruel chance! the town which did oppose
My strength so long, now yields to my dispose;
When overjoy'd with victory I fall
Dead at the foot of the surrender'd wall,
Without the usual ceremony, we
Have both fulfill'd the amorous mystery;
The action which we should have jointly done,
Each has unluckily perform'd alone;
The union which our bodies should enjoy,

The union of our eager souls destroy.
Our flames are punish'd by their own excess,
We'd had more pleasure had our loves been less.
She blush'd and frown'd, perceiving we had done
The sport she thought we scarce had yet begun.
Alas! said I, condemn yourself, not me,
This is th' effect of too much modesty.
Hence with that peevish virtue, the delight
Of both our victories was lost i' the fight;
Yet from my shame your glory does arise,
My weakness proves the vigour of your eyes:
They did consume the victim ere it came
Unto the altar, with a purer flame:
Phyllis, let then this comfort ease your care,
You'd been more happy had you been less fair.

THE LIBERTINE.

1.

SINCE death on all lays his impartial hand,
    And all resign at his command,
The Stoic too, as well as I,
With all his gravity must die:
Let's wisely manage the last span,
The momentary life of man,
And still in pleasure's circle move,
Giving t'our friends the days, and all our nights to
    love.

Chorus.

Thus, thus, whilst we are here, let's perfectly live,
And taste all the pleasures that nature can give;
Fresh heat when life's fading our wine will inspire,
And fill all our veins with a noble desire.

II.

When we are sapless, old and impotent,
Then we shall grieve for youth misspent:
Wine and woman only can
Cherish the drooping heart of man.
Let's drink until our blood o'erflows
Its channels and luxurious grows;
Then when our whores have drain'd each vein,
And the thin mass fresh spirits crave, let's drink again.

Chorus—Thus, thus, &c.

III.

The happy king, whom heaven itself call'd wise,
Saw all was vanity but dice;
His active mind, ever in quest of bliss,
Survey'd all things, and stuck to this.
Myriads of harlots round him strove,
Some sung, whilst others acted love.
Who shall our frailty then condemn,
Since one by heaven inspired left heaven to follow
     them?

Chorus—Thus, thus, &c.

FAIR Iris, all our time is spent
    In trifling, whilst we dally;
The lovers who're indifferent
    Commit the greatest folly.
Ah! stint not then the flowing pleasure
To such a wretched scanty measure;
Since boundless passion boundless joys will prove,
Excess can only justify our love.

EPHELIA'S LAMENTATION.[1]

HOW far are they deceived, who hope in vain
    A lasting lease of joys from love t'obtain!
All the dear sweets we promise or expect,
After enjoyment turn to cold neglect.
Could love a constant happiness have known,
The mighty wonder had in me been shown;
Our passions are so favoured by fate,
As if she meant them an eternal date.
So kind you look'd, such tender words you spoke,
'Twas past belief such vows should e'er be broke.

---

[1] Attributed to Etheredge by Mr. Ebsworth (*Roxburghe Ballads*, vol. iv. pp. 573-4), on the authority, doubtless, of Buckingham's couplet:

    Poor George grows old, his Muse is worn out of fashion;
    Hoarsely he sung Ephelia's Lamentation.
                          Epistle to Mr. Julian.

Fix'd on my eyes, how often did you say
You could with pleasure gaze an age away?
When thoughts too great for words had made you mute,
In kisses you would tell my hand your suit.
So great your passions were, so far above
The common gallantries that pass for love,
At worst, I thought, if you unkind should prove,
Your ebbing passion would be kinder far
Than the first transports of all others are.
Nor was my love or fondness less than yours,
In you I centred all my hopes of cures;
For you my duty to my friends forgot,
For you I lost—alas! what lost I not?
Fame, all the valuable things of life,
To meet your love by a less name than wife;
How happy was I then, how dearly blest,
When you lay panting on my tender breast,
Acting such things as ne'er can be express'd!
Thousand fresh looks you gave me every hour,
Whilst greedily I did those looks devour;
Till quite o'ercome with charms I trembling lay,
At every look you gave, melted away.
I was so highly happy in your love,
Methought I pitied them that dwelt above.
Think then, thou greatest, loveliest, falsest man!
How you have vow'd, how I have loved, and then,
My faithless dear! be cruel if you can.
How I have loved I cannot, need not tell;
For every act has shown I loved too well.
Since first I saw you I ne'er had a thought
Was not entirely yours; to you I brought

My virgin innocence and freely made
My love an offering to your noble bed.
Since when you've been the star by which I steer'd,
And nothing else but you I loved or fear'd.
Your smiles I only live by; and I must,
Whene'er you frown, be shatter'd into dust.
Oh! can the coldness which you show me now,
Suit with the generous heat you once did show?
I cannot live on pity or respect:
A thought so mean would my whole love infect;
Less than your love I scorn, sir, to expect.
Let me not live in dull indifferency,
But give me rage enough to make me die:
For if from you I needs must meet my fate,
Before your pity I would choose your hate.

DRYDEN TO ETHEREDGE.

TO you, who live in chill degree,
    As map informs, of fifty-three,[1]
And do not much for cold atone,
By bringing thither fifty-one,
Methinks all climes should be alike,
From tropic even to pole artique;
Since you have such a constitution
As nowhere suffers diminution.

---

[1] Not quite correct. Dryden probably wanted a rhyme to "degree;" or perhaps "fifty-three" was meant as a mild antithesis to "fifty-one."

You can be old in grave debate,
And young in love-affairs of state;
And both to wives and husbands show
The vigour of a plenipo:
Like mighty missioner you come
Ad partes Infidelium.
A work of wondrous merit sure,
So far to go, so much t'endure;
And all to preach to German dame,
Where sound of Cupid never came.
Less had you done, had you been sent
As far as Drake or Pinto went,
For cloves or nutmegs to the line a,
Or even for oranges to China.
That had indeed been charity,
Where lovesick ladies helpless lie,
Chapt, and, for want of liquor, dry;
But you have made your zeal appear
Within the circle of the Bear.
What region of the earth's so dull,
That is not of your labours full?
Triptolemus (so sung the Nine)
Strew'd plenty from his cart divine;
But spite of all these fable-makers,
He never sow'd an Almain acres.
No, that was left by fate's decree
To be perform'd and sung by thee.
Thou break'st through forms with as much ease
As the French king through articles.
In grand affairs thy days are spent,
In waging weighty compliment

With such as monarchs represent.
They whom such vast fatigues attend
Want some soft minutes to unbend,
To show the world that, now and then,
Great ministers are mortal men.
Then Rhenish rummers walk the round;
In bumpers every king is crown'd;
Besides three holy mitred Hectors,
And the whole college of Electors.
No health of potentate is sunk,
That pays to make his envoy drunk.
These Dutch delights I mention'd last
Suit not, I know, your English taste.
For wine, to leave a whore or play,
Was ne'er your Excellency's way.
Nor need this title give offence,
For here you were your Excellence;
For gaming, writing, speaking, keeping,
His Excellence for all—but sleeping.
Now if you tope in form, and treat,
'Tis the sour sauce to the sweetmeat,
The fine you pay for being great.
Nay, here's a harder imposition,
Which is indeed the Court's petition,
That, setting worldly pomp aside,
Which poet has at font denied,
You would be pleased in humble way
To write a trifle call'd a Play.
This truly is a degradation,
But would oblige the crown and nation
Next to your wise negotiation.

If you pretend, as well you may,
Your high degree, your friends will say
The Duke St. Aignion made a play.
If Gallic wit convince you scarce,
His Grace of Bucks has made a farce,
And you, whose comic wit is terse all,
Can hardly fall below *Rehearsal.*
Then finish what you have began,
But scribble faster if you can ;
For yet no George, to our discerning,
Has writ without a ten years' warning.

INDEX TO NOTES.

Baptiste, 339.
Barroy, 298.
Basset, 383.
Bear tavern, 127, 165.
Beaver, 176.
Bourée, 327.
Brussels, Diversions of, 268.
Bubble, 37.
Bussy-Rabutin, 324-5.

Calotte, 175.
Candale, Duke of, 337.
Chedreux, 298.
China orange, 218.
Compter, 50.
Coranto, 327.
Cornuel, Madame, 323.
Covent Garden shows, 178.

D'Ambois, 324.
Dill and Cucumbers, 371.
Dorset, Earl of, 3.
Drury Lane, 165.
Duke's House, 190, 396.

Eveillée, 323.

Farendon, 143.
Fleece tavern, 24.
Flûtes douces, 268.

Foxhall, 203.
French House, 127.

Gray's Inn Walks, 190.
"Great horse," 52.

Haggard, 161.
Hicks' Hall, 13.
High Park, 302.

King's House, 190.

Lambert, Michel, 338.
Lantrillou, 213.
Lincoln's Inn Fields, 91.
Locket's, 261.
London Bridge, 13.
Long's, 261.

Matadore, 267.
Merille, 337.
Middleton, Earl of, 377.
Mirror of knighthood, 96.
Mulberry Garden, 96.

Newcastle, Duchess of, 394.
New Exchange, 148.

Oblivion, Act of, 232.
Oliver's knights, 92.

Ombre, 184.
Orange essence, 161.

Pall Mall, 293.
Pancridge, 44.
Patches, 360.
Point, 135.
Pont Neuf, 52.
Premunire, 182.
Pulvilio, 309.

Rebate, 320.
Rose tavern, 47.
Ruelle, 338.

St. James's Street, 123.
Scroope, Sir Car, 358.
Sleeveless, 333.

Totnam, 245.

CHISWICK PRESS :—C. WHITTINGHAM AND CO., TOOKS COURT, CHANCERY LANE.

THE NEW EDITED AND COMPLETE EDITIONS
OF
The Elizabethan Dramatists.

This is the first instalment towards a collective edition of the Dramatists who lived about the time of Shakespeare. The type will be distributed after each work is printed.

One of the chief features of this New Edition of the Elizabethan Dramatists, besides the handsome and handy size of the volumes, will be the fact that *each Work will be carefully edited and new notes given throughout.*

ALGERNON CHARLES SWINBURNE

(IN THE *NINETEENTH CENTURY*, JANUARY 1886)

ON THE

Elizabethan Dramatists.

"If it be true, as we are told on high authority, that the greatest glory of England is her literature, and the greatest glory of English literature is its poetry, it is not less true that the greatest glory of English poetry lies rather in its dramatic than its epic or its lyric triumphs. The name of Shakespeare is above the names even of Milton and Coleridge and Shelley ; and the names of his comrades in art and their immediate successors are above all but the highest names in any other province of our song. There is such an overflowing life, such a superb exuberance of abounding and exulting strength, in the dramatic poetry of the half century extending from 1590 to 1640, that all other epochs of English literature seem as it were but half awake and half alive by comparison with this generation of giants and of gods. There is more sap in this than in any other branch of the national bay-tree ; it has an energy in fertility which reminds us rather of the forest than the garden or the park. It is true that the weeds and briars of the underwood are but too likely to embarrass and offend the feet of the rangers and the gardeners who trim the level flower-plots or preserve the domestic game of enclosed and ordered lowlands in the tamer demesnes of literature. The sun is strong and the wind sharp in the climate which reared the fellows and the followers of Shakespeare. The extreme inequality and roughness of the ground must also be taken into account when we are disposed, as I for one have often been disposed, to wonder beyond measure at the apathetic ignorance of average students in regard of the abundant treasure to be gathered from this widest and most fruitful province in the poetic empire of England. And yet, since Charles Lamb threw open its gates to all comers in the ninth year of the present century, it cannot but seem strange that comparatively so few should have availed themselves of the entry to so rich and royal an estate. Mr. Bullen has taken up a task than which none more arduous and important, none worthier of thanks and praise, can be undertaken by any English scholar."

14 King William Street, Strand, London, W.C.

Volumes now Ready of the new Edited and Complete Editions of the Elizabethan Dramatists.

Post 8vo, cloth. Published price, 7s. 6d. per volume *net*; also large fine-paper edition, medium 8vo, cloth.

The following are Edited by A. H. BULLEN, B.A. :—

THE WORKS OF GEORGE PEELE.	Two Volumes.
THE WORKS OF JOHN MARSTON.	Three Volumes.
THE WORKS OF THOMAS MIDDLETON.	Eight Volumes.
THE WORKS OF CHRISTOPHER MARLOWE.	Three Volumes.

Others in active preparation.

SOME PRESS NOTICES.

Athenæum.—" Mr. Bullen's edition deserves warm recognition. It is intelligent, scholarly, adequate. His preface is judicious. The elegant edition of the Dramatists of which these volumes are the first is likely to stand high in public estimation. . . . The completion of the series will be a boon to bibliographers and scholars alike."

Saturday Review.—" Mr. Bullen has discharged his task as editor in all important points satisfactorily, his introduction is well informed and well written, and his notes are well chosen and sufficient. . . . We hope it may be his good fortune to give and ours to receive every Dramatist, from Peele to Shirley, in this handsome, convenient, and well-edited form."

The Spectator.—" Probably one of the boldest literary undertakings of our time, on the part of publisher as well as editor, is the fine edition of the Dramatists which has been placed in Mr. Bullen's careful hands ; considering the comprehensiveness of the subject, and the variety of knowledge it demands, the courage of the editor is remarkable."

Notes and Queries.—" .·. . Appropriately, then, the series Mr. Bullen edits and Mr. Nimmo issues in most attractive guise is headed by Marlowe, the leader, and in some respects all but the mightiest spirit, of the great army of English Dramatists."

The Academy.—" Mr. Bullen is known to all those interested in such things as an authority on most matters connected with old plays. We are not surprised, therefore, to find these volumes well edited throughout. They are not overburdened with notes."

Scotsman.—" Never in the history of the world has a period been marked by so much of literary power and excellence as the Elizabethan period ; and never have the difficulties in the way of literature seemed to be greater. The three volumes which Mr. Nimmo has issued now may be regarded as earnests of more to come, and as proofs of the excellence which will mark this edition of the Elizabethan Dramatists as essentially the best that has been published. Mr. Bullen is a competent editor in every respect."

The Standard.—" Throughout Mr. Bullen has done his difficult work remarkably well, and the publisher has produced it in a form which will make the edition of early Dramatists of which it is a part an almost indispensable addition to a well-stocked library."

Pall Mall Gazette.—" . . . If the series is continued as it is begun, by one of the most careful editors, this set of the English Dramatists will be a coveted literary possession."

Daily Telegraph.—" The introduction to this new edition of Marston is of exceeding interest, and is honourable to the earnest spirit in which Mr. Bullen is steadfastly pursuing the object set before him in this notable series."

14 King William Street, Strand, London, W.C.

NEW ILLUSTRATED EDITION OF DR. DORAN'S GREAT WORK.

In Three Volumes, demy 8vo, Roxburghe binding, gilt top, price 54s. *net.*
Also large-paper copies, royal 8vo, with Portraits in duplicate.

"THEIR MAJESTIES' SERVANTS."
ANNALS OF THE ENGLISH STAGE
FROM
THOMAS BETTERTON TO EDMUND KEAN.
By DR. DORAN, F.S.A.

Edited and Revised by R. W. LOWE, from Author's Annotated Copy. With Fifty Copperplate Portraits and Eighty Wood Engravings.

SOME PRESS NOTICES.
Athenæum.

"It is well that in the issue of a new edition of 'Their Majesties' Servants,' which is one of the most esteemed of Dr. Doran's works, the task of supervision and correction has been assigned to one of the best informed and most earnest of our younger writers on dramatic subjects. Some of the most serious inaccuracies of the original are corrected, slight additions from the MSS. of Dr. Doran are supplied, and full indexes are appended to each of the volumes. With its admirable text and its delightful reproductions of old illustrations, it is the most attractive volume upon things histrionic that has yet appeared in England."

Saturday Review.

"Of all Dr. Doran's works, his 'Stage Annals' has been the most successful, and both the first and second editions have long been out of print. The first, indeed, has been in great request, especially for the purpose of what is known as book illustration. Such corrections as are made in the second edition Mr. Lowe, in the shape of notes, has incorporated with the original, and from the papers of Dr. Doran, to which he has had access. The illustrations meanwhile to the new edition enhance remarkably its value. No such collection of theatrical engravings is elsewhere to be obtained. It is difficult to know which most to praise, the views of old theatres and other scenes, &c., which, in the shape of head- or tail-pieces, are given to each chapter, or the portraits, all of which are interesting, and many of them admirable. Some of the scarcest and most desirable of histrionic portraits have been reproduced, and there is not a commonplace or indifferent plate in the series. The task of the publisher has been accomplished with equal care and taste, and the new Doran is a credit to a firm to which are owing many surpassingly handsome books."

Manchester Examiner.

"Dr. Doran was, in the best sense of the word, a popular writer; his style has the brightness, spontaneity, and picturesqueness which draw us to a book in our least studious hours; and no one knew better than he the value of a characteristic anecdote, or could tell it with greater crispness and vivacity. In these three volumes his varied gifts are seen at their best, and the book is one which can with pleasure be either read steadily through from beginning to end or taken up in that odd quarter of an hour which it is so difficult to utilise with pleasure and profit."

Notes and Queries.

"The works of Dr. Doran, with their pleasant blending of antiquarian information and social gossip, are well known. To a portion of them it will be good news that the scarcest and the most popular of these, the 'Annals of the Stage,' first published under the characteristic title of 'Their Majesties' Servants,' has now been reissued. Mr. Lowe's task has been discharged with commendable industry and acumen. His notes are condensed and to the point. They appear few and unobtrusive; they are, in fact, numerous and important. Difficult indeed is it to conceive a book of this class deserving higher praise or appealing to a larger public. It is pleasant to see an old favourite in so lovely and artistic a dress, and not less pleasant to think that the work is wholly English, and in design and execution owes nothing to a foreign source."

14 King William Street, Strand, London, W.C.

PRESS NOTICES OF "DORAN"—continued.

Pall Mall Gazette.

"Turning to the illustrations, we can only pronounce them by far the finest collection of English theatrical portraits ever issued in book form. They are well chosen and admirably reproduced. Scarcely any actor or actress of the first rank is omitted, and io almost all cases rare and little known portraits are preferred to the more hackneyed ones. How charming, for instance, are the Colley Cibber and the Mrs. Abingdon! How characteristic the Quin and Macklin, the George Frederick Cooke and the Robert William Elliston! How valuable the Mrs. Woffington, the Mrs. Yates, and the Mrs. Pritchard, the Harris as Wolsey, and the Kean as Shylock! Scarcely less interesting are the small woodcut head-pieces, printed on Japanese paper. They consist for the most part of pictures of old theatres and of scenes and characters from plays, curious as first-hand records of costume and gesture."

Birmingham Mail.

"Each volume contains a copious and exhaustive index, and the work has been annotated by reference to Dr. Doran's own MS. This history may fairly claim to rank as a standard work on the British drama, and no library can be considered complete without it. The previous editions have been long out of print, and command high prices, but Mr. Nimmo, by the care and special features he has lavished on this one, will make it outvie them in importance, and even render them incomplete and unsatisfactory by comparison."

The Graphic.

"Mr. Robert W. Lowe is already known through his work in connection with the bibliography of the stage, and there is probably no man in London better fitted for the task he has so successfully accomplished. His plan has been to reprint Dr. Doran's work exactly as it stood in the first edition, and to add a series of foot-notes correcting and explaining the text. Though some objection might possibly be taken to the scheme on which Dr. Doran planned his work, it is still the best popular book on the stage, and, with Mr. Lowe's notes, it will be long before it can be superseded."

Glasgow Herald.

"Dr. Doran was master of a singularly attractive style; he had studied the Restoration drama with a minuteness altogether exceptional, even among stage annalists; and if he was not lucky enough to discover any great mass of new material, he presented what was known in the most pleasing, orderly, and informing manner. An excellent and characteristic portrait of Dr. Doran is prefixed to the first volume of the 'Annals.' The editor, Mr. Lowe has with commendable taste confined himself for the most part to correcting those errors scarcely to be avoided by even an experienced writer among the confused, inaccurate, and contradictory documents of theatrical history."

Bookseller.

"The publication of a new edition of Doran's 'Annals of the Stage' partakes almost of the nature of an event in the world of books, and is one we could scarcely have passed over without notice. . . . Produced in such a delightful and fascinating shape, readers of Dr. Doran's work will be hard to please if they are not charmed with this edition of 'Their Majesties' Servants.'"

Scotsman.

"Histories of the stage are not rare; and although, as a rule, these are concerned more with the literature of the theatre than with players, some of them are based upon the biographical rather than the literary interest of their subject. Perhaps the most prominent of such histories is Dr. Doran's 'Annals of the English Stage;' it is a storehouse of information concerning the theatre as it existed in England during the seventeenth and eighteenth centuries."

North British Daily Mail.

"The intrinsic worth of this work has long been recognised, and in this new edition we have not only the revision of a careful editor, but also a series of illustrations of a very attractive character. The portraits are most interesting, and so are the numerous little pictures on Japanese paper; indeed, with regard to the latter, we have rarely seen anything finer. Altogether, the work in its present form is a most covetable one, and is sure to commend itself to the book-collector."

14 King William Street, Strand, London W.C.

A Bibliography of Theatrical Literature.

In demy 8vo, 400 pages, cloth, price 18s. net. Also, One Hundred Copies on fine deckle-edge royal 8vo paper, each numbered.

A BIBLIOGRAPHICAL ACCOUNT OF ENGLISH THEATRICAL LITERATURE
FROM THE EARLIEST TIMES TO THE PRESENT DAY.
By ROBERT W. LOWE.

SOME PRESS NOTICES.

Athenæum.

"It is a work of much industry and research, and will probably remain the standard bibliography of the stage. What further information is to he chronicled may be grafted on this stock. To the student and the collector the book has real value. The latter will prize the few quotations of sale prices Mr. Lowe has given, and will wish them more numerous."

Saturday Review.

"Mr. Lowe's bibliographical account of the stage forms a goodly volume of 384 pages, and describes, it may be estimated, nearly three thousand separate works. It is admirably furnished as regards cross-references and other means of facilitating use, and is a work of much labour and erudition. Further additions and emendations will doubtless be forthcoming. Meantime the contribution Mr. Lowe has made is important and welcome. His work is convenient in arrangement, and his own observations are pertinent."

Daily News.

"It is not a mere bibliography, but rather what is known as a '*catalogue raisonné*,' since a large number of the titles are accompanied by serviceable explanatory notes, together with mention of prices for which scarce works have been sold at more or less recent sales. It is a gracious task to render homage to the industry and the painstaking care displayed on every page of this volume."

Scotsman.

"The entries go as far back in point of time as the 'Coventry Mysteries,' and come down so near the present day as to include reference to the pamphlet containing the articles from the *Saturday Review* on the state of the London theatres which appeared last month, and the new edition of Dr. Doran's 'Annals of the Stage,' which was published last week. The work will be heartily welcomed by librarians and bookmen as a valuable product of bibliographical skill and industry. It is printed in a very elegant fashion, and published in a limited issue, and will probably soon become as scarce and high-priced as many of the books to which its pages give reference."

Glasgow Herald.

"It consists of about two thousand titles, the great majority of which are taken directly from the works described. These are arranged alphabetically, with exhaustive cross-references. Notes regarding each actor and actress are given, with an account of the occurrences to which particular works refer, special attention being paid to the less known and more curious pamphlets."

Pall Mall Gazette.

"Mr. Lowe's notes are, as a rule, eminently to the point, and add greatly to the value of his work. It is difficult to estimate the amount of patient labour that goes to the compilation of such a book as this, especially when it is the first of its kind; and Mr. Lowe's diligence, accuracy, and enthusiasm for his subject deserve the warmest recognition. The book is excellently printed and got up, the English edition being limited to 350 numbered copies, while 150 have been printed for America."

Manchester Examiner.

"This is a book the leaves of which can be turned over with considerable interest and no small amount of instruction by that miscellaneous-minded person, the general reader, and to the student of the special class of literature with which it deals it will be very valuable."

14 King William Street, Strand, London, W.C.

A New Volume of Elizabethan Lyrics.

Post 8vo, hand-made paper, 750 copies, each numbered, price 10s. 6d. *net.*
Also 250 large-paper copies, in half German calf, each numbered.

More Lyrics from the Song-Books of the Elizabethan Age.
Edited by A. H. BULLEN, B.A.

SOME PRESS NOTICES.
Scotsman.
"Mr. A. H. Bullen has found a happy hunting-ground for songs in the anthologies of the Elizabethan period. His first collection of lyrics rapidly won the favour of lovers of literature, and brought to the light of print many gems of excellent lustre that had lain hidden in the manuscripts hoarded by collectors. His reprint of 'England's Helicon' whetted the wholesome appetite for such good songs, and his new volume, 'More Lyrics from the Song-Books of the Elizabethan Age,' will go far to satisfy the demand for more of the same. This collection is issued in the same elegant form as the others—a form which reflects the highest credit upon the publisher of the book, and will make the volume prized by collectors of beautiful books."

Manchester Examiner.
"Mr. A. H. Bullen's new book, 'More Lyrics from the Song-Books of the Elizabethan Age,' is a worthy companion of the volume issued some months ago. Whilst that volume was still in the press the compiler was again gleaning where he had reaped, confident in the success of his first venture. The result is a rich store of lyrics which were absolutely unknown to the public, and of many of which even specialists were ignorant. Mr. Bullen has unearthed a large number of the poems from unique books in the British Museum, the Bodleian Library, the Royal College of Music, Mr. Halliwell-Phillipps' Library at Hollingbury Copse, and unpublished manuscripts."

Notes and Queries.
"From the same rich sources that have supplied him with the previous volume of 'Lyrics' Mr. Bullen has dug out yet further treasures. His earlier volume is already prized by the bibliophile and by the lover of poetry. The second forms a worthy companion. All but inexhaustible seems the supply of poetry of the Elizabethan era. Poem after poem that we come upon in these second gleanings is good enough in a later age to have won the writer a place among poets. Men such as Carew, for instance, have obtained a name as poets without writing anything equal to the best of Thomas Campion, whom Mr. Bullen has permanently rescued from practical oblivion."

Daily News.
"They are beautiful tunable pieces; they have the accent of that old day, a music like the jargoning of birds, artless trills that our later art 'never can recapture.' Such were our fathers' songs, and why are our modern songs, as a rule, such trash?"

14 King William Street, Strand, London, W.C.